JESSE LIBERTY'S
from scratch
PROGRAMMING SERIES

D1290726

The C++ Standard Library

from scratch

Pablo Halpern

201 West 103rd Street,
Indianapolis, Indiana 46290

The C++ Standard Library from Scratch

Copyright © 2000 by Pablo Halpern

International Standard Book Number: 0-7897-2128-7

Library of Congress Catalog Card Number: 99-62895

Printed in the United States of America

First Printing: November 1999

01   00   99   4   3   2   1

Trademarks

Warning and Disclaimer

Executive Editor
Tracy Dunkelberger

Acquisitions Editors
Holly Allender
Michelle Newcomb

Development Editors
Jeff Durham
Bryan Morgan

Managing Editor
Lisa Wilson

Project Editors
Sara Bosin
Tonya Simpson

Copy Editor
Michael Dietsch

Indexer
Heather McNeill

Proofreader
Billy Fields

Technical Editor
Paul Snaith

Technical Reviewer
Danny Kalev

Novice Reviewer
Stuart Snaith

Media Developer
Andrea Duvall

Interior Design
Sandra Schroeder
Anne Jones

Cover Design
Maureen McCarty
Anne Jones

Copy Writer
Eric Borgert

Layout Technicians
Tim Osborn
Mark Walchle

Contents at a Glance

Contents

Foreword

Welcome to *Jesse Liberty's Programming From Scratch series*. I created this series because I believe that traditional primers do not meet the needs of every student. A typical introductory computer programming book teaches a series of skills in logical order and then, when you have mastered a topic, the book endeavors to show how the skills might be applied. This approach works very well for many people, but not for everyone.

I've taught programming to over 10,000 students: in small groups, large groups, and through the Internet. Many students have told me that they wish they could just sit down at the computer with an expert and work on a program together. Rather than being taught each skill step-by-step in a vacuum, they'd like to create a product and learn the necessary skills as they go.

From this idea was born the *Programming From Scratch* series. In each of these books, an industry expert will guide you through the design and implementation of a complex program, starting from scratch and teaching you the necessary skills as you go.

You might want to make a *From Scratch* book the first book you read on a subject, or you might prefer to read a more traditional primer first and then use one of these books as supplemental reading. Either approach can work: Which is better depends on your personal learning style.

All the *From Scratch* series books share a common commitment to showing you the entire development process, from the initial concept through implementation. We do not assume you know anything about the subject: *From Scratch* means from the very beginning, with no prior assumptions.

Although I didn't write every book in the series, as series editor I have a powerful sense of personal responsibility for each one. I provide supporting material and a discussion group on my Web site (www.libertyassociates.com), and I encourage you to write to me at jliberty@libertyassociates.com if you have questions or concerns.

Thank you for considering this book.

Jesse Liberty

From Scratch Series Editor

About the Author

Pablo Halpern has been in the software industry for more than 17 years, working mostly in C and C++. As the senior consultant at Halpern-Wight Software, Inc., he provides training, mentoring, and programming expertise in C++ and object-oriented analysis and design for software development organizations large and small. Pablo is the author of a training course on the C++ Standard Library and has assisted in the development of other courseware for introductory and advanced C++ courses.

Pablo lives with his wife, Nancy, and his daughter, Julia, in the midst of the Massachusetts technology region, near Boston and Cambridge. He can be reached by email at phalpern@newview.org.

Dedication

This book is dedicated to my father, Teodoro Halpern, who taught me the value of eloquence.

Acknowledgments

Nonfiction books are never really written by one person. There are always collaborators, seen and unseen, who help make it happen. If you really want to know who wrote a book, look at the acknowledgements section, not just the cover.

I couldn't have written this book without the support of my wife and daughter. They had to put up with me as I got excited, then discouraged, and worked late at night and took a computer on vacation. Nancy had to take on an even larger burden of child care than usual, and Julia had to live with only half a father. I love you both very much. I couldn't have paid the bills without the fine folks at Ironbridge Networks, who hired me as a consultant even after I told them I would be preoccupied writing a book.

A special thanks to Jesse Liberty, the series editor of the *From Scratch* series, for having more confidence in my ability to complete this project than I had myself. Jesse roped me into writing this book, and I will never forgive him for that. Holly Allender was my first contact at Que and helped easy the pain of getting started. Thanks also to Paul Snaith for double-checking the material for accuracy and to the various editors who walked behind me and fixed my goofs.

Introduction

What Makes This Book Different?

This book is different from any primer on this topic *ever* written. Here's the difference: All other programming books start by teaching you simple skills that build in difficulty, adding skill on skill as you go. When you've learned all the skills, the books then demonstrate what you can do: a sample program.

This book does not start with a list of classes and functions; it starts with a project. You begin by analyzing and designing the project and then you implement that design. Standard library features are taught in the context of implementation; first you understand what you are trying to accomplish, and then you learn the skills and library features needed to get the job done.

Learning the Standard Library Doesn't Have to Be Difficult

Many people find the C++ Standard Library to be intimidating. I believe this is because most books and courses focus on the set of features supplied by the library, rather than on the problem these features help you solve. The C++ Standard Library is so large that trying to learn it this way is like trying to learn French by memorizing a French dictionary.

There are two ways to learn to speak a foreign language. One way is to memorize dozens of vocabulary words and practice declension of verbs. The other is to go to the country and interact with native speakers. Different people learn differently, but I can tell you that in my experience a week in France is worth two years in the classroom.

If I were going to teach you the C++ Standard Library and we worked together, I would not hand you a book at all. I'd sit down with you and we'd write a program together. Along the way, I'd teach you what you need to know, occasionally giving you short pieces to read to flesh out your understanding.

That is exactly how this book works: we'll sit down together and write a program, and along the way I'll teach you what you need to know. From the very first page, you will focus on understanding the problem you are trying to solve, and designing a solution, rather than on a list of features.

 Note   Because this book might be the first book you read after learning C++, I have included several excursions that review C++ concepts. If you are an old hand at C++ programming, simply skip these excursions.

Learning to Make Choices Among Library Constructs

One drawback of the other teaching approaches is that you get bombarded with a set of features with little guidance on how to choose among them. Because you are working through a real program, I can explain alternative ways of solving a problem and describe why we choose a particular solution. Returning to the foreign language analogy, you will learn not only the legal way to use library constructs, but the *idiomatic* use of those constructs.

 An *idiom* is a customary way of using a programming construct or feature. The meaning of an idiomatic construct is understood as a whole, without having to analyze the individual parts.

Using idioms reduces the amount of thinking you have to do and it makes your code easier to maintain by other people who understand the idioms.

Why Should I Learn the C++ Standard Library?

The official standard for the C++ language is a 776-page document (ISO/IEC 14882, 1998). About half of that document is devoted to the library of functions and classes that are provided with standard-conforming compilers. If you use C++ without understanding the Standard Library, you know only half the story.

 Tip   If you do not already know how to program in C++, put this book down right now. Run (do not walk) to the store where you bought this book and buy Jesse Liberty's *C++ from Scratch* (ISBN: 0-7897-2079-5). When you are finished reading *C++ from Scratch*, you can resume reading this book where you left off.

A large part of programming involves mundane tasks such as managing collections of objects, manipulating text strings, searching, sorting, and performing formatted input and output. Though conceptually simple, many of these tasks are tedious and some are hard to get right. Do you really want to implement a sort algorithm yourself? What are the chances of introducing a subtle bug that only shows up when, say, sorting arrays that contain three elements with the same value?

Proper use of the library increases the portability of your programs to different compilers and operating systems. The use of standard library classes for data interchange is becoming increasingly common as more and more third-party libraries use standard classes in their interfaces.

By learning about the Standard Library, you can avoid reinventing the wheel. The features of the Standard Library are there to make your programs easier to write and more robust. The people who maintain your code will thank you for using well-understood facilities instead of inventing your own. (Okay, they might not actually thank you, but they'll be grateful inside and at least they won't curse you.)

What Is the C++ Standard Library?

The C++ Standard Library is really two things. In the classical sense, it is a set of types and functions, which come ready-to-use with a *standards-conforming compiler*.

A *library* is a set of reusable components (classes, functions, macros, and so on) intended to help a programmer perform a set of tasks. A library can be special purpose (for example, Internet programming) or general purpose (for example, sorting).

A *standard library* is A library whose contents and behavior are described in a document issued by a standards body (for example, the International Standards Organization, ISO). Unless otherwise stated, "standard library" is used here as an easier way to say "C++ Standard Library"—that is, the library described in the ISO C++ standard.

A *standards-conforming compiler* is a compiler and library that correctly implements the behavior described in the ISO standard for the C++ language and library.

But the C++ Standard Library is also an *extensible framework* for creating additional library components. Most of your work with the Standard Library will not involve creating new components. But for those 10% of the cases where new components are needed, the power of the library proves to be extraordinary. It is the ability to create new library components that distinguishes skilled library users from novices. With this book, I hope to move you a substantial distance down the road toward being a skilled library user.

Parts of the Standard Library

Ten smaller libraries together comprise the C++ Standard Library. They are

1. The Language Support Library, which contains types and functions directly related to the language and compiler. For example, there are constants that define the range and precision of floating point numbers and functions for exiting a program.

2. The Diagnostics Library, which contains exception classes and other facilities for detecting and reporting errors.

3. The General Utilities Library, which contains useful facilities not easily categorized into one of the other libraries.

4. The Strings Library, for manipulating text strings.

5. The Localization Library, for handling international character sets and culturally specific formatting of things such as time, date, and currency.

6. The Containers Library, which provides generic containers for collecting objects.

7. The Iterators Library, for traversing items in a collection.

8. The Algorithms Library, which implements many commonly used data-manipulation algorithms.

9. The Numerics Library, which provides complex numbers, special numeric array types, and numeric algorithms.

10. The Input/Output Library, for performing portable formatted and unformatted input and output to files and other devices.

Which Parts Are Really Useful?

The ten libraries aren't equally useful. Some libraries you will use every day, whereas others you might never use. This book concentrates on the five libraries that I consider most useful in day-to-day use: Strings, Containers, Iterators, Algorithms, and Input/Output.

Conversely, not everything that could be useful was included in the Standard Library. The ISO (International Standards Organization) committee responsible for creating the International C++ Language Standard reviewed hundreds of proposals for features that could have been added to the standard. They attempted to include only those features that are of the most general use and that had well-constructed proposals.

In retrospect, many generally useful features were omitted, whereas other less generally useful features were included. As we go along, I will point out some of the more glaring omissions. I won't bore you with all the obscure features that are hardly ever used. In picking and choosing, I am in a sense second-guessing the ISO committee members that slaved over the standard for so long. This is my prerogative as an author with 20/20 hindsight and I make no apologies.

What About Those Library Features I Once Used in C?

If you programmed in C before learning C++, you are probably familiar with a number of library functions that are part of the C Standard Library. These functions—such as `printf`, `strcpy`, `atoi`, and so on—are still available to you in the C++ Standard Library and you will explore several of them in this book. Some parts of the C library, such as the input/output functions, are rarely used in C++ because more sophisticated components are available in the C++ library. Other parts of the C library, however, continue to be valuable for writing C++ programs.

The C Standard Library underwent a few changes when it was incorporated into the C++ Standard Library. To begin with, the header files have changed names. For example, `stdio.h` was renamed `cstdio`. The rule is the same for the other headers: Remove the `.h` and put a lowercase `c` in front.

Taking advantage of the capability to overload function names in C++, some functions were changed to make better use of `const`. For example, the C function

```
char* strchr(const char* s, char c);
```

has been replaced in C++ with the following two overloaded functions:

```
const char* strchr(const char* s, char c);
      char* strchr(      char* s, char c);
```

The first form searches for a character within an array of `const` characters and returns a `const` pointer to the first one. The second form works for a non-`const` array and returns a non-`const` pointer. This closes a `const`-safety hole in the C version of the function, which returned a non-`const` pointer into a potentially `const` array.

Overloading also provides multiple versions of floating-point math functions for the different size floating-point number types. For example, the C function

```
double sin(double);
```

has been replaced in C++ with

```
float sin(float);
double sin(double);
```

and

```
long double sin(long double);
```

Finally, all components inherited from the C library except macros have been put into the std namespace. (The macros from the C library are still available but, since macros do not obey scoping rules, they cannot be assigned to a namespace.) We delve further into the std namespace in the next chapter.

Is the Standard Library the Same as STL?

STL stands for *Standard Template Library*. The term refers to a set of interfaces and components developed by Alexander Stepanov and others working at AT&T Bell Laboratories and Hewlett-Packard Research Laboratories. Stepanov's goal was to realize the potential of generic programming to create a standard set of reusable components. Today, the STL comprises the Containers, Iterators, Algorithms, and some of the General Utilities libraries within the C++ Standard Library. In other words, STL is only a part of the Standard Library, albeit a very important part. Much of this book is devoted to understanding and using STL components.

An *interface* is any formal description of how a programmer or user gains access to the capabilities of a function, class, macro, or any other component of the system. Interface is an abstract programming concept, not a specific keyword C++ construct.

A *class interface* describes the set of public functions, types, and variables in a class.

A *function interface* describes the set of argument types and the return type for a function (that is, its prototype).

Design Goals of the STL

When the main ideas of the STL were presented to the C++ standardization committee in late 1993, they were received enthusiastically. So rare was it that a proposal could satisfy so many goals simultaneously. The STL successfully achieved the following design goals:

- **General usefulness**   When learned, STL components become part of the bread-and-butter of everyday programming. The STL uses templates to create components that can be applied to a wide range of programming problems.

- **Simplicity**   Although STL is not without complexity, the most commonly used components have small, easy-to-learn interfaces.

- **Efficiency**   The use of templates enables the library to be very efficient in runtime processing. Templates translate a general-purpose component at compile-time into a special-purpose implementation. In addition, the STL components provide specific performance guarantees, enabling you to choose the most efficient component for your task.

- **Flexibility**   The components of the STL are small and designed to be combined in infinite combinations. You can often change your mind and substitute one component for another with very little ripple effect on the code.
- **Extensibility**   The STL is not simply a bunch of components, but a set of *interfaces*. You can add new components to the framework merely by adopting the STL interfaces. Your new component will work seamlessly with the existing ones.

If you have been hearing a lot about the STL and were wondering what all the excitement was about, now you know. Anything that can promise this much is bound to cause excitement.

What Tools Do I Need?

Theoretically, you could read this book without ever touching a computer. However, to get the most out of it, you're going to want to compile some or all the sample code in the book, perhaps modifying it to experiment with the library features. I also suggest that you try to solve the exercises scattered throughout the book, usually at the end of chapters.

The code is available for download from the book's Web site at `http://www.mcp.com/product_support`. When you locate the URL, you'll be asked to enter the book's ISBN: Enter `0789721287`, and then click the Search button to go to this book's information page. There you will find one or more links to the code.

To compile and run the programs in this book, you will need a text editor or Integrated Development Environment (IDE), a modern C++ compiler, and the Standard Library itself.

What Compilers Will Work?

This book is based on the C++ language as standardized by the International Standards Organization (ISO) in July 1998. Theoretically, therefore, any standards-conforming compiler will work equally well. As of this writing, however, standards-conforming compilers are rare. Compilers vary as to which features of Standard C++ they have not yet implemented. Some compilers are so hopelessly behind that they cannot effectively support a commercial-grade version of the Standard Library. You should avoid any compiler that predates the December 1996 draft of the ISO standard. In fact, few compilers from before 1998 are usable with the Standard Library.

The examples in this book have been tested with the Microsoft Visual C++ 6.0 compiler on Windows and the GNU egcs 1.1.2 compiler on UNIX/Linux. The egcs compiler is the next-generation of the GNU compiler and is substantially closer to ISO conformance than the older GNU compiler. It is available free on the Web at `http://egcs.cygnus.com/`.

The other popular compiler that should work for Microsoft Windows is the Borland compiler that comes with C++ Builder 4.0. (This is not the Borland C++ 4.0 compiler, which is quite old and insufficient for supporting the Standard Library.) On UNIX and other operating systems, the compilers from KAI and those derived from the Edison Group compiler have received favorable reviews for standards conformance.

Because Sun's Solaris operating system is a popular software development platform, it is worth singling out the SunPro 5.0 compiler as another compiler you can use for programming with the Standard Library. The previous version of the SunPro compiler, 4.2, is marginally usable for Standard Library programming with some workarounds.

Compiler Notes

Even among the compilers listed earlier, there are errors, flaws, and idiosyncrasies that differ from compiler to compiler. In cases where I can identify these idiosyncrasies, I will flag them for you using a note that looks like this:

Compiler Note   The XYZ compiler fails to recognize the `#include` directive. The workaround is to concatenate all your source files and the Standard Library headers into a single, huge, monstrosity.

Some compiler notes will apply to a whole class of compilers (for example, pre-1998 compilers), whereas others will apply to a specific compiler. The examples in this book have not been compiled on every compiler on the market, or even on every compiler mentioned here. Take advantage of the tips in the Compiler Notes, but know that I have certainly missed many opportunities for enlightening you on potential compiler problems. If my Compiler Notes seem to be picking on the Microsoft compiler, it is only because it is the one on which I have done the most testing. The fact that Microsoft owns most of the world (or at least most of the market) also makes their compiler a reasonable subject for thorough coverage.

Where Do I Get the Standard Library?

Most of the compilers mentioned earlier come with their own implementation of the C++ Standard Library.

Compiler Note   The version of the Standard Library that comes with the Microsoft Visual C++ 6.0 and earlier compilers has some known bugs, at least one of which would prevent you from compiling the code in this book. Dinkumware, Ltd., the company that supplies the library to Microsoft, has fixed many of these bugs. A list of fixes is available on the Internet at `http://www.dinkumware.com/vc_fixes.html`. You can also purchase a complete, updated library through this Web site.

Some of the older compilers (for example, the SunPro 4.2 compiler) provide an implementation of streams but not of the STL or standard string class. You can get implementations for these parts of the library from various commercial and free sources, including those listed here.

Standard Template Library Adaptation Page

`http://www.stlport.org/`

The STLport project provides a port of the STL and standard string class for many different compilers at no cost. It is built on the commercial-grade SGI version of the library and should probably be the first place you look. Also contains links to other good sites.

ObjectSpace, Inc.

`http://www.objectspace.com`

ObjectSpace sells several class libraries for C++ and Java. Their very-portable version of the STL and strings library (Standards<Toolkit>) comes bundled with many of their C++ class libraries. ObjectSpace used to provide the library for free downloading, though that no longer seems to be the case.

Rogue Wave, Inc.

`http://www.roguewave.com/`

Like ObjectSpace, Rogue Wave sells several class libraries for C++, including a standard library. Beware that most of Rogue Wave's other products do not directly use the standard library, but instead use a proprietary library called Tools.h++, which is largely a set of wrapper classes designed to give STL classes an older-style, more limited interface. The Rogue Wave version of the standard library is bundled with a number of compilers.

A *wrapper* is a class or function intended only to provide a different interface to another class or function and that provides little new functionality.

Conventions Used in This Book

Some of the unique features in this series include the following:

The *Geek Speak* icon in the margin indicates the use of a new term. New terms will appear in the paragraph in *italics*.

how tōō
prō nouns′ it

> **How to Pronounce It**   You'll see an icon set in the margin next to a box that contains a technical term and how it should be pronounced. For example, "`cin` is pronounced *see-in*, and `cout` is pronounced *see-out*."

EXCURSIONS

Excursion

These are short diversions from the main topic being discussed, and they offer an opportunity to flesh out your understanding of a topic.

Sometimes an excursion is titled *The Gory Details*. This kind of excursion is used to introduce details that you probably don't want to know, but which you will be better off knowing. In general, these gory details do not affect the sample program.

With a book of this type, a topic can be discussed in multiple places as a result of when and where we add functionality during application development. To help make this all clear, I've included a Concept Web that provides a graphical representation of how all the programming concepts relate to one another. You'll find it on the inside cover of this book.

Notes give you comments and asides about the topic at hand, as well as full explanations of certain concepts.

Tips provide great shortcuts and hints on how to program in C++ more effectively.

Cautions warn you against making your life miserable and avoiding the pitfalls in programming.

In addition, you'll find various typographic conventions throughout this book:

- Commands, variables, and other code stuff appear in text in a special `mono-spaced font`.
- In this book, I build on existing listings as we examine code further. When I add new sections to existing code, you'll spot it in **`bold monospace`**.
- Commands and such that you type appear in `monospace`.
- Placeholders in syntax descriptions appear in a *`monospaced italic`* typeface. This indicates that you will replace the placeholder with the actual filename, parameter, or other element that it represents.

Getting Project Code and Support

As stated earlier, the code is available for download from the book's Web site at `http://www.mcp.com/product_support`. When you locate the URL, enter `0789721287` for the book's ISBN, and then click the Search button to go to this book's information page, where you will find one or more links to the code. You will find source code, a quick reference guide, exercises, errata, and links to help you get the most out of this book. Check back periodically for new information and links.

The source code on the Web is organized by chapter, with the final project source in the Chapter 10 Code section. Look for **Code Notes** in the text, which will direct you to the code directory for each set of listings.

Chapter 1

Introducing TinyPIM

As I mentioned in the introduction, we will work through a real program as we examine ways to use the standard library features. It is now time to introduce that program.

The sample program is a small PIM (Personal Information Manager) that we will name TinyPIM. A PIM is an electronic address book and date book, with other features to help you keep your life organized. A PIM can be as simple or as elaborate as you want, making it an excellent sample program. We will start out relatively simple and add bells and whistles as we go along.

Before we start coding, I will walk you through an abbreviated presentation of the analysis and design process for TinyPIM. Note that only my *presentation* is abbreviated, not the actual design process. Even though TinyPIM is not very large, it is large enough to benefit from a proper analysis and design process. Because this book is about the Standard Library, and not about object-oriented analysis and design, there is no need to go step-by-step through the whole process, however. The real design process required a number of iterations, with blind allies and reworks. Perhaps you are so smart that you could have produced this entire design all at once out of your head, but I certainly am not.

I used the Unified Modeling Language (UML) to document my analysis and design process. In my presentation, I describe just enough of UML for you to understand what I'm talking about. When requirements analysis was mostly complete, I created a top-level design. I refined my top-level design, adding detail, until I was ready to start coding. What I will present here makes the process look much more linear than it was in reality. When I actually wrote this program, I had to regularly modify the design and occasionally the requirements.

Unified Modeling Language (UML) is a popular notation for describing the design of an object-oriented program.

It is worth noting that I created the UML diagrams in this book using a tool called Rose from Rational Software. Some of the industry's top object-oriented methodology gurus work at Rational and invented UML from a number of different notations that preceded it. Check out `http://www.rational.com/`.

Requirements Analysis

Requirements analysis is the process of understanding the customer's needs and how the computer program will fulfill those needs. I broke up the analysis phase into two parts: a "Requirements Statement," which is a short, high-level description of the program from the customer's point of view, and a set of "Use Cases" that describe a number of things the user might do when interacting with the program and how the system would react.

Requirements Statement

1. TinyPIM will provide a basic address book and appointment calendar. The address book will enable the user to store and edit phone numbers and addresses, look them up by name, or perform simple searches. Index views will enable the user to pick entries from a list.

2. The appointment calendar will enable the user to store and edit appointments or calendar events. Events can be viewed in month-at-a-time, week-at-a-time, day-at-a-time, or single-event views. Each view shows successively more detail about the individual events.

3. The first version of TinyPIM will use a primitive command-line interface.

4. The first version of TinyPIM will use a simple in-memory storage system.

5. The program will be designed and implemented in such a way as to permit the following future enhancements:

   - Replacing the command-line interface with either a graphical interface or a Web interface

   - Adding a permanent (flat-file or database) storage system for TinyPIM data

   - Adding a to-do-list function

6. The program will be implemented in such a way as to show off the facilities in the C++ Standard Library.

This last requirement will have a significant effect on our design. Although I tried to design this program as if I really wanted to write it as cleanly and effectively as possible, there will be times where I make unusual design decisions because it lets me use a feature of the standard library that I would otherwise not need. I will also choose one implementation and then change my mind in order to show alternative ways of getting something accomplished using the standard library. Given the purpose of this book, the requirement that I show off the C++ Standard Library is really the main requirement. The other requirements are in service of this one.

Use Cases

Now that you have a basic understanding of what we are building, look at a few situations that we need to handle. During the design process, I started with high-level *use cases* where I described an action on the part of the user, often without knowing what TinyPIM's reaction should be. Then I refined the use cases, adding detail, answering questions, combining or splitting use cases, and figuring out what the program should do in each situation. I will spare you all the intermediate steps and simply present to you the detailed use cases.

 Use case is the description of a specific interaction between the system being designed and one or more of the *actors* with which the system interacts.

 An *actor* is something outside of the system that interacts with it. An actor can be a person, a peripheral device, another computer, and so on.

how tōō prō nouns' it	**Use case** rhymes with *goose chase*. Here, *Use* is being used as an adjective, not a verb (that is, pronounce it *Yoos*, not *Yooz*).

Data Entry Use Cases

1. The user wants to create a new address record. The program prompts for last name, first name, phone number, and address. The last name is the only required field.
2. The user wants to edit an existing address record. The user selects a record using one of the search or list functions and then modifies one or more fields.
3. The user wants to delete an address record. The user selects a record using one of the search or list functions and tells the system to delete it.
4. The user wants to schedule an appointment. The system prompts the user for start and end dates and times and a description of the appointment.

5. The user wants to edit an existing appointment record. The user selects an appointment using one of the search or list functions and then modifies any or all of the fields.

6. The user wants to delete an appointment. The user selects an appointment using one of the search or list functions and then chooses to delete it.

Searching and Listing Use Cases

7. The user wants to search for one or more address records by name. The program prompts for the first part of the last name and, optionally, the first name. If there is no match, entries with last names that start with the search string are presented to the user for selection. If there are multiple matches, they are all presented to the user for selection.

8. The user wants to search for address records containing a specified string anywhere in the record. The system lists all matching records.

9. The user wants to see all her appointments for the day. The system lists the first line of each appointment.

10. The user wants to see all her appointments for the week. The system lists the first line of each appointment.

11. The user wants to see which days of the month she has appointments. The system displays a calendar with special markings on each day that has appointments.

12. The user wants to see all her appointments for the next day or week. The system provides an easy way to specify these common dates and displays a brief description of each appointment in the date range.

13. The user wants to see all her appointments for a different day, week, or month. The system provides a way to specify the desired time period.

Error Handling Use Cases

14. The user enters an address record for a duplicate name by accident. The user doesn't realize that this is a duplicate. The system gives the user the option of canceling the entry.

15. The user enters an address record for a duplicate name on purpose. The user deliberately enters an address record using a name that already exists because she knows two people with identical names.

These use cases give us a more detailed understanding of what the program will do. As we proceed with design and implementation, we will be guided by these use cases, even if we don't refer to them directly.

Class Design

I begin the design of the project by breaking it up into logical pieces called packages. I will then go into each package in detail.

Top-Level Logical View

Based on the requirements statement, I chose to divide the project into three packages, representing the core functions of the PIM, the user interface, and the persistence (file or database storage) mechanism. Although the persistence package will not be part of our first version, I include the diagram because its eventual inclusion might influence our design decisions. Figure 1.1 shows a package-level class diagram for TinyPIM.

Figure 1.1

Package-level design.

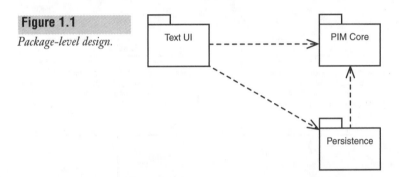

In the UML diagram in Figure 1.1, each file folder represents a package of classes. The dotted arrows connecting the boxes represent the *using* relationship. In other words, the Text UI package *uses* the PIM Core and Persistence packages.

The three packages should be as loosely coupled as possible, in order to meet the requirements that both the user interface and the persistence system be replaceable at a future date. It is especially significant that the PIM Core does not use either of the other two packages. This means that the core of the program will be virtually unaffected by changes in the other two packages.

The separation of the program into loosely coupled packages imposes another restriction on the design. The objects flowing between the packages must be relatively simple in nature. Imagine that the text user interface is eventually replaced by a Web browser. The PIM Core would probably be connected to the browser by means of an Internet connection. Because the user interface and the PIM Core would no longer be part of the same physical program, it would not be possible to pass pointers between the two parts. Instead, each package would need to convert the data into a sequence of bytes that could easily be converted back to meaningful data by the other package. Data objects containing pointers, virtual functions, and so on would be difficult to manage. Similarly, the persistence package may be implemented using a relational database, where complex data structures imply complex database schemas. I will touch on this point again as I move through the design and implementation.

A Short Course in UML

A UML diagram for the PIM Core package is shown in Figure 1.2.

Figure 1.2

Class diagram for PIM core.

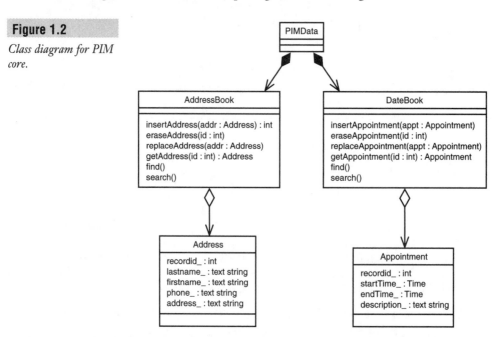

Figure 1.2 is called a *class diagram*. It describes the members of each class and the relationships between objects (instances) of those classes. Each box represents a class. The boxes are subdivided into three sections. The top section is the class name, the middle section is the set of member variables (state variables), and the bottom section is the list of member functions. The level of detail shown in a class diagram need only be sufficient to communicate the design. I could teach you a lot of UML here—including a notation for public, private, and protected—but we'll get to those details when we write the code. For now, I'll show you enough to get started.

Notice in Figure 1.2 that Address and Appointment seem to have no member functions and that AddressBook and DateBook seem to have no data members. PIMData seems to be a totally empty class! There are two reasons for this. The first has to do with the notation itself. The relationships between the classes imply certain data members. Thus, PIMData must contain at least two data members: one for the AddressBook and one for the DateBook object logically contained within it. UML allows you to name these associations and thus effectively name the member variables. But that gets me to the second reason why some things seem to be missing: I don't find them interesting at this point in the design. An important attribute of UML is that you make your diagrams readable by leaving out detail. The same part of the program can appear in multiple diagrams, each detailing a different aspect of the design. In particular, I left out simple accessors to member variables.

The lines connecting the classes represent relationships between objects of those classes. An arrowhead on one end of a relationship indicates that the association is one-way. Thus, an AddressBook object knows which Address objects it is associated with, but not the other way around. The small diamonds denote whole-part relationships. An Address object is *part of* an AddressBook object, which is in turn *part of* a PIMData object. The difference between solid and hollow diamonds is fairly subtle. Solid diamonds indicate *composition*, where the contained object only exists as long as the composite object exists. Hollow diamonds indicate *aggregation* where the two objects exist independently. In practice, it is often difficult at this stage to determine whether composition or aggregation is more appropriate, so I wouldn't worry about it.

An asterisk on one end of a relationship indicates that there can be multiple instances of that object for each instance of the other object in the relationship. An AddressBook contains many Addresses, for example. When we get to coding these classes, we will find some standard library facilities to be well-suited for representing these different types of relationships.

TinyPIM Core Package

Now that you know a little about UML class diagrams, let's examine Figure 1.2. The PIM Core package, as the name implies, is the guts of TinyPIM. It contains objects for the address book and date book and also describes the types of objects stored in the address book and date book. The address book and date book are each represented as a class with an obvious name. The PIMData object collects these two into a single composite object that represents all the user's data as a single object.

The AddressBook and DateBook classes each contain zero or more instances of Address or Appointment records, respectively. They also supply interfaces for inserting, removing, replacing, and accessing these records. Additionally, they supply interfaces for finding a specific record and searching for records containing a string. Because the user interface is the main client for the search functions, we need not get into the details of arguments and return values for them until we finish specifying and designing the user interface.

The `Address` class is a basic data container, with fields to hold a unique ID as well as the last name, first name, phone number, and address of a person or company. These name and address fields are all text strings, whose representation we will explore as we get to coding. I could have broken an `Address` into more fields—for example, work number, home number, fax number, email address, and so on—but all these additional fields would be similar to the ones I already defined and would add little to the educational value of the example. The Address class contains three possible key fields: `recordId_`, `lastname_`, and `firstname_`. As it turns out, we will need to use all these as key fields to implement different parts of the program's function. This presents an interesting challenge that we will meet using standard library facilities at coding time.

The `Appointment` class is also a basic data container. Here, the key fields are `recordId_`, `startTime_`, and possibly `endTime_`. The `startTime_` and `endTime_` fields are of type `Time`, which is another class I will have to define.

One more thing about the `Address` and `Appointment` classes: Objects of these two classes are used throughout TinyPIM, including in the `Text UI` and `Persistence` packages. The current design for these classes contains basic types such as text strings and `Time` values. The only member functions we know of at this point are basic accessors. This simplicity serves us in case we find ourselves transmitting these objects over a network or storing them in a relational database.

Text UI Package

The `Text UI` package will be responsible for interacting with the user. It will make heavy use of the input and output facilities in the standard library. The system's interaction with the user will consist of displaying menus, prompting for and accepting menu choices, and prompting for and accepting address and appointment data. To make such a primitive system usable requires a small amount of complexity in the design.

Menu Classes

Figure 1.3 describes the portion of the class design for the `Text UI` package that handles menu interactions.

Figure 1.3 uses a couple more elements of the UML notation. The large, hollow, triangular arrow heads indicate a *generalization/specialization* relationship. In this case, `Menu` is a *generalization* (also known as a super class or base class) of the `MainMenu`, `AddressBookMenu`, and `DateBookMenu` classes. The other side of the same relationship is the *specialization* role. I say that AddressBookMenu is a specialization (also known as a *subclass* or *derived class*) of Menu and thus inherits from Menu. Note that the inheritance relationship is a relationship between *classes* whereas all the other relationships are between *objects*.

Figure 1.3

Class diagram for Text
IU *menus.*

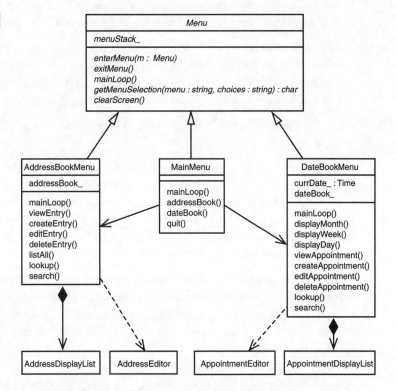

The four boxes at the bottom of Figure 1.3 also represent classes, but no member variables or function sections are shown. This is a shorthand way of indicating the existence of a class without showing any detail about it. I will present class diagrams that show more detail about these four classes later in this chapter.

The Menu class is an *abstract class* that contains common utilities for displaying menus and handling the user response. The mainLoop virtual function must be implemented by each derived class to actually do the work that the menu is designed to do. The getMenuSelection and clearScreen functions encapsulate the part of menu handling that is common to all the menu classes. The program maintains a menu stack. (The menu stack is unrelated to the subroutine call stack.) When a submenu is needed, it is pushed on to the stack using the enterMenu function; when the submenu exits, it is popped from the stack using the exitMenu function. When the stack is empty, the program exists. Don't confuse a submenu with a subclass. Any menu can be a submenu of any other menu simply by pushing it on to the menu stack. There is no need for them to have an inheritance relationship.

An *abstract class* is a class that exists solely as a generalization of its subclasses. All instances of an abstract class must belong to one if its subclasses. In C++ an abstract class is usually indicated by the presence of a *pure virtual function*.

A *pure virtual function* is a virtual function that might not have an implementation. The declaration of a pure virtual function ends with = 0. A class containing a pure virtual function cannot create objects. However, its derived classes can override the pure virtual function with normal virtual functions, thus making them *concrete classes*.

A *concrete class* is a class that can be used to create real objects. The opposite of an abstract class.

The main menu simply gives the user the choice of entering the address book application or the date book application or else quitting the program. If the user chooses to go to the address book, the AddressBookMenu gets pushed on to the menu stack. Likewise for the date book and the DateBookMenu. The AddressBookMenu and DateBookMenu classes define their own mainLoop functions and also functions for each of the operations you can select from the menu.

The AddressBookMenu and DateBookMenu each need to display a list of entries. This list could be the entire set of entries or a subset of entries selected by some search criteria. Because the screen is limited in size, a long list must be broken up into screenfuls that can be paged up or down. In addition, each entry is numbered so that the user can choose to view, edit, or delete an entry by number. The task of managing the lists of entries is delegated to the AddressDisplayList and AppointmentDisplayList classes, which we need to examine in more detail.

Editor Classes

When the user wants to create or edit an entry in either the address book or date book, an AddressEditor or AppointmentEditor class is used to handle the editing interactions with the user. Figure 1.4 shows a top-level design for the editor classes.

The basic structure of the editors is simple. The Editor base class supplies functions for editing a single-line field (such as last name) or a multiline field (such as address). It also keeps a status for reporting whether the user completed the edit or aborted. The derived classes keep a copy of the record being edited and provide a main function that uses editSingleLine and editMultiLine, as appropriate. As we will see, the challenge in implementing the editor classes is in using the string and input/output facilities of the standard library to handle the myriad strange things that a user could enter in the editSingleLine and editMultiLine functions.

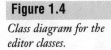
Figure 1.4

Class diagram for the editor classes.

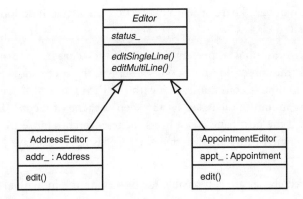

Display List Classes

In Figure 1.5, we return to the classes that display lists of Address or Appointment entries.

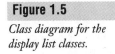
Figure 1.5

Class diagram for the display list classes.

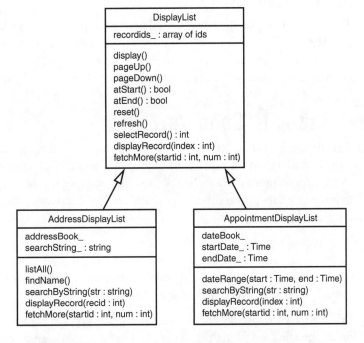

The general design of the display list puts most of the hard work into the DisplayList base class. There are functions for displaying the current subset of entries, moving to the next or previous page (screenful), resetting the list to the beginning, refreshing the list by refetching the data records, and selecting a specific record by number. There are also two protected virtual functions that are provided by the derived classes.

A `DisplayList`'s job is to present a subset of the `Address` or `Appointment` records to the user. If the subset doesn't fit on one screen, the user can page up or down to see more. To minimize communication with the PIM Core (still keeping that network connection in mind), the `DisplayList` keeps a cache of record IDs for records it has displayed. If the next page is not in its cache, it fetches more from the PIM Core. The basic logic is the same whether the records being displayed are `Address` objects or `Appointment` objects.

The derived classes are responsible for displaying the individual records in a short (one-line) format when `displayRecord` is called. They are also responsible for fetching a block of record IDs from the PIM Core when `fetchMore` is called. The other data members and member functions control which subset of records `fetchMore` will retrieve. I will go into more detail as we get ready to implement this.

Persistence Package

The persistence package is responsible for storing the contents of the address book and date book in a disk file or database and reading it back in. Because persistence is not part of the first version of TinyPIM, I am content to just acknowledge it as an eventual part of the system and will not go any deeper into its design.

Am I Ready to Code Yet?

This design is far from complete. We have only created class diagrams, which are static and don't give us much information about how each class does its job or how it interacts with other classes. To have a complete design would require Sequence diagrams or Collaboration diagrams (which are UML diagrams that show the flow of messages between classes).

The truth is we haven't even really finished the analysis portion of this project. A complete analysis would describe everything the program does, down to the keystroke level. Theoretically, we couldn't implement anything until we knew how it should respond to every type of stimulus.

What do we do now? I could continue to guide you through a more detailed functional specification of the project and a more detailed design. I could take you down to individual data structures and algorithms. But I won't do that. Instead, we'll finish the specification and design process as we go along. As we prepare to implement each component, we'll refine our definition of what it should do and, if necessary, draw a few more diagrams to refine the design.

1

This model of approaching a project is called *incremental development*. Using the incremental development model, we visit the specification, design and implementation phases of development repeatedly for each small part. This kind of development is gaining popularity as an alternative to the old "waterfall" model that requires a complete, up-front specification and design of the entire program before a single line of code can be written. Incremental development has numerous advantages, such as enabling your experience implementing one part of the project to influence the design of the next part. But that's not why I'm using it. I'm using it because I don't want to bore you any more. Like you, I'm anxious to do some C++ coding with the standard library. So get to it!

Implementing the Address Class with Text Strings

An Address object holds the data for a single entry in the address book. This type of object doesn't actually *do* much; it simply holds data. All the data members of the Address class are text strings. In implementing Address, therefore, we concentrate on finding the best way to represent text strings.

Using Fixed-Length Strings

We begin by defining the Address class using fixed-length, null-terminated character arrays to hold string values. This introduces you to the facilities in the standard library that help you manipulate character arrays as text strings. Some consider these facilities, which are inherited from the C Standard Library, to be obsolete holdovers from C. Although it is worth understanding them because they are useful and efficient, at the end of this exercise, you'll be glad that the C++ Standard Library provides a better way to represent a string.

Declaring Class Address

My first cut at defining the Address class is shown in Listing 2.1. I used fixed-length character arrays to hold text fields for first and last name, phone number, and address. Note that the line numbers are for our convenience and are not a part of the actual code.

Code Note Listings 2.1 through 2.3 correspond to files on the companion Web page in the Chapter 2 Code\strcpy Version directory. The files in this directory can be compiled and linked together to create an executable program. (See the end of the Introduction for information on accessing this book's companion Web page.)

Listing 2.1   The Address Class Using Fixed-Length Character Arrays

```
 1:  // TinyPIM (c) 1999 Pablo Halpern. File Address.h
 2:
 3:  #ifndef Address_dot_h
 4:  #define Address_dot_h 1
 5:
 6:  // Address class implemented using fixed-length strings
 7:  class Address
 8:  {
 9:  public:
10:    // Constructor
11:    Address();
12:
13:    // Field accessors
14:    const char* lastname() const { return lastname_; }
15:    void lastname(const char*);
16:
17:    const char* firstname() const { return firstname_; }
18:    void firstname(const char*);
19:
20:    const char* phone() const { return phone_; }
21:    void phone(const char*);
22:
23:    const char* address() const { return address_; }
24:    void address(const char*);
25:
26:  private:
27:    // Enumerate string lengths
28:    enum { namelen = 16, phonelen = 16, addrlen = 100 };
29:
30:    // Data Fields
31:    char lastname_[namelen];
32:    char firstname_[namelen];
33:    char phone_[phonelen];
34:    char address_[addrlen];
35:  };
36:
37:  #endif // Address_dot_h
```

This class is a basic container class. It doesn't do anything except hold data. The only member functions are accessors used to set and retrieve the data fields in the address.

2

Let me first describe data members. Line 28 defines constants for the field lengths. It is considered good practice to use named constants for things such as array lengths so that changing a single constant definition can change the length throughout the program. By making these constants private enumerations instead of #define macros, we get the safety and modularity that comes with making them private members of the Address class.

Compiler Note ISO Standard C++ allows and encourages the following alternative method of defining constants within class definitions:

```
static const int namelen = 16;
static const int phonelen = 16;
static const int addrlen = 100;
```

Unfortunately, most current compilers do not yet support this syntax for static member constants, although they have always supported it for static file-scope constants.

The address fields are stored in fixed-length, classic (C-style), null-terminated character strings, as defined in lines 31–34. The characters in the string simply occupy sequential locations in the array. Of the 16 characters reserved for lastname_, at most 15 of them can contain text, in order to leave room for the null terminator.

EXCURSION

A Quick Review of Null-Terminated Character Strings

A *null-terminated character string* is a common representation of text strings consisting of a sequence of characters ending with a null character. The *null character* is a character with an integer value of zero. In C and C++, a null character is represented by the character literal, \0. The length of a null-terminated character string does not include the null terminator itself.

A *null-terminated character string* is a sequence of characters ending with a null character.

A *null character* is a character with value zero (\0, a NUL in the ASCII character set). Do not confuse with NULL (the null pointer).

A null-terminated character string is stored in an array of char. A string declared as char string[15] could have up to 14 characters, plus the null terminator. In the context of a function call, the C and C++ languages arrays are passed as pointers to their first element. Thus, a char* can also be a null-terminated character string. You must never forget, however, that a pointer must point to something. You cannot use a pointer to char as a null-terminated character string unless it actually points to a character in an array. Failing to set a pointer to allocated storage would cause the program to reference random memory and crash.

A string in double quotes is called a *string literal*. The string literal, `"hello"`, has type, `const char[6]` (the sixth character is for the null-terminator). Because of the automatic relationship between arrays and strings, you often see code such as `const char* p = "hello";`, where p points to the *h* in *hello*.

A *string literal* is a sequence of characters appearing within double quotes in a program. The compiler generates a null-terminated character string for each string literal.

Line 11 declares a constructor that makes all the fields empty on initialization. An empty string simply has the null terminator in the first position. There is nothing special to clean up when the Address object is destroyed, so we don't need to define an explicit destructor. The compiler-generated copy constructor and assignment operators are also acceptable for this class.

Line 14 defines an inline read-accessor to return the value in the `lastname_` field. The return value is a pointer to a `const` character array so that the caller cannot modify the last name through this interface. Line 15 declares a write-accessor for the last name field. Similar accessors exist for all the other fields (lines 17–24).

Up until now, we have not used any part of the standard library. In fact, we have not even used the `#include` directive. Look now at Listing 2.2, the implementation file for this simple class, where we use the `strcpy` function from the standard library to copy strings.

Listing 2.2   Implementation of Address Class Using Fixed-Length Character Arrays

```
 1:  // TinyPIM (c) 1999 Pablo Halpern. File Address.cpp
 2:
 3:  #include "Address.h"
 4:  #include <cstring>
 5:
 6:  Address::Address()
 7:  {
 8:     // Initialize all strings to empty.
 9:     lastname_[0] = firstname_[0] = phone_[0] = address_[0] = '\0';
10:  }
11:
12:  void Address::lastname(const char* s)
13:  {
14:     std::strcpy(lastname_, s);
15:  }
16:
17:  void Address::firstname(const char* s)
18:  {
19:     std::strcpy(firstname_, s);
20:  }
21:
22:  void Address::phone(const char* s)
23:  {
24:     std::strcpy(phone_, s);
```

2

```
25:  }
26:
27:  void Address::address(const char* s)
28:  {
29:    std::strcpy(address_, s);
30:  }
```

Line 4 includes the header that declares the standard library functions for manipulating null-terminated strings. The angle brackets (<>) tell the compiler that we are looking for a standard library header. Using the angle brackets instead of straight quotes shortens the compiler's search. The language standard even allows the contents of the standard headers to be built into the compiler, rather than read from a file.

Note Always use angle brackets (<>) for including headers from the standard library. Always use straight quotes ("") for including headers that are not part of the standard library.

If you have been programming in C or C++ for awhile, you might be surprised to see `<cstring>` instead of `<string.h>`. This is a relatively recent change to the library specification. The ISO committee decided to drop the `.h` suffix because of an existing lack of consistency in the industry regarding C++ header file suffixes. (Some compiler vendors used `.h`, others used `.hxx`, and still others used `.hpp`.) By stripping the suffix off entirely, they made all vendors equally unhappy. The leading `c` in the name indicates that this particular part of the library was inherited from the C language.

The general rule is this: All elements from the C Standard Library are also present in the C++ Standard Library. The C header filenames are altered by prepending a lowercase `c` and removing the `.h` suffix.

Note **Compiler Note** Some vendors' libraries do not yet use the new naming conventions. You might have to add the `.h` suffix and remove the c prefix. A better approach is to create the header files yourself using the new names. Your customized header files would simply `#include` the vendor-supplied ones.

Line 9 in the constructor initializes all the string members to be empty by putting a null terminator in the first position of each character array. Properly initializing all character arrays is vital to the correct operation of the library functions that operate on them. Unfortunately, the compiler does not store any useful default values in character array class members.

Line 14 uses the first library function, std::strcpy. The strcpy function is defined in the <cstring> header. The std:: prefix means that it, along with all other identifiers in the standard library, belongs to namespace std.

EXCURSION
A Quick Review of Namespaces

Namespaces were added to the C++ language a few years ago but have only recently been implemented by major compiler vendors. A namespace is defined in code like the following:

```
namespace stuff {
  int g();
  extern int x;
  class A
  {
  public:
    int f() { return g() + x; }
  };
}
```

At first glance, namespace stuff looks a lot like a class definition. However, stuff is not a type; it is just a group of related names. The stuff namespace declares three namespace identifiers: g, x, and A. Outside of the namespace you use the *namespace-qualified* names, stuff::g, stuff::x, and stuff::A. Within the namespace, the namespace qualifier is not needed, as seen in function stuff::A::f, which refers to g and x without the qualifier.

Unlike classes, a namespace is not limited to a single declarative unit. You can add more declarations to an existing namespace by "reopening" the namespace as follows:

```
namespace stuff
{
  enum colors { red, green, blue };
}
```

The type colors and the constants red, green, and blue are now part of namespace stuff along with g, x, and A. This allows namespaces to be split across multiple header files.

The purpose of namespaces is to prevent name collisions between pieces of code that comes from different sources. The object-oriented nature of C++ encourages the use of reusable, third-party libraries. If the third party uses a descriptive name such as print, you don't want it to conflict with a print in your own code or in another third party's code. A library vendor can prevent these collisions by enclosing their library in a distinctive namespace based, for example, on the name of the company that wrote the library. The standards committee chose std for the name of their namespace and, because it is enshrined in the standard, nobody else can use the same name.

There are three techniques for reducing the burden that namespaces impose on the user of a library. The first is namespace aliasing, which looks like this:

```
namespace mlnn = my_long_namespace_name;
```

2

With this declaration, you can say `mlnn::f()` instead of `my_long_namespace_name::f()`. If this is still too long for you, you can import specific names into your scope with the `using` declaration. For example,

```
using stuff::g;
```

enables you to use `g()` instead of `stuff::g()`. This is particularly useful for names you use frequently. As a last resort, you can import an entire namespace with the `using` directive:

```
using namespace stuff;
```

The `using` directive gives you access to all the identifiers in namespace `stuff` without using the qualified names. Use `using` with care. Anytime you import a name into your scope, you risk causing a name conflict or ambiguity. Exposing the contents of an entire namespace with the `using` directive is especially dangerous because a new name could be added to the namespace, creating an ambiguity in code that once compiled.

To use functions, types, and variables from the standard library, we must qualify them with the `std::` namespace name or else use the `using` declaration. The `lastname` write-accessor could also have been written as

```
void Address::lastname(const char* s)
    {
      using std::strcpy;      // Import std::strcpy
      strcpy(lastname_, s);    // Use strcpy without std::
    }
```

Or, using the `using` namespace directive

```
using namespace std;      // Import all std symbols
void Address::lastname(const char* s)
{
  strcpy(lastname_, s);    // Use strcpy without std::
}
```

The latter approach allows you to use any symbol in the standard library without the `std::` prefix. Remember, however, that the standard library introduces many new identifiers that were not present in older C++ libraries. Some of these identifiers are simple words such as copy, set, and map. The chance that a name in the standard library will conflict with a global name in your application is thus much higher than it was in prestandard C++, when the library was smaller. In general, importing the entire `std` namespace into the global scope is discouraged except as a way to get older code to compile on newer compilers with a minimum of fuss.

 Note

Concept With the exception of macros, all identifiers in the C++ Standard Library, *including those inherited from C*, belong to the `std` namespace.

At this point, you might be saying to yourself, "Yuck! You want me to stick an unwieldy std:: in front of *every* use of a standard library facility, even cout?" Don't despair. My personal experience is that when you get used to it, you start to like it. It really makes the code easier to read by documenting every use of the standard library. Following my advice, the venerable "hello world" program would look like this:

```
#include <iostream>
int main()
{
  std::cout << "Hello, world" << std::endl;
  return 0;
}
```

Given the frequency with which cout and endl are used in real code, you would be forgiven if you wrote:

```
#include <iostream>
using std::cout;
using std::endl;
int main()
{
  cout << "Hello, world" << endl;
  return 0;
}
```

Compiler Note   Some compilers do not yet support namespaces or don't define the std namespace. If you want to write code for these compilers that will also compile on more modern compilers, you can add the following macro to your source files:

```
#ifdef _NO_NAMESPACES_
#define std
#endif
```

You would need to define NO_NAMESPACES somewhere, probably on the compiler command line. This definition is done for you in some versions of the standard library (including the popular freeware SGI version).

The library that ships with the Microsoft Visual C++ compiler, version 6.0, *does* put library elements in namespace std, but *does not* do this for those parts of the library that are inherited from C. The only workaround is to not use std:: in front of function names that come from C. Complain to Microsoft.

The prototype for std::strcpy is as follows:

```
namespace std {
  char* strcpy(char* to, const char* from);
}
```

This function is probably already familiar to many of you. It makes a copy of a null-terminated string by copying the sequence of characters starting at the location pointed to by from to the location pointed to by to. Copying stops after the null character has been copied. If the character sequences pointed to by to and from overlap, or if the character array pointed to by to is not large enough to hold the resulting string, *undefined behavior* results because strcpy does not perform error checking.

Undefined behavior is the result of applying certain unsanctioned operations. A common type of undefined behavior is a program crash, which sometimes occurs after the program is in the customer's hands.

The return value of strcpy is its first argument—that is, a pointer to the new copy. Note that strcpy copies characters into an existing character array. It does not allocate any memory.

Now, back to line 14 in Listing 2.2, we see that the Address::lastname(const char*) function works by copying the sequence of characters being passed in through the s argument to the member variable, lastname_. The other write-accessors work in exactly the same way, copying their input string into a member variable.

Listing 2.3 shows a small test program for the Address class.

Listing 2.3   Test Program for the Address Class

```
 1:   // TinyPIM (c) 1999 Pablo Halpern. File test1.cpp
 2:
 3:   #include <iostream>
 4:
 5:   #include "Address.h"
 6:
 7:   void dump(const Address& a)
 8:   {
 9:      std::cout << a.firstname() << ' ' << a.lastname() << '\n'
10:               << a.address() << '\n' << a.phone() << '\n'
11:               << std::endl;
12:   }
13:
14:   int main()
15:   {
16:      Address a;
17:      a.lastname("Smith");
18:      a.firstname("Joan");
19:      a.phone("(617) 555-9876");
20:      a.address("The Very Big Corporation\nSomewhere, MA 01000");
21:      dump(a);
22:
23:      // Add phone extention
24:      a.phone("(617) 555-7777 ext. 112");
25:      dump(a);
26:
27:      return 0;
28:   }
```

Line 3 includes the input/output stream header. Again, we follow the standard convention of using angle brackets and omitting the .h extension. Because this header is not inherited from C, there is no c prefix. The <iostream> header defines the core parts of the standard stream library, including the global streams, cin, cout, and cerr. I will discuss the standard stream library in more depth when we implement the editor classes in Chapter 5. For now, we will simply use the cout stream and the endl end-of-line manipulator.

Lines 7–12 implement a dump function by simply outputting each member of the address to the standard output stream, cout, with both cout and endl, prefixed by the std:: namespace qualifier.

Line 16 creates an Address object and lines 17–20 set the fields of the address. Note that the street address contains an imbedded newline (\n), making it a two-line address. The first address object is printed out by calling the dump function at line 21.

At line 24 we change the phone number in the Address object and then print it again at line 25.

When we look at the output of the test program in Listing 2.4, we see that things aren't quite right.

Listing 2.4   Output of Test Program

```
1:  Joan Smith
2:  The Very Big Corporation
3:  Somewhere, MA 01000
4:  (617) 555-9876
5:
6:  Joan Smith
7:  xt. 112
8:  (617) 555-7777 ext. 112
```

The program does not work exactly as it should. The initial Address object prints out just fine in lines 1–4. For the modified address, we see that the name and phone number print out correctly at lines 6 and 8. But at line 7 something goes wrong. The address field appears to be corrupt. In fact, it seems to contain the last few characters from the phone field. What happened?

The problem stems from the fact that the phone number we are trying to set is longer than the array of characters allocated to hold it. Because of the semantics of arrays and pointers in C++ (and C), the strcpy function does not know the physical size of the target character array. As a result, if the target array is shorter than the source string (including its null terminator), the copying continues past the end of the target array. In this example, the memory immediately following the phone_ member is the address_ member. In most compilers, the result is what we saw earlier: The address_ member is overwritten with the end of the phone_ string. However, the result of writing past the end of any array is technically undefined behavior, so the program could do anything, including crash at run time.

Fortunately, as veteran C programmers know, the standard library provides a more robust form of strcpy known as strncpy, with the following prototype:

```
char* strncpy(char* to, const char* from, size_t n);
```

The additional parameter, n, of type std::size_t indicates the maximum number of characters to copy. Using strncpy judiciously can prevent undefined behavior. Listing 2.5 shows a quick fix to the program. Changes appear in **boldfaced type**.

Code Note Listing 2.5 corresponds to one of the files on the companion Web page in the Chapter 2 Code\strncpy Version directory. The files in this directory can be compiled and linked together to create an executable program.

Listing 2.5 Using strncpy to Avoid Writing Past the End of Arrays

```
 1:  // TinyPIM (c) 1999 Pablo Halpern, File Address.cpp
 2:
 3:  #include <cstring>
 4:
 5:  #ifndef _MSC_VER
 6:  // These declarations for non-Microsoft compiler. Not needed
 7:  // for MSC because these functions are not in namespace std
 8:  // in the MSC compiler.
 9:  using std::strncpy;
10:  #endif
11:
12:  #include "Address.h"
13:
14:  Address::Address()
15:  {
16:    // Initialize all strings to empty.
17:    lastname_[0] = firstname_[0] = phone_[0] = address_[0] = '\0';
18:  }
19:
20:  void Address::lastname(const char* s)
21:  {
22:    strncpy(lastname_, s, namelen);
23:  }
24:
25:  void Address::firstname(const char* s)
26:  {
```

continues

Listing 2.5   continued

```
27:    strncpy(firstname_, s, namelen);
28:  }
29:
30:  void Address::phone(const char* s)
31:  {
32:    strncpy(phone_, s, phonelen);
33:  }
34:
35:  void Address::address(const char* s)
36:  {
37:    strncpy(address_, s, addrlen);
38:  }
```

No changes are needed to Address.h or to the main program because the class interface is the same. The only thing we change is the implementation of the write-accessor functions.

At lines 22, 27, 32, and 37, we replace strcpy with strncpy. The strncpy function is exactly like strcpy except that it takes a third parameter that indicates the length of the receiving array. Strncpy never copies more than the number of characters specified, ensuring that we don't write past the end of the arrays.

Lines 5–10 are a partial workaround for the Microsoft C++ compiler. The library that comes with the MSC compiler (version 6.0) doesn't put functions from the C library into namespace std. In order to write portable code, we conditionally import std::strncpy into the global namespace, making it available without the std:: prefix. This use of the using declaration is done only for compilers that are *not* the Microsoft compiler. In lines 22, 27, 32, and 37, we use strncpy without the std:: prefix, which now works for most compilers, thanks to the using declaration.

Using the same main program as before, we get the output shown in Listing 2.6.

Listing 2.6   Output of Program Using strncpy

```
 1:  Joan Smith
 2:  The Very Big Corporation
 3:  Somewhere, MA 01000
 4:  (617) 555-9876
 5:
 6:  Joan Smith
 7:  The Very Big Corporation
 8:  Somewhere, MA 01000
 9:  (617) 555-7777 The Very Big Corporation
10:  Somewhere, MA 01000
11:
```

Things are getting better, but are not yet quite right. In lines 1–4, we see that this change does not break any previously working code, which is always a good thing.

2

In lines 7 and 8, we see that the address_ field prints out correctly, so things seem to be improving over the previous version. However, in lines 9 and 10 we see something very strange. If you look carefully, you can see that the phone number is truncated after the e and that both lines of the address are appended to the end.

To understand what is happening, step through the call to a.phone ("(617) 555-7777 ext. 112"). (You can step through in your debugger while following this discussion, if you want.) The call to strncpy copies 16 characters from the input string to the phone_ array, filling it up with the characters (617) 555-7777 e. What is missing is the null terminator. As a result, the stream output keeps reading until it finds a null character in memory, which happens to be at the end of the address_ field. Reading past the end of an array is just as much undefined behavior as writing past the end of an array, so the program could have crashed while trying to output the results.

To get rid of this new occurrence of undefined behavior, we must make sure that every string is null-terminated after using strncpy. Listing 2.7 is one more attempt to get it right.

 Note   **Code Note**   Listing 2.7 is one of the files on the companion Web page in the Chapter 2 Code\strncpy fixed directory. The files in this directory can be compiled and linked together to create an executable program.

Listing 2.7   Fix Address Class to Add Null Terminator

```
 1:  // TinyPIM (c) 1999 Pablo Halpern. File Address.cpp
 2:
 3:  #include <cstring>
 4:
 5:  #ifndef _MSC_VER
 6:  using std::strncpy;
 7:  #endif
 8:
 9:  #include "Address.h"
10:
11:  Address::Address()
12:  {
13:    // Initialize all strings to empty.
14:    lastname_[0] = firstname_[0] = phone_[0] = address_[0] = '\0';
15:  }
16:
17:  void Address::lastname(const char* s)
18:  {
19:    strncpy(lastname_, s, namelen - 1);
```

continues

Listing 2.7   continued

```
20:       lastname_[namelen - 1] = '\0';
21:   }
22:
23:   void Address::firstname(const char* s)
24:   {
25:     strncpy(firstname_, s, namelen - 1);
26:     firstname_[namelen - 1] = '\0';
27:   }
28:
29:   void Address::phone(const char* s)
30:   {
31:     strncpy(phone_, s, phonelen - 1);
32:     phone_[phonelen - 1] = '\0';
33:   }
34:
35:   void Address::address(const char* s)
36:   {
37:     strncpy(address_, s, addrlen - 1);
38:     address_[addrlen - 1] = '\0';
39:   }
```

Line 31 copies one fewer character from s into phone_ in order to leave room for the null terminator. At line 32, we add a null terminator at the end of the string, in case the part of s that we copied doesn't include a trailing null.

The final output is shown in Listing 2.8.

Listing 2.8   Output of Program After Adding Null Terminators

```
1:  Joan Smith
2:  The Very Big Corporation
3:  Somewhere, MA 01000
4:  (617) 555-9876
5:
6:  Joan Smith
7:  The Very Big Corporation
8:  Somewhere, MA 01000
9:  (617) 555-7777
10:
```

At line 9 we see that the phone number was changed without corrupting other fields and without losing the null terminator. However, the phone number that we were trying to set has now been truncated to only 15 characters, excluding the null terminator (the 15th character is a space after the last 7). The phone extension has been chopped off entirely. The program is very simple, but we are at the limit of what we can accomplish using fixed-length strings. Summarized, the advantages of using fixed-length character arrays to store character strings are

- The implementation is very simple.
- Memory management is trivial: The character arrays automatically get created and destroyed along with the enclosing object.

The disadvantages of fixed-length character arrays are

- It is easy to make subtle errors related to array length and null termination.
- If the programmed maximum length for the string is too short, the program loses information (or generates an error).
- The amount of memory dedicated to a fixed-length character array is constant, thus wasting memory if the string stored in it is much shorter than the maximum length.

Next, we will remedy some of these shortcomings by using dynamically allocated character arrays. As we shall see, for each shortcoming we cure, a new one crops up.

Switching to Dynamically Allocated Character Arrays

Before I introduce the string class library, I want to illustrate one more point using null-terminated character strings. We solve the functional problems with the fixed-length character arrays by dynamically allocating character arrays on the heap. By allocating the characters on demand, we can allocate exactly enough storage for the number of characters being stored. It sounds easy, but there lurk a number of sneaky problems. Understanding these problems and their solutions helps you understand the purpose for many of the components in the standard library as well as gives you a feel of how and when to use them.

If you are a veteran C++ programmer, you are likely to already be familiar with the solutions to the problems described here. In that case, you might want to skim this section and read the summary at the end.

Using Pointers to Dynamically Allocated Memory

When working with strings, we would like to allocate only enough memory to hold the text of a given string. The typical way to do this is to allocate memory off the heap and retain just a pointer to the first character of the allocated block. Listing 2.9 shows a new version of `Address.h` using pointers to dynamically allocated memory.

Note

Code Note   Listings 2.9 through 2.11 correspond to files on the companion Web page in the Chapter 2 Code\dynamic version directory. The files in this directory can be compiled and linked together to create an executable program.

Listing 2.9   Definition of Address Using Dynamically Allocated Character Arrays

```cpp
 1:  // TinyPIM (c) 1999 Pablo Halpern, File Address.h
 2:
 3:  #ifndef Address_dot_h
 4:  #define Address_dot_h 1
 5:
 6:  // Address class using dynamically allocated strings
 7:  class Address
 8:  {
 9:  public:
10:    // Constructor
11:    Address();
12:
13:    // Destructor
14:    ~Address();
15:
16:    // Copy constructor and assignment
17:    Address(const Address&);
18:    const Address& operator=(const Address&);
19:
20:    // Field accessors
21:    const char* lastname() const { return lastname_; }
22:    void lastname(const char*);
23:
24:    const char* firstname() const { return firstname_; }
25:    void firstname(const char*);
26:
27:    const char* phone() const { return phone_; }
28:    void phone(const char*);
29:
30:    const char* address() const { return address_; }
31:    void address(const char*);
32:
33:  private:
34:    // Variable-length data fields
35:    char* lastname_;
36:    char* firstname_;
37:    char* phone_;
38:    char* address_;
39:
40:    // Private function for making a copy of a string:
41:    char* dup(const char* s);
42:  };
43:
44:  #endif // Address_dot_h
```

2

Lines 35–38 replaced each array of characters with a pointer. Recall that in C and C++, an array of objects can be represented by a pointer to the first object in the array. Experienced C and C++ programmers know that the appearance of char* almost always represents a (null-terminated) string of characters. Because the character arrays can be of any length, we no longer need the enumeration that defines the maximum string lengths.

In line 41 we declare a private function used to create a duplicate of a string on the heap. The return value of dup is a pointer to an array of characters allocated from the heap using new[] and containing a copy of the characters in s (including the null terminator). You'll see how dup works when we get to the implementation.

Line 14 declares the Address destructor. Now that we are allocating memory from the heap, a destructor is needed to make sure the memory is returned to the heap when the Address object is destroyed. The presence of a destructor alerts us to the need for a *copy constructor* and *assignment operator*, which we declare on lines 17 and 18, in addition to the default constructor at line 11. The need for these will become clearer when we get to the implementation.

 A *default constructor* is a constructor that can be called with no arguments. If no constructor (default or otherwise) is declared for a class, the compiler will generate one that calls the default constructor for all of its base classes and data members.

 A *copy constructor* is a constructor that can be called with an object of the same class as its only argument. The purpose of the copy constructor is to construct a copy of another object. If no copy constructor is declared for a class, the compiler will generate one that calls the copy constructor for all of its base classes and data members.

 An *assignment operator* is the = operator. Used to copy the value of one object to another of the same type. If no assignment operator is declared for a class, the compiler will generate one that calls the assignment operator for all of its base classes and data members.

Notice that none of the other public members of the Address class have changed. In other words, the *interface* to Address is stable, even though its *implementation* is different.

Listing 2.10 shows the new version of Address.cpp. Most of the file has changed, so it wouldn't be very instructive to bold the changes.

Listing 2.10   Implementation of Address Using Dynamically Allocated Character Arrays

```
1:  // TinyPIM (c) 1999 Pablo Halpern, File Address.cpp
2:
3:  #include <cstring>
4:
```

continues

Listing 2.10   continued

```
 5:  #ifndef _MSC_VER
 6:  using std::strcpy, std::strlen;
 7:  #endif
 8:
 9:  #include "Address.h"
10:
11:  // Constructor
12:  Address::Address()
13:    : lastname_(new char[1]),
14:      firstname_(new char[1]),
15:      address_(new char[1]),
16:      phone_(new char[1])
17:  {
18:    // Initialize all strings to empty.
19:    lastname_[0] = firstname_[0] = phone_[0] = address_[0] = '\0';
20:  }
21:
22:  // Destructor
23:  Address::~Address()
24:  {
25:    // Clean up memory
26:    delete[] lastname_;
27:    delete[] firstname_;
28:    delete[] phone_;
29:    delete[] address_;
30:  }
31:
32:  char* Address::dup(const char* s)
33:  {
34:    // Allocate space for string, including NUL terminator
35:    char* ret = new char[strlen(s) + 1];
36:
37:    // Copy contents into newly allocated string
38:    strcpy(ret, s);
39:
40:    return ret;
41:  }
42:
43:  // Copy constructor
44:  Address::Address(const Address& a2)
45:    : lastname_(0), firstname_(0), phone_(0), address_(0)
46:  {
47:    // Use assignment operator to do the hard work
48:    *this = a2;
49:  }
50:
51:  // Assignment operator
52:  const Address& Address::operator=(const Address& a2)
53:  {
54:    if (this != &a2)
55:    {
56:      lastname(a2.lastname_);
```

```
57:        firstname(a2.firstname_);
58:        phone(a2.phone_);
59:        address(a2.address_);
60:      }
61:
62:      return *this;
63:   }
64:
65:   void Address::lastname(const char* s)
66:   {
67:      if (lastname_ != s)
68:      {
69:        delete[] lastname_;
70:        lastname_ = dup(s);
71:      }
72:   }
73:
74:   void Address::firstname(const char* s)
75:   {
76:      if (firstname_ != s)
77:      {
78:        delete[] firstname_;
79:        firstname_ = dup(s);
80:      }
81:   }
82:
83:   void Address::phone(const char* s)
84:   {
85:      if (phone_ != s)
86:      {
87:        delete[] phone_;
88:        phone_ = dup(s);
89:      }
90:   }
91:
92:   void Address::address(const char* s)
93:   {
94:      if (address_ != s)
95:      {
96:        delete[] address_;
97:        address_ = dup(s);
98:      }
99:   }
```

Lines 13–16 allocate an initial array of characters for each string member. We start with just enough space to hold the null terminator. The body of the constructor is unchanged. In lines 23–30, the destructor frees all the memory that was owned by this Address object.

The dup function copies a string on the heap. We need to allocate enough storage for the characters in the string plus an additional one for the null terminator. We do that at line 35. The std::strlen function is another function declared in <cstring>.

It returns the number of characters in a null-terminated string up to but not including the null terminator. Because of the using declaration in line 6, we don't need to use the std:: prefix for strlen.

In line 38, we use strcpy to copy s into the newly allocated array. Note that using strncpy here would be redundant and inefficient because we know that the target array is large enough to hold all the characters in s. Line 40 returns the newly copied string.

Memory Leaks and Duplicate Deletes

Forget about the copy constructor and assignment operators for a moment and get to the write accessors. It is tempting to write the lastname(const char* s) function as follows:

```
void Address::lastname(const char* s) { lastname_ = s; }
```

In other words, we could simply copy the pointer. But this creates a serious problem. If we assume s points to Jones and lastname_ points to Doe, we have the situation in Figure 2.1 before the assignment.

Figure 2.1

Pointer values before changing lastname_.

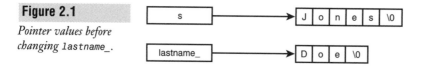

After the assignment, both pointers would point to the same value, as shown in Figure 2.2.

Figure 2.2

Pointer values after pointer assignment.

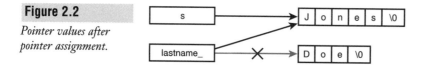

This situation causes two problems. First, the old value of lastname_ is lost, producing *orphaned memory* and a *memory leak*. More importantly, the destructor for the Address object will try to free the memory now pointed to by lastname_. But we have not established ownership of this memory. Indeed, other Address objects might contain pointers to this same memory. If more than one Address object attempts to free the same memory, the result is (you guessed it) undefined behavior.

 Orphaned memory is memory on the heap that is not referenced by any pointer. This memory can never be freed back to the heap.

 A *memory leak* is a bug in a program that keeps memory allocated even when it is no longer used. A recurrent memory leak will eventually use up all available memory.

Once this happens, subsequent memory allocations will fail, possibly leading to a crash and/or lost data.

If we want to avoid both memory leaks and undefined behavior, we must make sure that we do a *deep copy* of the character strings. In other words, we must not copy the pointers but the objects they point to. Furthermore, before modifying a pointer, we must free the memory it used to point to. The correct behavior is illustrated in Figure 2.3.

Figure 2.3

Pointer values after a deep copy.

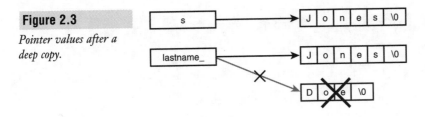

After the deep copy, each pointer points to a separate chunk of memory. Modifying or deleting one does not affect the other. The memory previously referenced in lastname_ is released back to the heap.

Creating a *deep copy* means making a copy of all the indirect subobjects in an object so that the original and the copy do not share references to the same subobjects.

Returning to the actual implementation of lastname(const char*) at line 69 in Listing 2.10, we free the old memory used by lastname_ before assigning it a new value. This avoids the memory leak. Then, at line 70, we use dup to make a new copy of the string pointed to by s and store the result in the lastname_.

Self Assignment

Line 67 contains a curious test. What happens if you have two references to Address objects, a and b, and you want to make a and b have identical lastname fields? The logical statement that would do this would be

```
a.lastname(b.lastname())
```

But what if the context were such that a and b could refer to the same object? Line 69 would delete the lastname_ array and then line 70 would try to copy the deleted array! The test in line 67 prevents this problem by checking that the two pointers are not identical before doing anything. If they are identical, you are assigning a string to itself and nothing needs to be done. The firstname, phone, and address write-accessors work exactly like the lastname write-accessor function.

Copy Constructors and Assignment Operators

Go back now and look at the assignment operator and copy constructor, which are restated in Listing 2.11. If we did not define these copy operations, the compiler would have generated member-by-member copies. In other words, each pointer member would be copied from one `Address` object to another. The result would be the orphaning and undefined behavior we saw in Figure 2.2. Thus, it is critical that we define our own copy operations to perform deep copies on all the member pointers.

Listing 2.11   Copy Constructor and Assignment Operator

```
43:   // Copy constructor
44:   Address::Address(const Address& a2)
45:     : lastname_(0), firstname_(0), phone_(0), address_(0)
46:   {
47:     // Use assignment operator to do the hard work
48:     *this = a2;
49:   }
50:
51:   // Assignment operator
52:   const Address& Address::operator=(const Address& a2)
53:   {
54:     if (this != &a2)
55:     {
56:       lastname(a2.lastname_);
57:       firstname(a2.firstname_);
58:       phone(a2.phone_);
59:       address(a2.address_);
60:     }
61:
62:     return *this;
63:   }
```

In the assignment operator, line 54 contains a test much like the one we saw at line 67. It makes the assignment a *no-op* if you try to assign an `Address` object to itself. This is a normal part of most assignment operators, both to avoid unnecessary work and to prevent the kinds of problems that we addressed at line 67. In this case, it would be harmless to leave this test out, but we include it in order to keep the idiom whole.

A *no-op (also Noop)* is an operation having the net effect of doing nothing.

Lines 56–59 call the write-accessor functions, which make a deep copy of each string field. After the copy operation is complete, the two `Address` objects contain the same data, but do not share any memory. The copy constructor uses the assignment operator to do most of the work. In line 48, we simply call the assignment operator to do the deep copies. But first we give the pointers initial null values, at line 45. It is common to call the assignment operator from within the copy constructor, but the step of initializing pointer members is often forgotten, leading to mysterious crashing bugs.

Note

> You might be surprised to see me use a raw zero (0) as the null pointer, instead of using the NULL macro. In the early days of C, it was often necessary to define NULL as something other than just 0. This led to coding rules that said "Thou shalt always use NULL to represent the null pointer." Because C was standardized in 1990, NULL and 0 have been interchangeable. Furthermore, NULL requires that you include a header file. Beware religious dogmatism in coding rules.

Because the Address public interface has not changed, we can use the same test program that we've been using all along. The output looks like Listing 2.12.

Listing 2.12   Output of Program Using Dynamically Allocated Character Arrays

```
 1:  Joan Smith
 2:  The Very Big Corporation
 3:  Somewhere, MA 01000
 4:  (617) 555-9876
 5:
 6:  Joan Smith
 7:  The Very Big Corporation
 8:  Somewhere, MA 01000
 9:  (617) 555-7777 ext. 112
10:
```

Line 9 shows the improvement. Now that the phone number string is dynamically sized, there is no more truncation.

Summary: Implementing Dynamically Allocated Strings

Eureka! Things are looking good. We have implemented the Address class using dynamically allocated null-terminated character strings. We have no bugs or memory leaks that we know of, and we are able to handle strings of arbitrary length. In moving from fixed-length character arrays to dynamically allocated character arrays, we not only had to add the dynamic allocation code itself, we also had to make the following adjustments:

- We added a destructor to free the strings that belong to the Address object.

- We added a copy constructor and an assignment operator to make sure that two Address objects do not share the same memory (or else they will both try to free it in their respective destructors).

- We had to modify the write-accessors to free the old value of a string before creating a new value.

- We had to be very careful to make sure all pointers were initialized (for example, to NULL).

We've now exhausted the C approach to strings. It is time to examine an easier way using more advanced features of the C++ Standard Library.

A Much Simpler Implementation of Address Using the String Class Library

If you have a good sense of programming aesthetics, you should be uncomfortable with the previous solution. There is an awful lot of code for such a simple class. The duplication of similar code is relatively high and the chance of making a mistake is likewise high.

Introducing the String Class

What we would like to do is encapsulate all this memory allocation, deallocation, and copying into a nice string class. Fortunately, the standard library has already done this for us. Let's reimplement the Address class using the standard string class. Listing 2.13 shows the new class definition.

 Note   **Code Note**   Listings 2.13 through 2.15 correspond to files on the companion Web page in the Chapter 2 Code\Strings version directory. The files in this directory can be compiled and linked together to create an executable program.

Listing 2.13   Definition of the Address Class Using the Standard string Class

```
1:  // TinyPIM (c) 1999 Pablo Halpern, File Address.h
2:
3:  #ifndef Address_dot_h
4:  #define Address_dot_h 1
5:
6:  #include <string>
7:
8:  // Address class implemented using std::string class
9:  class Address
10: {
11: public:
12:    // The following are automatically generated by the compiler:
13:    // Address();
14:    // ~Address();
15:    // Address(const Address&);
```

```
16:     // Address& operator=(const Address&);
17:
18:     // Field accessors
19:     std::string lastname() const { return lastname_; }
20:     void lastname(const std::string&);
21:
22:     std::string firstname() const { return firstname_; }
23:     void firstname(const std::string&);
24:
25:     std::string phone() const { return phone_; }
26:     void phone(const std::string&);
27:
28:     std::string address() const { return address_; }
29:     void address(const std::string&);
30:
31:  private:
32:     // Data Fields
33:     std::string lastname_;
34:     std::string firstname_;
35:     std::string phone_;
36:     std::string address_;
37:  };
38:
39:  #endif // Address_dot_h
```

The first thing we need to do if we want to use standard strings is to include the standard string header, which we do at line 6. This header defines a class, string, in namespace std. As the name implies, string is an encapsulation of a character string.

In the comments at lines 12–16, we assert that we don't need to create a default constructor, destructor, copy constructor, or assignment operator because the compiler will do this automagically for us. I will say more about this later in this chapter.

At lines 19 and 20, we changed the lastname function to return a string value for read access and take a string parameter for write-access. We made the same change for all the other accessors. "But wait," you say, "you're changing the interface. That's cheating!" Perhaps that's true, but there are two mitigating factors. The first is that if we had known about the string class when we first started, we would have used it instead of raw character pointers. One important quality of standard library elements is that they are *standard*. This means that you can (or should be able to) count on them being present in the compile environment. The second mitigating factor is that this change in interface has very little effect on the use of this object in practice, as we'll see shortly.

We changed all the data members to be of type std::string, which, of course, is the class that encapsulates all the copying and memory management that we did manually before. The implementation of string is not the concern, but it might be implemented in a manner very similar to the way we implemented dynamically allocated strings. On the other hand, it is common to implement string classes using efficiency tricks to reduce the number of memory allocation, deallocation, and copying operations. The fact that string is an abstraction in the library frees us from dealing with the complexities of its implementation.

The implementation file is shown in Listing 2.14.

Listing 2.14   Implementation of `Address` Using the Standard `string` Class

```
 1:  // TinyPIM (c) 1999 Pablo Halpern, File Address.cpp
 2:
 3:  #include "Address.h"
 4:
 5:  void Address::lastname(const std::string& s)
 6:  {
 7:     lastname_ = s;
 8:  }
 9:
10:  void Address::firstname(const std::string& s)
11:  {
12:     firstname_ = s;
13:  }
14:
15:  void Address::phone(const std::string& s)
16:  {
17:     phone_ = s;
18:  }
19:
20:  void Address::address(const std::string& s)
21:  {
22:     address_ = s;
23:  }
```

Where's the rest? Could the whole implementation be so small? At last we have an implementation that reflects the inherent simplicity of the Address class. The key to this breakthrough is in the proper value semantics of the string class. At line 7, we see this in action. In order to copy the value of one string to another, we simply assign it. The string class' assignment operator does the rest. No calls to strcpy, no allocations, no deallocations, and *no pointers!*

Note

Concept   Many facilities of the standard library have the effect of reducing your dependence on raw pointers. Because the use of pointers is one of the most error-producing parts of programming in C++, liberal use of these facilities can prevent introducing a substantial number of bugs in a large project.

It's worth taking a closer look at strings and how they're used.

A Natural Interface

Unlike arrays, standard strings are first-class objects. Most of their behavior is what you would intuitively expect if string were a built-in type. For example, the default value of a string is empty. As you have already seen, they have logical copy semantics. The expression *string1* == *string2* returns true if the two strings match, character-by-character (and the opposite for *string1* != *string2*). The comparison operators <, >, <=, and >= all perform a lexicographic comparison of the two strings and return the expected Boolean results.

I Don't Remember Allocating Any Memory

Return to the issue of the Address class constructors, destructors, and assignment. If we don't declare any constructors for the Address class, the compiler generates a default constructor and a copy constructor for us. In the case of the default constructor, the compiler-generated version simply calls the default constructor for each data member. The effect is that the Address object is full of empty fields, precisely what we want. The compiler-generated copy constructor calls the copy constructor for each member variable, one-by-one. Again, this is exactly what we want.

If we don't declare a destructor, the compiler automatically generates one that calls the destructor for each data member. All of Address's data members are of type string so when an Address object is destroyed, all its string members automatically clean up after themselves.

Finally, if we don't declare a copy assignment operator, the compiler generates one that does a member-by-member copy assignment. Like the copy constructor, we rely on the logical copy semantics of string to make this work exactly as we want.

In the case of the default constructor, the savings in effort are due to the logical default initialization semantics of the string class. In the case of the destructor, copy constructor, and copy assignment operator, the savings in effort are due to string's transparent handling of memory.

An Easy Replacement

Return to the Address class test program. Now that we changed the public interface of Address to be based on string instead of char*, what do we need to change in the main program? The answer, surprisingly is *nothing at all!* In Listing 2.15, look at the main program again and see what happens when we use the new Address class.

Listing 2.15   Test Program for Address

```
 1:  // TinyPIM (c) 1999 Pablo Halpern. File test1.cpp
 2:
 3:  #include <iostream>
 4:
 5:  #include "Address.h"
 6:
 7:  void dump(const Address& a)
 8:  {
 9:    std::cout << a.firstname() << ' ' << a.lastname() << '\n'
10:              << a.address() << '\n' << a.phone() << '\n'
11:              << std::endl;
12:  }
13:
14:  int main()
15:  {
16:    Address a;
17:    a.lastname("Smith");
18:    a.firstname("Joan");
19:    a.phone("(617) 555-9876");
20:    a.address("The Very Big Corporation\nSomewhere, MA 01000");
21:    dump(a);
22:
23:    // Add phone extention
24:    a.phone("(617) 555-7777 ext. 112");
25:    dump(a);
26:
27:    return 0;
28:  }
```

In lines 9–11, we output each field in the `Address` object. Looking at the first part of the statement, we see `std::cout << a.firstname()`. This expression works because `<string>` extends the I/O system with insertion and extraction operators that work with string objects. Effectively, a string can output itself and the result is what you would expect. We have substituted a string for a `char*` in this context without any change in the code. This is part of the power of the type-based I/O system in the standard library. You will learn more about type-based I/O when we start implementing classes for date and time.

At line 17, we pass a literal string, `"Smith"`, into a function that expects a string argument. A literal string has type `const char[]`, which is converted to a pointer of type `const char*` when it is passed as an argument to a function. The `string` class has a conversion constructor that accepts a `const char*` and constructs a string object with the same character sequence (but does not include the trailing null character). The result is that we can use a string literal or a `char*` in almost any context where a string value or `const` string reference is expected. Thus, the main program does not need to change at all in the transition from `char*` to `string`. The C++ *string* class provides an easy transition from *C-style strings*.

A *C-style string (or just C string)* is a null-terminated character string. The only type of string known to the C language.

 A *C++ string* is an object of type `std::string`. The preferred way to represent strings in the C++ language.

The results of running the program are identical to the results of running the hand-crafted, dynamically allocated string version (Listing 2.12).

From String Objects Back to Null-Terminated Strings

I will take a moment now to burst a bubble that is probably forming in your head about now. Just because a `char*` can be transparently converted to a string doesn't mean that it works the other way around. People who are used to working with some third-party, nonstandard `string` classes are often disappointed by the lack of automatic conversion from C++ strings to C strings (that is, `std::string::operator const char*() const`). However, the standardization committee made a well-reasoned decision not to include such a conversion in the `string` class. I will attempt to explain the logic for this deliberate omission so that you will not mutter curses under your breath every time you use the `string` class. This discussion should also teach you something about pointer ownership that will serve you in understanding other parts of the standard library.

Assume for a moment that there is a conversion operator in `string` that returns a `const char*`. The first question you should always ask when a function returns a pointer is Who owns the memory pointed to by that pointer? One possibility is that the conversion function creates a new character array on the heap and that it is the client's job to free the memory. Listing 2.16 would then be valid code.

Listing 2.16   Hypothetical Code Using Conversion from `string` to `const char*`

```
1:  extern void f(const char*);
2:  std::string s("hello world");
3:  const char* p = s; // Convert s to a const char*
4:  f(p);          // Pass p to another function
5:  delete[] p;    // Don't forget to free the memory!
```

Line 1 declares a function that takes a C-style string. At line 2, we use the existing conversion constructor to initialize a string from a `const char*`. At line 3, we convert it back to a `const char*` using a hypothetical conversion operator that returns an array allocated from the heap. At line 4 we call function `f`, passing it the array returned by the conversion at line 3. At line 5 we free the memory used by this array. The likelihood of an error that results in a memory leak is enormous. For example, Listing 2.17 is an attempt to do the same thing as Listing 2.15, but in a more concise manner. Unfortunately, it accidentally orphans memory.

Listing 2.17   A Memory Leak Caused by the Conversion Operator

```
1:   extern void f(const char*);
2:   std::string s("hello world");
3:   f(s);    // s is converted to a temp const char*
```

At line 3, s is converted from string to const char* totally transparently as a side effect of calling f(const char*). The resulting pointer is stored in an unnamed temporary variable that is passed to function f. Because the pointer is unnamed, there is no way to delete it when we're finished, and memory gets orphaned in a very subtle way.

Okay, so assume instead that the const char* resulting from an automatic conversion continues to belong to the string object itself. Using this definition, the character array would be destroyed automatically when the string that owned it was destroyed. What would the innocent-looking code in Listing 2.18 do?

Listing 2.18   Another Possible Definition for the Conversion Operator

```
1:   extern void f(const char*);
2:   extern std::string g();
3:   const char* p = g();    // Convert result of g()
4:   f(p);    // Use converted string?
```

At line 2 we declare a function, g, which returns a string by value. At line 3, we call g and convert the resulting string to a character pointer, p, using a hypothetical conversion operator that retains ownership of the resultant array. At line 4, we pass this pointer, p, to f. However, the string returned by g() is stored in an unnamed temporary variable and goes out of scope at the end of statement 3. Destroying the temporary variable also destroys the character array that was produced by the conversion (because the temporary variable "owns" the character array). By the time we pass p to f() at line 4, p points to deallocated storage and the behavior is undefined.

There is no reasonable definition for operator const char* that would prevent innocent-looking code from having either memory leaks or undefined behavior. The standardization committee decided that such constructs are simply too dangerous, even for C++.

Nonetheless, there are some times when you absolutely need to convert a string in to a plain character array. For example, to call functions written in C or other languages, it is usually necessary to use a simple character array to represent strings. Even some parts of the C++ standard library use C-style strings instead of the string class. (The fstream constructor is one such surprising case.) So what can you do?

Listing 2.19 is a rewrite of Listing 2.17, using the copy member function of string.

2

Listing 2.19   Converting a String Using the copy Function

```
1:   extern void f(const char*);
2:   extern std::string g();
3:   char p[100];
4:   p[g().copy(p, 99)] = '\0';      // Convert result of g()
5:   f(p);     // Use converted string
```

In line 3 we create p as an array of characters, instead of as a pointer. We could also have allocated p from the heap, instead. Line 4 is a bit complicated. We call g and then call the copy function on the results. The copy function takes three parameters: a character array, a length for the character array, and a position within the string to start copying. The last parameter defaults to zero, so we don't need to specify it. The copy function copies characters from the string to the character array up to the smaller of the size of the character array or the length of the string. It returns the number of characters copied. We take this return value and use it as an index to the proper location of the null terminator. Line 4 is approximately equivalent to the following three lines:

```
std::string temp1 = g();
int temp2 = temp1.copy(p, 99);
p[temp2] = '\0';
```

You're probably thinking "there's got to be an easier way." Yes, there is. Listing 2.20 shows similar code rewritten using the c_str member function.

Listing 2.20   Converting a String Using the c_str Function

```
1:   extern void f(const char*);
2:   extern std::string g();
3:   f(g().c_str());    // convert string and use conversion
```

In line 3, we convert the result of calling g to a C-style string and pass the pointer to f. The pointer returned by c_str points to a (const) null-terminated character array that is *owned by the string object*. The important thing to remember is that any change to the string object (including destruction) renders the pointer invalid. Thus, the code in Listing 2.21 will not work correctly.

Listing 2.21   Improper Use of the c_str Function

```
1:   extern void f(const char*);
2:   extern std::string g();
3:   const char* p = g().c_str();     // Convert temporary to const char*
4:   f(p);                    // oops! p is invalid
```

In Listing 2.21, we have exactly the same problem as we had with Listing 2.18. In line 3, we call c_str and store the result in p. But the destruction of the temporary string makes p invalid at the end of the very same expression. When we pass p to f in line 4, we cause undefined behavior. The difference between Listings 2.20 and 2.21 is that in the latter, we store the result of calling c_str in a named variable. Between the time we store the pointer and the time we use it, it gets invalidated.

 Tip   Avoid storing the result of calling c_str because it's hard to track when it will be invalidated.

If they have the same invalidation problem, then what is the difference between the hypothetical conversion operator in Listing 2.18 and the c_str function? The only difference is syntactic. The conversion operator can be invoked invisibly, sabotaging the innocent programmer. When you call c_str, the conversion is no longer invisible, and you are no longer innocent. Explicitness makes all the difference. If you can't keep track of pointer invalidations, it is safer to use the copy function.

In the interest of completeness, I'll mention the data function. The data member function of string works just like c_str except that it doesn't put the null terminator on the end of the string. This is useful if your string contains binary data rather than text. Because a string object does not rely on a null terminator, it can contain characters of any value, including the null character.

The Project So Far

We now have an Address class that stores the information needed for an entry in the address book. Along the way, we included library headers and used namespace std. We manipulated null-terminated character strings using library functions strcpy, strncpy, and strlen inherited from C.

When we wanted more power, we implemented dynamically allocated null-terminated character strings. Then, when that approach turned out to be complex and error prone, we reimplemented Address using the standard string class. The string class freed us from memory management headaches and proved to be easy to create, destroy, and copy.

Our next task will be to create an address book class to hold our Address objects. Along the way, we will use container class templates, which are the core of the STL portion of the C++ Standard Library. After that, we will create an editor for the Address objects. As we progress, we will use more features of strings, including functions that chop up and concatenate strings as well as input and output operations on strings.

Chapter 3

Creating the AddressBook Using Container Classes

Now that we have an Address class that we're happy with, we need to collect the addresses into an address book. According to our design we need functions to insert, erase, replace, and retrieve addresses in the address book. We will need to store our Address objects in some sort of container that permits these kinds of operations.

A *container* is an object that holds a collection of other objects.

In this section, we will define the AddressBook class and try out different containers to hold the Address objects within AddressBook objects.

Adding an Integer ID to the Address Class

Because it is possible to have entries in our address book for two people with exactly the same name, we distinguish our Address entries using a unique integer identifier. An Address object is assigned an ID when it is first inserted into an AddressBook object and this ID is used to retrieve, replace, or erase the Address entry thereafter. We reserve the special ID value of zero for an Address that has not yet been assigned an ID. Listing 3.1 shows the changes needed in the Address class.

Except where otherwise noted, the listings in this chapter correspond to files on the companion Web page in the Chapter 3 Code\Vector version directory. The files in this directory can be compiled and linked together to create an executable program. (See the end of the Introduction for information on accessing this book's companion Web page.)

Listing 3.1   Adding an ID Field to the Address Class

```
 1:  // TinyPIM (c) 1999 Pablo Halpern. File Address.h
 2:
 3:  #ifndef Address_dot_h
 4:  #define Address_dot_h 1
 5:
 6:  #include <string>
 7:
 8:  // Address class implemented using std::string class
 9:  class Address
10:  {
11:  public:
12:     // Default constructor initializes recordId to 0
13:     // and all strings to empty.
14:     Address::Address() : recordId_(0) { }
15:
16:     // The following are automatically generated by the compiler:
17:     // ~Address();
18:     // Address(const Address&);
19:     // Address& operator=(const Address&);
20:
21:     // Field accessors
22:     int recordId() const { return recordId_; }
23:     void recordId(int i) { recordId_ = i; }
24:
25:     std::string lastname() const { return lastname_; }
26:     void lastname(const std::string&);
27:
28:     std::string firstname() const { return firstname_; }
29:     void firstname(const std::string&);
30:
31:     std::string phone() const { return phone_; }
32:     void phone(const std::string&);
33:
34:     std::string address() const { return address_; }
35:     void address(const std::string&);
36:
37:  private:
38:     // Data Fields
39:     int         recordId_;
40:     std::string lastname_;
41:     std::string firstname_;
42:     std::string phone_;
43:     std::string address_;
44:  };
45:
46:  #endif // Address_dot_h
```

Line 39 declares our new identification field. In line 14, we introduce a default constructor that initializes the recordId_ to zero. In lines 22 and 23, we define read and write accessors for the recordId_ field.

The AddressBook Class

Let's begin by defining the AddressBook class's public interface. We will then experiment with ever more sophisticated implementations of AddressBook, all without changing the public interface. We will, however, add to the public interface later in our development of TinyPIM. Listing 3.2 shows a public interface that allows inserting, erasing, replacing, and accessing Address objects. We will wait until we do a more detailed design of the user interface components in Chapter 6, "An Enhanced AddressBook Using Algorithms and Sorted Containers," before we define the interfaces for searching for addresses within an address book.

Listing 3.2   Interface to the AddressBook Class

```
 1: // TinyPIM (c) 1999 Pablo Halpern. File AddressBook.h
 2:
 3: #ifndef AddressBook_dot_h
 4: #define AddressBook_dot_h
 5:
 6: #include "Address.h"
 7:
 8: class AddressBook
 9: {
10: public:
11:   AddressBook();
12:   ~AddressBook();
13:
14:   // Exception classes
15:   class AddressNotFound { };
16:   class DuplicateId { };
17:
18:   int insertAddress(const Address& addr, int recordId = 0)
19:     throw (DuplicateId);
20:   void eraseAddress(int recordId) throw (AddressNotFound);
21:   void replaceAddress(const Address& addr, int recordId = 0)
22:     throw (AddressNotFound);
23:   const Address& getAddress(int recordId) const
24:     throw (AddressNotFound);
25:
26: private:
27:   // Disable copying
28:   AddressBook(const AddressBook&);
29:   AddressBook& operator=(const AddressBook&);
30: };
31:
32: #endif // AddressBook_dot_h
```

In lines 15 and 16, we declare a couple of exception classes that will be thrown in case an address lookup fails or a duplicate ID is discovered.

An *exception* is an unusual condition (usually an error) that is handled outside the normal flow of control.

 Throwing an exception is the process of initiating exception processing. Throwing an exception is sort of like using a long-range `goto` statement to the exception processing code.

 An *exception class* is a class used as the parameter to a `throw` statement. The `throw` statement uses an exception class object to communicate with the exception processing code.

If you are not well-versed in C++ exception handling, don't worry too much. I will be using it sparingly and you can probably gloss over most such occasions.

At lines 18 and 19 we see the interface to the `insertaddress` function. In addition to the `Address` argument, this function accepts an optional parameter for the record ID. A record ID of 0 means that the `insertAddress` function should generate a new ID for the `Address` record. There will be rare cases (related to reading records from a file or database) where we will want to specify the record ID for the new record. Only in these rare cases will `insertAddress` be called with a nonzero value for `recordId`. Should a record ID be specified and conflict with an address already in the address book, `insertAddress` will throw a `DuplicateId` exception.

The rest of the functions use a record ID to designate an `Address` object with the `AddressBook` object. If a nonexistent record ID is specified, those functions throw an `AddressNotFound` exception. On line 10, we declare `eraseAddress`, which removes an address from the address book. The `replaceAddress` function on lines 21 and 22 allows an address to be modified by completely replacing the record in the address book. If the `recordId` argument to `replaceAddress` is 0 (the default), the record ID is taken from the `Address` argument. We use `getAddress`, declared in lines 23 and 24, to retrieve an address by ID.

At this point, we don't have any reason to make `AddressBook` copyable, so we declare the copy constructor and assignment operators to be private in lines 28 and 29, respectively. This frees us from worrying about implementing proper copy semantics.

Conspicuously absent from our interface are functions that look up an address by name. We will return to these functions as we discover our needs and learn more about the data structures that we might want to use in our interface.

Implementing AddressBook Using Vector

Let's return briefly to the design of `AddressBook`. Figure 3.1 shows a small piece of our UML class diagram, showing the relationship between `AddressBook` and `Address`.

Figure 3.1

The relationship between AddressBook *and* Address.

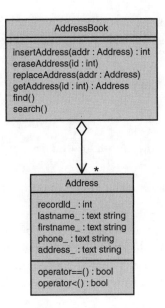

```
          AddressBook
─────────────────────────────────
insertAddress(addr : Address) : int
eraseAddress(id : int)
replaceAddress(addr : Address)
getAddress(id : int) : Address
find()
search()
```

```
           Address
─────────────────────────
recordId_ : int
lastname_ : text string
firstname_ : text string
phone_ : text string
address_ : text string
─────────────────────────
operator==() : bool
operator<() : bool
```

The AddressBook has a one-to-many compositional relationship to Address. On a data-structure level, we will need to store multiple Address objects in some container within the AddressBook object. This is the most critical part of the AddressBook data structure. One obvious candidate for this container is a plain old array of Addresses. An array is an example of a *sequence* container: a container that holds its elements in a linear order determined by the code that uses it. The standard library supplies several other sequence containers that make the job of using sequences easier.

 Note

Concept   The appearance of a one-to-many relationship in a class diagram almost always indicates the need for a container within the object on the singular side of the relationship. The container classes in the standard library make implementing these relationships easier.

Properties of the Old-Fashioned Array Implementation

Don't worry, I'm not about to introduce an elaborate implementation of AddressBook based on simple arrays, only to discard it in favor of some standard library class. However, it is worth discussing the properties of an array-based implementation so that you can better understand the motivations behind certain standard library idioms.

In Listing 3.3, we amend our `AddressBook` interface with some data elements. (This is a hypothetical change and does not show up as an actual file on the companion Web page.)

```
1:   class AddressBook
2:   {
3:   public:
4:       // ... Public interface as described in Listing 3.2
5:   private:
6:       enum { numAddresses = 100 };
7:       Address addresses_[numAddresses];
8:   };
```

Line 6 declares the size of the array that will hold the addresses, and line 7 declares the array itself. Right away we see a limitation to the array approach: It has a fixed size. If we want more than `numAddresses` addresses in our address book, we have no place to store the excess. If we have many fewer than `numAddresses` addresses, space is wasted.

We could replace our `addresses_` member with a pointer to a dynamically allocated array that we would reallocate as needed to make it grow. This would require memory management and careful attention to the constructor and destructor. It is a fair amount of work to get the dynamic sizing correct. In addition, any array will have some number of unused elements (unless we reallocate the array for every insertion and deletion). It is inefficient to be constructing `Address` objects in these unused elements.

Some of these issues should sound familiar. The limitations of fixed-sized arrays and the headaches of dynamically allocated and sized arrays are exactly the same problems we encountered when trying to represent strings effectively. It is unnecessary to take the array implementation to its logical conclusion. We understand the issues well enough to stop here and look for a better way. The standard `string` class saved us from the limitations and drudgery of raw character arrays. We'll look to the standard library again to supply us with classes that do the same thing for arrays of arbitrary type.

Declaring a Vector of Address Objects

We will now implement `AddressBook` using the standard library's `vector` container class template. A vector acts like an array except that it grows automatically as you add elements. Like the `string` class, a vector manages memory automatically and transparently. Listing 3.4 shows the new version of the `AddressBook` header file.

Listing 3.4   The AddressBook Class Using Vectors

```
1:  // TinyPIM (c) 1999 Pablo Halpern. File AddressBook.cpp
2:
3:  #ifndef AddressBook_dot_h
4:  #define AddressBook_dot_h
5:
6:  #include <vector>
7:  #include "Address.h"
8:
9:  class AddressBook
10: {
11: public:
12:   AddressBook();
13:   ~AddressBook();
14:
15:   // Exception classes
16:   class AddressNotFound { };
17:   class DuplicateId { };
18:
19:   int insertAddress(const Address& addr, int recordId = 0)
20:     throw (DuplicateId);
21:   void eraseAddress(int recordId) throw (AddressNotFound);
22:   void replaceAddress(const Address& addr, int recordId = 0)
23:     throw (AddressNotFound);
24:   const Address& getAddress(int recordId) const
25:     throw (AddressNotFound);
26:
27:   // Test routine to print out contents of address book
28:   void print() const;
29:
30: private:
31:   // Disable copying
32:   AddressBook(const AddressBook&);
33:   AddressBook& operator=(const AddressBook&);
34:
35:   static int nextId_;
36:   std::vector<Address> addresses_;
37:
38:   // Get the index of the record with the specified ID.
39:   // Returns notFound if not found.
40:   int getById(int recordId) const;
41:   enum { notFound = -1 };
42: };
43:
44: #endif // AddressBook_dot_h
```

At line 28, we declare a print member function, which we will use for testing. The print function displays the contents of the address book to the standard output device and will not be needed in the final version of TinyPIM. At line 35, we declare a static integer, nextId, which holds the value of the next unused recordId. Each time a new Address object is added to the address book, this variable is incremented to generate a new unique ID. Remember that static variables are shared by all instances of a class. Thus, two `AddressBooks` could never generate the same ID. If we ever need to create two `AddressBook` objects, we can copy records from one into the other without fearing an ID collision.

In line 36, we declare `addresses_` to be a vector of `Address` objects. The standard vector class *template* was made available by including the appropriate header on line 6. The type of object contained in the vector is provided as a *template parameter* when `vector` is *instantiated* on line 36. For the moment, think of `addresses_` as an array of `Address` objects.

 A *template* is a pattern or boilerplate that generically describes a family of possible classes or functions. (See the excursion, "A Quick Review of Templates," later in this chapter.)

 A *template parameter* is a compile-time parameter appearing within angle brackets (< >) after a template name. Template parameters can be types or values, depending on the template.

 Template instantiation is a class or function generated from a template. A template instantiation is produced at compile time by supplying template parameters to a template.

In line 40, we declare a private utility function, `getById`, which searches for an address object within the `addresses_` vector. The return value of `getById` will be the *index* of the found address object. Vectors, like arrays, can be indexed using integer subscripts. The first element in `addresses_` is `addresses[0]`, the second element is `addresses[1]`, and so on. A vector can never have a negative element index so we use -1 as a special return value for `getById` that means that the address was not found. In line 41, we give a name, `notFound`, to this special value.

EXCURSION

A Quick Review of Templates

The use of templates is ubiquitous in the standard library. A quick overview of templates is in order to make sure we have a common understanding of how they work and the terminology used.

A template is a boilerplate description used to create a class or function. It is important to note that a class template is *not* an actual class and a function template is *not* an actual function (although we often describe them that way in casual conversation). Within the template, there are named parameters that represent "blanks" in the actual implementation. When we use a template, we supply types or values that "fill in the blanks" in the template definition, somewhat like expanding a macro.

Templates enable us to describe a data structure or algorithm in a generic way, independent of the actual data it will be working with. For example, the class template, `vector`, describes a class where elements can be inserted, removed, and retrieved, regardless of the actual type of elements. Similarly, the `sort` template function describes how to sort a sequence of elements, regardless of their types.

When we supply parameters to a template, the compiler creates a real class or function to work with the actual data. We use the word *instantiate* to describe the process of creating an actual class from a class template or an actual function from a function template. Template instantiation takes place at compile time. We instantiate a class template by supplying *template parameters* in angle brackets after the template name (for example, `vector<int>`). We instantiate a function template by supplying function arguments the way we would for a normal function. The compiler *deduces* the function template parameters and instantiates the function at compile time. Thus using a template is a two-step process: first we instantiate the template at compile time, and then we use the instantiated class or function at runtime. Listing 3.5 shows a small sample of code using templates.

Listing 3.5   A Small Template Example

```
 1:  // Template declarations */
 2:  template <class T> class mytmplt { /* ... class def ... */ };
 3:  template <class A, class B> B func(A a, B b);
 4:
 5:  // Some class declaration (not necessarily a template)
 6:  class myclass { /* ... class def ... */ };
 7:
 8:  int main()
 9:  {
10:    // Use class template
11:    mytmplt<int> v;
12:
13:    // Use function template
14:    myclass x;
15:    int ret = func(x, 5);
16:
17:    // ...
18:  }
```

In line 2, we declare a class template called `mytmplt` that takes one parameter, T. The T parameter is declared as being of type `class`. In spite of this designation, T can be the name of any type: built-in type or user-defined class. (Modern compilers also permit the more descriptive keyword, `typename`, to be used instead of `class` for declaring template parameters.)

In line 11, we instantiate `mytmplt`, creating a new class, `mytmplt<int>`, which we use to create a variable, v. Although we typically express both instantiation and variable creation in a single line of code, it is important to keep these two steps separate in your mind. In line 15, we instantiate `func`, creating a new function, `func<myclass,int>`, which we call with arguments x and 5. Notice that the compiler deduced the template parameters by looking at the arguments. (x is of type `myclass`, which corresponds to template parameter A, and 5 is of type `int`, which corresponds to template parameter B.) Again, the instantiation and execution of the function template are two steps that appear as only one expression in the code. The instantiation process for this example is illustrated in Figure 3.2.

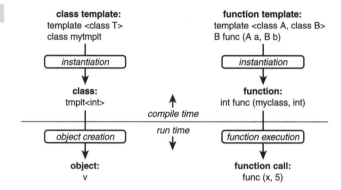

Figure 3.2

Two-step template use corresponding to Listing 3.5.

Using the Vector as an Expandable Array

The first function we will implement in our `AddressBook` class is `insertAddress`, which inserts addresses into the address book. Listing 3.6 shows our implementation of `insertAddress` using the `addresses_` vector.

Listing 3.6   Implementation of the `insertAddress` Function

```
 1: // TinyPIM (c) 1999 Pablo Halpern
 2:
 3: #ifndef _MSC_VER
 4: #pragma warning(disable : 4786)
 5: #endif
 6:
 7: #include <iostream> // For print() function
 8:
 9: #include "AddressBook.h"
10:
11: int AddressBook::nextId_ = 1;
12:
13: AddressBook::AddressBook()
14: {
15: }
16:
17: AddressBook::~AddressBook()
18: {
19: }
20:
21: int AddressBook::insertAddress(const Address& addr,
22:                                int recordId) throw (DuplicateId)
23: {
24:   if (recordId == 0)
25:     // If recordId is not specified, create a new record id.
26:     recordId = nextId_++;
27:   else if (recordId >= nextId_)
28:     // Make sure nextId is always higher than any known record id.
29:     nextId_ = recordId + 1;
30:   else if (getById(recordId) != notFound)
```

```
31:        // Explicitly-specified ID is not unique
32:        throw DuplicateId();
33:
34:     // Append record onto vector.
35:     addresses_.push_back(addr);
36:
37:     // Assign an Id to the record
38:     addresses_.back().recordId(recordId);
39:
40:     return recordId;
41:  }
```

Compiler Note   In lines 3–5, we turn off warning 4786 if we are using the Microsoft VC compiler. Leaving this warning on will cause the compiler to complain about the very long names generated internally when instantiating templates. This warning is about a limitation in the Microsoft compiler (actually, the debugger) and not about anything wrong with the code. The compiler gets so verbose about this problem, that the real errors get lost in the verbiage. I always prefer to turn this warning off.

In lines 13–19, we define a constructor and a destructor that do nothing. The constructor implicitly calls the default constructor for `vector`. Like `string`, `vector` automatically initializes itself to contain no elements. The destructor for `vector` makes sure all elements of the vector are destroyed and that memory is returned to the heap. It is unnecessary for our `AddressBook` destructor to do anything explicit to free memory because it implicitly calls the destructor for the `addresses_` vector.

EXCURSION

The Gory Details: Default Allocator Parameters

The `vector` template actually has two parameters: the type of element and an *allocator* class. An allocator is an object that is used to allocate memory. The allocator parameter to `vector` (and all other container classes) is used internally by the vector to allocate memory for its elements. A standard allocator is automatically provided as a default argument for the container. When you declare a `std::vector<Address>`, the compiler actually compiles `std::vector<Address, std::allocator<Address> >`. Most of the time, this makes no difference to you. However, most debuggers display the long name, including the allocator parameter, when displaying container classes. Often, you will see the long name in compiler or linker error messages, too, so it is good to understand what is going on.

Strings are even worse. A `std::string` is really just a typedef for `std::basic_string<char,char_traits<char>,allocator<char> >`. Some day, compilers and debuggers will be smarter about displaying the short name instead of the long name.

Allocators give the programmer a great deal of control. Writing your own allocator, however, is an advanced concept and beyond the scope of this book.

Lines 24–26 generate a unique ID for each `Address` object for the common case where an explicit ID is not specified (`recordId` is zero). In line 26, the `Address` is given an ID value of `nextId_`, and then `nextId` is incremented. However, if the caller specified a specific record ID, we need to make sure that no other `Address` records could have that ID. If the specified record ID is larger than any record ID seen so far, it is certainly unique but we must update or ID generator, `nextId_`, so that it can never generate the same ID again. The assignment in line 29 updates `nextId_` so that it is one larger than the largest ID seen so far.

One more situation that must be handled is an explicit `recordId` that is smaller than the largest seen so far. The only way to make sure it is unique in this case is to search for the record ID among the `Address` records already in the address book and throw an exception if a record is found that already has the specified ID. We do this in lines 30–32. The call to `getById` is expected to return `notFound`, or else we have a duplicate ID. We will look at the implementation of `getById` in a moment.

The heart of the `insertAddress` function is line 35. Here we use the `push_back` function of `vector` to append an element to the end of `addresses_`. The `push_back` function is fast, effectively operating in *constant time*. Vectors are design to enable fast insertion and removal of elements at the end of the sequence.

 Constant time is the performance classification of an operation that takes approximately the same amount of time regardless of the number of elements currently in the container. Computational mathematicians refer to this as "Order 1" or "O(1)." Constant time is the most desirable performance metric because the program remains fast even as the container grows.

Now `addr` has been copied into the vector, but it has not been assigned a record ID. In line 38, we get a reference to the last element of the vector using the `back` function. Since we just appended our `Address` object to the vector, `back` returns the object we just appended. We then set the record ID by calling `recordId` on the result of `back`. The `back` function also operates in constant time. We finish the `insertAddress` function by returning the record ID to the caller at line 40.

EXCURSION

The Gory Details: Constructing Only Needed Elements

You might notice that an obvious implementation of `vector` would be a dynamically-allocated array. However, when you allocate an array of elements, all the elements get constructed at once. Not only is this a wasteful use of processing time, but it requires that the element type have a default constructor. It would be preferable to construct only the elements that are in use without reallocating the dynamic array for every element insertion. The containers in the standard library do this by allocating *raw* (unstructured) memory and then constructing individual elements as needed in the raw memory. When an object is removed from the container, the destructor is called on the removed element. This also eliminates the artificial requirement that the element type have a default constructor.

Accessing Elements from the Vector

The addRecord function depends on the getById to test for duplicate IDs. The implementation of getById is shown in Listing 3.7, which is a continuation of Listing 3.6.

Listing 3.7   Implementation of the getById Function

```
42:
43:  int AddressBook::getById(int recordId) const
44:  {
45:    for (int i = 0; i < addresses_.size(); ++i)
46:      if (addresses_[i].recordId() == recordId)
47:        return i;
48:
49:    return notFound;
50:  }
```

This code is almost identical to what you would expect if addresses_ were an array instead of a vector. We loop through all the elements, comparing each element's record ID with the one we are searching for. In line 45, we call addresses_.size() to get the number of elements in the vector. All container classes in the standard library supply a size function that returns the number of elements in the container. In this case, we are using size to calculate the termination condition of our for-loop.

In line 46, we use the index operator (operator[]) to access individual elements of the vector. The index operator also works in constant time, giving us *random access* to the elements. We call the recordId function on the result of the index operation and return the index, i, if we have a match for the record ID. If the loop terminates without finding a match, we return notFound in line 49.

Random access is the capability to retrieve elements from a collection in constant time, regardless of the order in which they are retrieved.

The getById function is declared const. This means that we have read-only access to the members of the AddressBook object. Thus, to access our vector, all the vector operations we invoke must be const. The size function of vector is const because it does not modify the vector. The index operator has both const and non-const versions; the non-const version returns a reference to a modifiable object and the const version returns a const reference, so the caller cannot modify an element in a const vector. This type of interface has a quality known as *logical constness*. Logical constness means that a const container behaves like a container of const elements. There are const and non-const variants of all the operations that return a reference to a container's element. All the containers in the standard library exhibit logical constness.

> **Concept**   The containers in the standard library exhibit a quality known as *logical constness*. A const container behaves as if all its elements were also const.

Removing Address Records

Sooner or later, we will have a falling out with a friend and decide to erase his or her address from our address book. To do this, we'll need the support of our container classes. We continue our implementation with Listing 3.8, the eraseAddress function.

Listing 3.8   The eraseAddress Function of AddressBook

```
51:
52:  void AddressBook::eraseAddress(int recordId)
53:    throw (AddressNotFound)
54:  {
55:    int index = getById(recordId);
56:    if (index == notFound)
57:      throw AddressNotFound();
58:
59:    // Move element from end of vector to location being erased.
60:    addresses_[index] = addresses_.back();
61:
62:    // Remove the now unused last element of the vector.
63:    addresses_.pop_back();
64:  }
```

The eraseAddress function takes a record ID input parameter. In line 52, we use our getById function to get the index of the element in our vector containing the Address we want to erase. Lines 56 and 57 do an error check to make sure we have a valid ID.

At line 60, we get fancy. Erasing an element in the middle of a vector would be expensive because all the other elements in the vector would have to be moved forward one position. Instead, we copy the last element into the position we are vacating (line 60) and then remove the (now duplicate) last element in line 63. This takes advantage of the fact that removing the last element of a vector is a constant-time operation. The pop_back function is the easiest way to remove the last element of a vector. pop_back calls the destructor on the last element of the vector and removes it from the vector. There is no return value from pop_back.

Finishing Our Implementation

Listing 3.9 shows the rest of our vector-based implementation of AddressBook.

Listing 3.9   Rest of AddressBook Implementation

```
65:
66:  void AddressBook::replaceAddress(const Address& addr, int recordId)
67:    throw (AddressNotFound)
68:  {
69:    if (recordId == 0)
70:      recordId = addr.recordId();
71:
72:    int index = getById(recordId);
73:    if (index == notFound)
74:      throw AddressNotFound();
75:
76:    addresses_[index] = addr;
77:    addresses_[index].recordId(recordId);
78:  }
79:
80:  const Address& AddressBook::getAddress(int recordId) const
81:    throw (AddressNotFound)
82:  {
83:    int index = getById(recordId);
84:    if (index == notFound)
85:      throw AddressNotFound();
86:
87:    return addresses_[index];
88:  }
89:
90:  void AddressBook::print() const
91:  {
92:    std::cout << "*****************************************\n";
93:    for (int i = 0; i < addresses_.size(); ++i)
94:    {
95:      const Address& a = addresses_[i];
96:      std::cout << "Record Id: " << a.recordId() << '\n'
97:                << a.firstname() << ' ' << a.lastname() << '\n'
98:                << a.address() << '\n' << a.phone() << '\n'
99:                << std::endl;
100:   }
101: }
```

The replaceAddress function uses the record ID already stored in the addr argument unless a non-zero recordId argument is passed in. Lines 69 and 70 set recordId to the correct value. Lines 72–74 are the same error check we used in eraseAddress. In line 76, we use the index operator again. But this time, we are not operating on a const object. Therefore, the reference returned by the index operator is modifiable and we assign it the value of the addr parameter. In line 77, we call the non-const recordId function on the reference returned by the index operator.

The `getAddress` function in lines 80–88 is simply a wrapper around the `getById` function, adding an error check in lines 84 and 85. The `print` function in lines 90–101 is a simple loop like we used in `getById`. To avoid indexing the vector repeatedly, we briefly hold on to the reference returned by the index operator in line 95. The reference, a, is used to access the attributes of the selected `Address` object in each iteration of the loop (lines 96–98).

Does It Work?

We must test our implementation of `AddressBook`. To do this, we create a test program as shown in Listing 3.10.

Listing 3.10   Test Program for `AddressBook`

```
1:   // TinyPIM (c) 1999 Pablo Halpern. File AddressBookTest.cpp
2:
3:   #include <iostream>
4:   #include "AddressBook.h"
5:
6:   int main()
7:   {
8:      AddressBook book;
9:
10:     Address a;
11:     a.lastname("Smith");
12:     a.firstname("Joan");
13:     a.phone("(617) 555-9876");
14:     a.address("The Very Big Corporation\nSomewhere, MA 01000");
15:
16:     Address b;
17:     b.lastname("Adams");
18:     b.firstname("Abigale");
19:     b.phone("(212) 555-3734");
20:     b.address("743 Broadway\nNew York, NY");
21:
22:     Address c;
23:     c.lastname("Neighborhood Video");
24:     c.phone("555-FILM");
25:
26:     int a_id = book.insertAddress(a);
27:     int b_id = book.insertAddress(b);
28:     int c_id = book.insertAddress(c);
29:     std::cout << "*** Three Address Entries ***\n";
30:     book.print();
31:
32:     // Address d has same name as b
33:     Address d;
34:     d.lastname("Adams");
35:     d.firstname("Abigale");
36:     d.phone("(508) 555-4466");
```

```
37:     d.address("1 Small St.\nMarlboro, MA 02100");
38:
39:     // Insert address with duplicate name
40:     int d_id = book.insertAddress(d);
41:     std::cout << "*** After adding a duplicate Abigale Adams ***\n";
42:     book.print();
43:
44:     // Erase an address
45:     book.eraseAddress(a_id);
46:     std::cout << "*** After erasing Joan Smith ***\n";
47:     book.print();
48:
49:     // Replace an address
50:     c.address("22 Main St.\nMy town, MA 02200");
51:     book.replaceAddress(c, c_id);
52:     std::cout << "*** After replacing Neighborhood Video ***\n";
53:     book.print();
54:
55:     // Get and print address
56:     const Address& d2 = book.getAddress(d_id);
57:     std::cout << "*** Copy of d: ***\n"
58:               << d2.firstname() << ' ' << d2.lastname() << '\n'
59:               << d2.address() << '\n' << d2.phone() << '\n'
60:               << std::endl;
61:
62:     return 0;
63:   }
```

Our test program exercises the various functions in the AddressBook. Lines 10–28
create and insert three different Address objects into the AddressBook object. We
print the results in line 30. In lines 33–40, we prove to ourselves that we can insert
an entry with the same name as one already in the address book. We add a new entry
in line 50 and then replace that entry in the address book in line 51. Finally, we
retrieve an address from the address book in line 56. If all goes well, the address
printed in lines 57–60 will match the address that was inserted at line 40. This test
program is minimal, but it provides a good sanity check as we modify the implementation. The output from our test program is shown in Listing 3.11.

Listing 3.11 Output of the Test Program

```
 1:   *** Three Address Entries ***
 2:   *****************************************
 3:   Record Id: 1
 4:   Joan Smith
 5:   The Very Big Corporation
 6:   Somewhere, MA 01000
 7:   (617) 555-9876
 8:
 9:   Record Id: 2
10:   Abigale Adams
```

continues

Listing 3.11   continued

```
11:  743 Broadway
12:  New York, NY
13:  (212) 555-3734
14:
15:  Record Id: 3
16:   Neighborhood Video
17:
18:  555-FILM
19:
20:  *** After adding a duplicate Abigale Adams ***
21:  ******************************************
22:  Record Id: 1
23:  Joan Smith
24:  The Very Big Corporation
25:  Somewhere, MA 01000
26:  (617) 555-9876
27:
28:  Record Id: 2
29:  Abigale Adams
30:  743 Broadway
31:  New York, NY
32:  (212) 555-3734
33:
34:  Record Id: 3
35:   Neighborhood Video
36:
37:  555-FILM
38:
39:  Record Id: 4
40:  Abigale Adams
41:  1 Small St.
42:  Marlboro, MA 02100
43:  (508) 555-4466
44:
45:  *** After erasing Joan Smith ***
46:  ******************************************
47:  Record Id: 4
48:  Abigale Adams
49:  1 Small St.
50:  Marlboro, MA 02100
51:  (508) 555-4466
52:
53:  Record Id: 2
54:  Abigale Adams
55:  743 Broadway
56:  New York, NY
57:  (212) 555-3734
58:
59:  Record Id: 3
60:   Neighborhood Video
61:
```

```
62:    555-FILM
63:
64:    *** After replacing Neighborhood Video ***
65:    *****************************************
66:    Record Id: 4
67:    Abigale Adams
68:    1 Small St.
69:    Marlboro, MA 02100
70:    (508) 555-4466
71:
72:    Record Id: 2
73:    Abigale Adams
74:    743 Broadway
75:    New York, NY
76:    (212) 555-3734
77:
78:    Record Id: 3
79:     Neighborhood Video
80:    22 Main St.
81:    My town, MA 02200
82:    555-FILM
83:
84:    *** Copy of d: ***
85:    Abigale Adams
86:    1 Small St.
87:    Marlboro, MA 02100
88:    (508) 555-4466
89:
```

The program does what we said it would. Entries are inserted, replaced, erased, and retrieved from an AddressBook object. We made no effort to keep the entries in alphabetical order and right away we see that they are not. Up until line 43, it looks as though the entries will be ordered by ascending record ID. Even that ordering disappears, however, as soon as we erase an entry, as seen in lines 45–62. It is certainly desirable for an address book to keep entries alphabetically, so we'll make this a new requirement and we'll look at implementing it next.

Next Steps

In addition to a working Address class, we now have a working AddressBook that allows addresses to be inserted, erased, and modified using an integer record ID. We first explored the possibility of using plain arrays to hold the Address objects in our address book, but opted instead to use the standard library's vector template container class.

A vector is one of several sequence containers provided by the standard library. We used the push_back, pop_back, back, and size member functions as well as the index operator to access the elements of the vector as a dynamically-sized array.

We also constructed a basic test program for AddressBook that will serve us as we refine its implementation. The current implementation, though usable, does not keep address entries in any useful order. Our next step will be to explore an alternative implementation that keeps entries in alphabetical order. In the process, we will learn about the list container class template and about iterators.

In this chapter

- *Introducing the List Container*
- *Implementing* AddressBook *Using the List Container*
- *Traversing the List Using Iterators*
- *Keeping the List Sorted*

Chapter 4

An Alternative Implementation Using a List Container

At first glance, it looks as though we have a pretty efficient implementation of AddressBook. After all, we used push_back, pop_back, back, and operator[], all of which are constant-time functions. However, every one of our public functions uses the private getById function, which performs a linear search over the entire collection, looking for a match. This gives getById *linear time* performance. Therefore, all the operations on AddressBook have linear time performance. For large address books, this could become a performance problem. (I might exaggerate a bit to make a point. Although it is very unlikely that a real user would have so many address entries that the user would notice a performance degradation from inserting into the middle of a vector, there are real applications where this would be an unacceptable performance hit.)

Linear time is the performance classification of an operation whose time required is directly proportional to the number of elements in the container, on average. Computational mathematicians refer to this as "Order n" or "O(n)."

In addition, the vector implementation has the limitation of not keeping the entries alphabetized. Ideally, we would like to insert each element in its correct alphabetical order. The problem is that inserting into the middle of a vector is a linear-time operation, thus making insertAddress twice as slow as it already is. What if we could find another container that will give us performance that is no worse than linear time when looking for duplicate record IDs, but will allow faster insertion into the middle of the sequence? This should enable us to keep the container alphabetized.

> **Note**
>
> **Concept**   Often, more than one of the containers in the C++ Standard Library will meet your needs. Deciding which one to use often involves choosing among different performance trade-offs. Because the interfaces are similar, switching between container classes is usually not difficult.

Introducing the List Container

The standard library provides another container class template called `list`. The `list` and `vector` container class templates are both *sequence containers*. A sequence container is one in which the programmer chooses the place where a new element will be inserted: at the beginning, end, or somewhere in the middle. The standard specifies three sequence containers: `vector`, `list`, and `deque`.

From an interface standpoint, `list` and `deque` have a lot in common with `vector`. The `size`, `empty`, `push_back`, `pop_back`, and `back` functions have the same meaning and performance characteristics for all of them. All have default constructors that create an empty container and destructors that destroy all their contents. All have copy constructors and assignment operators that copy the entire contents of the container. As we will soon see, they also have `insert` and `erase` functions that work the same way (although not with the same performance characteristics).

The standard defines these operations in a unified way, making it easy to change your mind and substitute one container for another. There are certain requirements for all these operations (and more) that are segregated into a separate "requirements" section in the standard. Any class that meets the requirements is considered a standards-conforming container, even if the class itself is not part of the standard. This notion of presenting open requirements and supplying components that meet these requirements is seen throughout the standard library. This is what makes the standard library extensible. We'll return to extensibility later. For now, we'll take advantage of the similarity between container types to help us remember how they work.

Implementing AddressBook Using the List Container

Let's first replace the `vector` with `list` in our `AddressBook` class, as shown in Listing 4.1.

Note

> **Code Note:** Except where otherwise noted, Listings 4.1 through 4.10 correspond to files on the companion Web page in the `Chapter 4 Code\List Version` directory. The files in this directory can be compiled and linked together to create an executable program. (See the end of the Introduction for information on accessing this book's companion Web page.)

4

Listing 4.1   The `AddressBook` Class Using List Instead of Vector

```
1:  // TinyPIM (c) 1999 Pablo Halpern. File AddressBook.h
2:
3:  #ifndef AddressBook_dot_h
4:  #define AddressBook_dot_h
5:
6:  #include <list>
7:  #include "Address.h"
8:
9:  class AddressBook
10: {
11: public:
12:    AddressBook();
13:    ~AddressBook();
14:
15:    // Exception classes
16:    class AddressNotFound { };
17:    class DuplicateId { };
18:
19:    int insertAddress(const Address& addr, int recordId = 0)
20:      throw (DuplicateId);
21:    void eraseAddress(int recordId) throw (AddressNotFound);
22:    void replaceAddress(const Address& addr, int recordId = 0)
23:      throw (AddressNotFound);
24:    const Address& getAddress(int recordId) const
25:      throw (AddressNotFound);
26:
27:    // Test routine to print out contents of address book
28:    void print() const;
29:
30: private:
31:    // Disable copying
32:    AddressBook(const AddressBook&);
33:    AddressBook& operator=(const AddressBook&);
34:
35:    static int nextId_;
36:    std::list<Address> addresses_;
42: };
43:
44: #endif // AddressBook_dot_h
```

The public interface has not changed. The only change so far is that we include the list header in line 6 and we use `std::list` for our `addresses_` member in line 36.

Traversing the List Using Iterators

We turn our attention now to the `insertAddress` function. Let's first look at what it looked like in our `vector` implementation. This code formed part of Listing 3.6 and the relevant code fragment is repeated here in Listing 4.2.

Listing 4.2   Old Implementation of `insertAddress` Function Using Vectors

```
 1:  int AddressBook::insertAddress(const Address& addr,
 2:                                 int recordId) throw (DuplicateId)
 3:  {
 4:    if (recordId == 0)
 5:      // If recordId is not specified, create a new record id.
 6:      recordId = nextId_++;
 7:    else if (recordId >= nextId_)
 8:      // Make sure nextId is always higher than any known record id.
 9:      nextId_ = recordId + 1;
10:    else if (getById(recordId) != notFound)
11:      // Explicitly-specified ID is not unique
12:      throw DuplicateId();
13:
14:    // Append record onto vector.
15:    addresses_.push_back(addr);
16:
17:    // Assign an Id to the record
18:    addresses_.back().recordId(recordId);
19:
20:    return recordId;
21:  }
```

The core part of this function, lines 15 and 18, will work unchanged. The only problem area is line 10. Lists, unlike vectors, do not support indexing and do not provide random access to elements. Therefore, a function such as `getById`, which returns an index, does not make sense. In the case of vector, we were always indexing sequential elements, not really taking advantage of the random access nature of indexing. Although `list` does not support random access, it (and every other container) does support sequential access using a helper class called an *iterator*.

An iterator is like a cursor or pointer that "points" to an element in a container. Incrementing the iterator advances it to the next element. Decrementing it moves it back to the previous element. All standard library container classes provide an iterator type for traversing the elements in the collection. They also provide a function, begin, which returns an iterator to the first element in the collection as well as a function, end, which points *one past the last* element in the collection.

Rewriting our insertAddress function using iterators, we get the code in Listing 4.3.

Listing 4.3   The insertAddress Function Using List Iterators (from AddressBook.cpp)

```
 1:  int AddressBook::insertAddress(const Address& addr,
 2:                                 int recordId) throw (DuplicateId)
 3:  {
 4:    if (recordId == 0)
 5:      // If recordId is not specified, create a new record id.
 6:      recordId = nextId_++;
 7:    else if (recordId >= nextId_)
 8:      // Make sure nextId is always higher than any known record id.
 9:      nextId_ = recordId + 1;
10:    else
11:    {
12:      // Make sure we don't have a duplicate ID
13:      for (std::list<Address>::iterator i = addresses_.begin();
14:           i != addresses_.end(); ++i)
15:        if (i->recordId() == recordId)
16:          // Explicitly-specified ID is not unique
17:          throw DuplicateId();
18:    }
19:
20:    // Append record onto vector.
21:    addresses_.push_back(addr);
22:
23:    // Assign an Id to the record
24:    addresses_.back().recordId(recordId);
25:
26:    return recordId;
27:  }
```

In line 13, the phrase std::list<Address>::iterator refers to the iterator class belonging to the list<Address> instantiation of the list template. This iterator type is different from both std::list<int>::iterator or std::vector<Address>::iterator. Each instantiation of each container class template has its own iterator type.

The for loop in lines 13 and 14 is a typical idiomatic use of iterators. Figure 4.1 illustrates what is going on. The initialization part of the for loop declares an iterator, i, pointing to the first element of addresses_. The increment part of the for loop advances i to the next element. The test part of the for loop will terminate the loop when i has advanced past the end of the list.

Figure 4.1

Iterators into the
addresses_ list.

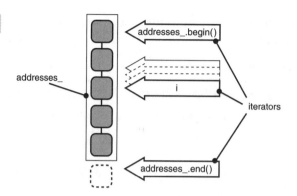

> **Tip**   Unless you need to use the result of an increment operation in a larger expression, prefer pre-increment to post-increment. For iterator classes, the post-increment operator requires creating an unnecessary temporary copy of the iterator. Thus, ++iter is more efficient than iter++.

In line 15 of Listing 4.3, we use the iterator to call the recordId function for an element of the list. We *dereference* the iterator with the -> operator, as if it were a pointer. If the recordId matches the current item, we know we have a duplicate and we throw an exception. Our whole loop has the effect of searching through the array looking for an Address object having a record ID that duplicates the one supplied by the caller.

Dereference means to take an object that refers to another object (for example, a pointer or iterator) and obtain the object to which it refers.

One way to think about iterators is as a type of *smart pointer*. We could write a very similar for loop for operating on an array instead of a list and using pointers instead of iterators, as shown in Listing 4.4. (This is sample code and is not part of the project on the Web page.)

A *smart pointer* is a class object that behaves like a pointer in that it can be dereferenced with operator* or operator->. Smart pointers can use arbitrarily sophisticated logic to reference or manipulate the pointed-to object.

Listing 4.4   Using Pointers as Iterator

```
1:  Address myarray[5];
2:  Address* begin = &myarray[0];
3:  Address* end = &myarray[5];
4:  for (Address* p = begin; p != end; ++p)
5:    if (p->recordId() == recordId)
6:      throw DuplicateId();
```

The actual for loop in Listing 4.4 is almost identical to the for loop in Listing 4.3. We initialize our pointer, p, to the beginning of our array and then increment it until it goes past the end of the array. Figure 4.2 shows the relationship between the variables.

Figure 4.2

Pointers used like iterators.

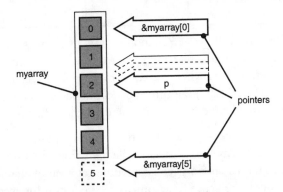

Iterators were modeled after pointers. They provide the important operators that work on pointers: ++, --, ==, !=, *, and ->. Some iterators also provide the operators +, -, +=, -=, <, >, <=, and >=. In all cases, these operators work the same way as they would for a pointer into an array. According to the requirements in the standard, a pointer into an array meets the requirements of an iterator and can therefore be used as an iterator. Later, we will take advantage of the fact that pointers *are* iterators.

 Note   **Concept**   Iterators point to elements in a collection the same way pointers point to elements in an array.

Erasing Elements Using Iterators

We could erase elements with almost exactly the same code we used for the vector implementation of AddressBook. The back and pop_back functions would work exactly the same way for the list as they did for the vector. However, we can get the job done more easily using the erase member function, as shown in Listing 4.5.

Listing 4.5   The `eraseAddress` Function Using `list<Address>::erase` (from AddressBook.cpp)

```
 1:  void AddressBook::eraseAddress(int recordId)
 2:    throw (AddressNotFound)
 3:  {
 4:    for (addrlist::iterator i = addresses_.begin();
 5:         i != addresses_.end(); ++i)
 6:      if (i->recordId() == recordId)
 7:        break;
 8:
 9:    if (i == addresses_.end())
10:      throw AddressNotFound();
11:
12:    addresses_.erase(i);
13:  }
```

Lines 4 and 5 make up the same for loop we saw in `insertAddress`. Lines 6 and 7 will stop looping if we find a matching record. If we never find a matching record ID, the loop will terminate when i is equal to `addresses_.end()`. This is another common idiom: When searching through a container, the end iterator is used to indicate the not-found condition. Lines 9 and 10 check for the not-found condition.

The real work of the `eraseAddress` function is done in line 12. Here the erase member function of `list` removes the desired element from the list and calls its destructor. The `list` container supports constant-time removal of elements from the middle of the list. Although the erase function is also supported for vectors and deques, the performance is only linear time, on average. (You can erase the last element of a vector in constant time.) The erase function is overloaded so that it can also be called with two iterators. When called that way, it erases all the elements from the first iterator up to, but not including, the second iterator.

Modifying Elements Using Iterators

The `replaceAddress` function is shown in Listing 4.6. Here we use the iterator to modify a specific element in the container.

Listing 4.6   The `replaceAddress` Function Using Iterators (from AddressBook.cpp)

```
 1:  void AddressBook::replaceAddress(const Address& addr, int recordId)
 2:    throw (AddressNotFound)
 3:  {
 4:    if (recordId == 0)
 5:      recordId = addr.recordId();
 6:
 7:    for (addrlist::iterator i = addresses_.begin();
 8:         i != addresses_.end(); ++i)
 9:      if (i->recordId() == recordId)
```

```
10:        break;
11:
12:    if (i == addresses_.end())
13:      throw AddressNotFound();
14:
15:    *i = addr;
16:    i->recordId(recordId);
17: }
```

Lines 7–12 are the same as what we saw for eraseAddress. We loop through the Address elements, looking for one with the matching record ID and throwing an exception if it is not found. At the end of this sequence (if we did not throw an exception), we have an iterator i, which points to the matching element. In line 15, we dereference the iterator and assign the element a new value through the reference returned by operator*. In line 16, we call a function, recordId, which modifies the element pointed to by i. An iterator thus provides a mechanism for modifying selected elements in a container.

Iterating Through const Containers

The next function we want to implement is getAddress. Our first attempt looks a lot like eraseAddress except that instead of erasing the element, we simply return it to the caller. This is shown in Listing 4.7.

Listing 4.7   A First Attempt at the getaddress Function

```
1:  const Address& AddressBook::getAddress(int recordId) const
2:     throw (AddressNotFound)
3:  {
4:     for (addrlist::iterator i = addresses_.begin();
5:          i != addresses_.end(); ++i)
6:       if (i->recordId() == recordId)
7:         break;
8:
9:     if (i == addresses_.end())
10:       throw AddressNotFound();
11:
12:     return *i;
13: }
```

Lines 4–10 are identical to eraseAddress (Listing 4.5). In line 12 we dereference the iterator and return the reference to the actual Address object to the caller.

There is one problem with this code: It won't compile. The getAddress function is declared const, making the addresses_ data member const in this context. If we were to be able to obtain a normal iterator into this const container, it would violate logical const safety by allowing the caller to modify the container through the iterator, the way we did in replaceAddress.

To better understand this const-ness problem, let's return to our pointer analogy. If addresses_ were an array of Address, we would iterate over its elements using a pointer to Address (that is, Address*). If we only had a const (read-only) view of addresses_ we would iterate over its elements using a pointer to const Address (that is, const Address*). What we need is an iterator that works like a const pointer. The name of the type we want is const_iterator. The meaning of const_iterator is the same as iterator except that dereferencing it produces a const reference. Thus, it is not possible to modify a container element using a const iterator. Listing 4.8 shows a rewrite of getAddress using const iterators.

Listing 4.8 Corrected Version of getAddress Function (from AddressBook.cpp)

```
 1:  const Address& AddressBook::getAddress(int recordId) const
 2:    throw (AddressNotFound)
 3:  {
 4:    for (addrlist::const_iterator i = addresses_.begin();
 5:        i != addresses_.end(); ++i)
 6:      if (i->recordId() == recordId)
 7:        break;
 8:
 9:    if (i == addresses_.end())
10:      throw AddressNotFound();
11:
12:    return *i;
13:  }
```

The only thing we changed was line 4, where we now use const_iterator instead of iterator. When called on a const container, begin and end return const iterators. In this function, i is a const iterator. In line 12, we dereference the iterator, producing a const reference to Address that we return to the caller. Just like pointers, it is possible and safe to convert a regular (mutable) iterator to a const iterator, but not vice-versa. This way, any operation that doesn't modify a container can be written in terms of const iterators, even if the container itself is not const.

At this point we notice that the code in lines 4–10 of Listing 4.8 shows up repeatedly. We can factor this code out into a private utility function, getById. In Listing 4.9 we declare this function in the class definition.

Listing 4.9 Declaration of getById Functions

```
 1:  // TinyPIM (c) 1999 Pablo Halpern. File AddressBook.h
 2:
 3:  #ifndef AddressBook_dot_h
 4:  #define AddressBook_dot_h
 5:
 6:  #include <list>
 7:  #include "Address.h"
 8:
 9:  class AddressBook
```

```
10:  {
11:  public:
...      // Public section is unchanged
29:
30:  private:
31:      // Disable copying
32:      AddressBook(const AddressBook&);
33:      AddressBook& operator=(const AddressBook&);
34:
35:      static int nextId_;
36:
37:      typedef std::list<Address> addrlist;
38:      addrlist addresses_;
39:
40:      // Get the index of the record with the specified ID.
41:      // Returns end() if not found.
42:      addrlist::iterator       getById(int recordId)
43:        throw (AddressNotFound);
44:      addrlist::const_iterator getById(int recordId) const
45:        throw (AddressNotFound);
46:  };
47:
48:  #endif // AddressBook_dot_h
```

In line 37, we define addrlist as a shorthand for std::list<Address>. The getById function declared in lines 42 and 43 returns an addrlist::iterator, which is the same as std::list<Address>::iterator. The returned iterator points to the element with the specified record ID. If the record ID is not found, it throws an AddressNotFound exception. Lines 44 and 45 declare another version of getById. This version is declared const and is thus callable from within const functions. It returns a const iterator instead of a modifiable iterator.

The full implementation of AddressBook using a list implementation is shown in Listing 4.10.

Listing 4.10   List Implementation of AddressBook

```
1:  // TinyPIM (c) 1999 Pablo Halpern. File AddressBook.cpp
2:
3:  #ifndef _MSC_VER
4:  #pragma warning(disable : 4786)
5:  #endif
6:
7:  #include <iostream> // For print() function
8:
9:  #include "AddressBook.h"
10:
11:  int AddressBook::nextId_ = 1;
12:
```

continues

Listing 4.10   continued

```
13:   AddressBook::AddressBook()
14:   {
15:   }
16:
17:   AddressBook::~AddressBook()
18:   {
19:   }
20:
21:   int AddressBook::insertAddress(const Address& addr,
22:                       int recordId) throw (DuplicateId)
23:   {
24:     if (recordId == 0)
25:       // If recordId is not specified, create a new record id.
26:       recordId = nextId_++;
27:     else if (recordId >= nextId_)
28:       // Make sure nextId is always higher than any known record id.
29:       nextId_ = recordId + 1;
30:     else
31:     {
32:       for (addrlist::iterator i = addresses_.begin();
33:            i != addresses_.end(); ++i)
34:         if (i->recordId() == recordId)
35:           throw DuplicateId();
36:     }
37:
38:     // Append record onto vector.
39:     addresses_.push_back(addr);
40:
41:     // Assign an Id to the record
42:     addresses_.back().recordId(recordId);
43:
44:     return recordId;
45:   }
46:
47:   AddressBook::addrlist::iterator
48:   AddressBook::getById(int recordId) throw (AddressNotFound)
49:   {
50:     for (addrlist::iterator i = addresses_.begin();
51:          i != addresses_.end(); ++i)
52:       if (i->recordId() == recordId)
53:         return i;
54:
55:     throw AddressNotFound();
56:   }
57:
58:   AddressBook::addrlist::const_iterator
59:   AddressBook::getById(int recordId) const throw (AddressNotFound)
60:   {
61:     for (addrlist::const_iterator i = addresses_.begin();
62:          i != addresses_.end(); ++i)
```

```
63:        if (i->recordId() == recordId)
64:          return i;
65:
66:      throw AddressNotFound();
67:  }
68:
69:  void AddressBook::eraseAddress(int recordId)
70:      throw (AddressNotFound)
71:  {
72:      addrlist::iterator i = getById(recordId);
73:      addresses_.erase(i);
74:  }
75:
76:  void AddressBook::replaceAddress(const Address& addr, int recordId)
77:      throw (AddressNotFound)
78:  {
79:      if (recordId == 0)
80:        recordId = addr.recordId();
81:
82:      addrlist::iterator i = getById(recordId);
83:
84:      *i = addr;
85:      i->recordId(recordId);
86:  }
87:
88:  const Address& AddressBook::getAddress(int recordId) const
89:      throw (AddressNotFound)
90:  {
91:      return *getById(recordId);
92:  }
93:
94:  void AddressBook::print() const
95:  {
96:      for (addrlist::const_iterator i = addresses_.begin();
97:          i != addresses_.end(); ++i)
98:      {
99:        const Address& a = *i;
100:       std::cout << "Record Id: " << a.recordId() << '\n'
101:               << a.firstname() << ' ' << a.lastname() << '\n'
102:               << a.address() << '\n' << a.phone() << '\n'
103:               << std::endl;
104:    }
105: }
```

Analyzing Listing 4.10 briefly, we see getById defined in lines 47–56. Lines 50–52 are a copy of the for loop we've seen before except that if we find the record ID we are looking for, we simply return it in line 53. If we ever get to line 55, it means the record ID was not found and we throw an exception. Lines 58–67 are another implementation of getById containing exactly the same code as lines 47–56, except that we used a const iterator instead of a regular iterator. This makes it possible to call this version of getById() from within another const method.

In lines 72 and 82, we simply substituted a call to getById for the explicit loop we had before. The result of getById is an iterator pointing to the Address object we are looking for (or else getById would have thrown an exception). In line 91, we implement getAddress as a simple call to getById, dereferencing the returned iterator to get the Address reference.

In lines 96 and 97, we implement print using an iterator for loop instead of an indexing for loop (because indexing doesn't work for list objects). In line 99 we dereference the iterator instead of indexing a vector.

The output in Listing 4.11 is almost identical to the vector version.

Listing 4.11   Output of List Version of AddressBook

```
 1:  *** Three Address Entries ***
 2:  Record Id: 1
 3:  Joan Smith
 4:  The Very Big Corporation
 5:  Somewhere, MA 01000
 6:  (617) 555-9876
 7:
 8:  Record Id: 2
 9:  Abigale Adams
10:  743 Broadway
11:  New York, NY
12:  (212) 555-3734
13:
14:  Record Id: 3
15:   Neighborhood Video
16:
17:  555-FILM
18:
19:  *** After adding a duplicate Abigale Adams ***
20:  Record Id: 1
21:  Joan Smith
22:  The Very Big Corporation
23:  Somewhere, MA 01000
24:  (617) 555-9876
25:
26:  Record Id: 2
27:  Abigale Adams
28:  743 Broadway
29:  New York, NY
30:  (212) 555-3734
31:
32:  Record Id: 3
33:   Neighborhood Video
34:
35:  555-FILM
36:
37:  Record Id: 4
```

```
38:   Abigale Adams
39:   1 Small St.
40:   Marlboro, MA 02100
41:   (508) 555-4466
42:
43:   *** After erasing Joan Smith ***
44:   Record Id: 2
45:   Abigale Adams
46:   743 Broadway
47:   New York, NY
48:   (212) 555-3734
49:
50:   Record Id: 3
51:    Neighborhood Video
52:
53:   555-FILM
54:
55:   Record Id: 4
56:   Abigale Adams
57:   1 Small St.
58:   Marlboro, MA 02100
59:   (508) 555-4466
60:
61:   *** After replacing Neighborhood Video ***
62:   Record Id: 2
63:   Abigale Adams
64:   743 Broadway
65:   New York, NY
66:   (212) 555-3734
67:
68:   Record Id: 3
69:    Neighborhood Video
70:   22 Main St.
71:   My town, MA 02200
72:   555-FILM
73:
74:   Record Id: 4
75:   Abigale Adams
76:   1 Small St.
77:   Marlboro, MA 02100
78:   (508) 555-4466
79:
80:   *** Copy of d: ***
81:   Abigale Adams
82:   1 Small St.
83:   Marlboro, MA 02100
84:   (508) 555-4466
85:
```

In lines 44–59, notice that in that the Address entries appear in increasing order of record ID. This stands in contrast to the vector version where, after an erase, the entries appeared in no particular order. This might not seem like much of an advantage at this point, but it does show how the ability to quickly insert and erase elements in the middle of a list increases our options for keeping our list ordered in some way. We will use this ability to keep our list sorted. The trade-off is that we can't access an element at random using its index.

Keeping the List Sorted

So far, our list implementation of `AddressBook` is no more efficient than our vector implementation. Both require linear searches to find elements and both use constant-time operations to insert and remove elements. However, the list has opened up the possibility of keeping the list ordered in some meaningful way. We will now take the implementation one step further by keeping our list alphabetized.

Adding Relational Operators to Our `Address` Class

To keep a container sorted, we must be able to compare any two objects and determine which should come first in the sort order. The most common way we do this is to use relational operators (<, >, ==, and so on), which provide a "natural" sort order for the objects concerned. Our `Address` class does not provide relational operators yet, so we define them in Listing 4.12.

 Note

Code Note: Except where otherwise noted, Listings 4.12 through 4.15 correspond to files on the companion Web page in the `Chapter 4 Code\Sorted List Version` directory. The files in this directory can be compiled and linked together to create an executable program.

Listing 4.12   Relational Operators for the `Address` Class (Appended to Address.h)

```
1:  bool operator==(const Address&, const Address&);
2:  bool operator< (const Address&, const Address&);
3:
4:  #include <utility>
5:  using namespace std::rel_ops;
```

Line 1 declares an equality operator for `Address`. It will return true if two `Address` objects have the same last name, first name, phone number, and address. Line 2 declares a less-than operator for `Address`. It will return true if the last name of the first `Address` object is less than the last name of the second `Address` object. If both objects have the same last name, the first names are compared. In other words, the less-than operator will return true if the first Address object comes before the second one in normal alphabetical order. The less-than operator ignores the phone number and address fields.

The utility header included in line 5 defines a namespace, std::rel_ops, which is a small namespace nested within namespace std. In line 6, we put all the identifiers from namespace std::rel_ops into global scope. This namespace contains template definitions for the relational operators !=, >, <=, and >=. When we bring these definitions into our scope with the using directive, any class that defines == and < will automatically be usable with the other four relational operators. Note that the using directive applies to the entire scope; it does not work on a per-class basis.

Warning   In some situations, especially with nonconforming compilers, using std::rel_ops will cause overloading ambiguities in cases where a class already has relational operators defined. The code in Listing 4.12 is for instructional purposes and should not necessarily be considered good practice.

The definitions of operators != and < for Address objects are shown in Listing 4.13.

Listing 4.13   Implementation of Relational Operators for Address (from Address.cpp)

```
 1: bool operator==(const Address& a1, const Address& a2)
 2: {
 3:   return (a1.lastname() == a2.lastname() &&
 4:           a1.firstname() == a2.firstname() &&
 5:           a1.phone() == a2.phone() &&
 6:           a1.address() == a2.address());
 7: }
 8:
 9: bool operator< (const Address& a1, const Address& a2)
10: {
11:   if (a1.lastname() < a2.lastname())
12:     return true;
13:   else if (a2.lastname() < a1.lastname())
14:     return false;
15:   else
16:     return (a1.firstname() < a2.firstname());
17: }
```

The implementation is straightforward. The equality operator in lines 1–7 returns true if all the member variables compare equal. The less-than operator in lines 9–17 checks the last names first. If neither last name is less than the other, it compares the first names. Note that neither operator function needs to be a *friend* of the Address class because they both work entirely by using public accessors.

A *friend* is a function or class that is allowed to access the private members of another class. A function or class is granted friendship by declaring it as such using the friend keyword within the grantor's definition. (Look up friend in a good C++ text-book for more information.)

Inserting Address Objects in Alphabetical Order

Our task now is to insert our Address objects in alphabetical order. An entry is in alphabetical order if it is the same or compares greater than the entry before it *and* it is the same or compares less than the entry after it. Therefore, in order to insert in alphabetical order, we should insert before the first entry that compares larger than the one we are inserting. We do this by adding a loop to our insertAddress function, as shown in Listing 4.14.

Listing 4.14   Alphabetical insertAddress Function (from AddressBook.cpp)

```
 1:    int AddressBook::insertAddress(const Address& addr,
 2:                                    int recordId) throw (DuplicateId)
 3:    {
 4:      if (recordId == 0)
 5:        // If recordId is not specified, create a new record id.
 6:        recordId = nextId_++;
 7:      else if (recordId >= nextId_)
 8:        // Make sure nextId is always higher than any known record id.
 9:        nextId_ = recordId + 1;
10:      else
11:      {
12:        for (addrlist::iterator i = addresses_.begin();
13:             i != addresses_.end(); ++i)
14:          if (i->recordId() == recordId)
15:            throw DuplicateId();
16:      }
17:
18:      addrlist::iterator i;
19:      for (i = addresses_.begin(); i != addresses_.end(); ++i)
20:        if (addr < *i)
21:          break;
22:
23:      // Insert record into vector.
24:      i = addresses_.insert(i, addr);
25:
26:      // Assign an Id to the record
27:      i->recordId(recordId);
28:
29:      return recordId;
30:    }
```

In line 18, we declare an iterator that will point to the element before which we want to insert. We find that element by looping through the list in line 19 and terminating the loop when we find an element that compares larger than `addr` (lines 20 and 21). At line 24, we call the `insert` member function of `list` to insert `addr` before the element pointed to by `i`. The return value of `insert` is an iterator to the newly inserted element. In line 27, we use this iterator to set the `recordId` of the new element. All sequence containers provide an insert function that works the same way. However, of the standard sequence containers, only `list` accomplishes the insert in constant time (`vector` and `deque` insert in linear time).

What happens if the loop in lines 19–21 reaches the end of the list, as would happen if `addr` were larger than any element already in `addresses_`? The loop will terminate with `i` equal to `addresses_.end()`. Inserting at this location is exactly the same as calling `push_back`—that is, it inserts the new element after the last element of the list. Because the new element is larger than any other in the list, inserting at the end is exactly what we want in this case. This would also happen if `addresses_` were empty.

We are not quite finished yet. Although we are inserting in alphabetical order, the ordering could be messed up by modifying an entry's name fields using `replaceAddress`. The simplest way to fix this is to make `replaceAddress` erase the old entry and insert the new one, as shown in Listing 4.15.

Listing 4.15   Changed `replaceAddress` to Maintain Sorted Order

```
1:   void AddressBook::replaceAddress(const Address& addr, int recordId)
2:     throw (AddressNotFound)
3:   {
4:     if (recordId == 0)
5:       recordId = addr.recordId();
6:
7:     eraseAddress(recordId);
8:     insertAddress(addr, recordId);
9:   }
```

This version of `relaceAddress` could be a bit inefficient in the case where the name fields don't change. We could make it more efficient by checking for this common special case, but we won't bother for now.

The output of our test program for the improved `AddressBook` is shown in Listing 4.16.

```
 1:  *** Three Address Entries ***
 2:  Record Id: 2
 3:  Abigale Adams
 4:  743 Broadway
 5:  New York, NY
 6:  (212) 555-3734
 7:
 8:  Record Id: 3
 9:   Neighborhood Video
10:
11:  555-FILM
12:
13:  Record Id: 1
14:  Joan Smith
15:  The Very Big Corporation
16:  Somewhere, MA 01000
17:  (617) 555-9876
18:
19:  *** After adding a duplicate Abigale Adams ***
20:  Record Id: 2
21:  Abigale Adams
22:  743 Broadway
23:  New York, NY
24:  (212) 555-3734
25:
26:  Record Id: 4
27:  Abigale Adams
28:  1 Small St.
29:  Marlboro, MA 02100
30:  (508) 555-4466
31:
32:  Record Id: 3
33:   Neighborhood Video
34:
35:  555-FILM
36:
37:  Record Id: 1
38:  Joan Smith
39:  The Very Big Corporation
40:  Somewhere, MA 01000
41:  (617) 555-9876
42:
43:  *** After erasing Joan Smith ***
44:  Record Id: 2
45:  Abigale Adams
46:  743 Broadway
47:  New York, NY
48:  (212) 555-3734
49:
50:  Record Id: 4
```

```
51:   Abigale Adams
52:   1 Small St.
53:   Marlboro, MA 02100
54:   (508) 555-4466
55:
56:   Record Id: 3
57:    Neighborhood Video
58:
59:   555-FILM
60:
61:   *** After replacing Neighborhood Video ***
62:   Record Id: 2
63:   Abigale Adams
64:   743 Broadway
65:   New York, NY
66:   (212) 555-3734
67:    output
68:   Record Id: 4
69:   Abigale Adams
70:   1 Small St.
71:   Marlboro, MA 02100
72:   (508) 555-4466
73:
74:   Record Id: 3
75:    Neighborhood Video
76:   22 Main St.
77:   My town, MA 02200
78:   555-FILM
79:
80:   *** Copy of d: ***
81:   Abigale Adams
82:   1 Small St.
83:   Marlboro, MA 02100
84:   (508) 555-4466
85:
```

A quick perusal of the output should convince you that the entries are inserted in alphabetical order and that they remain alphabetical through erasure and replacement of entries.

Next Steps

Our address book now keeps entries sorted alphabetically. We did this by using the list container class template instead of vector, taking advantage of the fact that list has operations for fast insertion and removal of elements in the middle. When we switched container types, we lost the ability to randomly access elements by index. To traverse our list, we had to learn about iterators and their pointer-like behaviors. We also learned a bit about the trade-offs in choosing a container type.

Our next task is to create an editor for our `Address` objects, so we can create new entries to insert into our address book. As we progress, we will use more features of `string`, including functions that chop-up and concatenate strings, as well as input and output operations on strings.

Chapter 5

Editing Addresses with Strings and I/O

Now we shift our attention away from the core classes to the user interface classes. The user will be composing and modifying the address book entries by means of some kind of editor. The editor must enable the user to enter text for each of the four fields in an Address object. The editor should also enable the user to modify an existing Address object without reentering all the fields.

A Specification for Editor Operation

In Chapter 1, "Introducing TinyPIM," we did a top-level requirements analysis for TinyPIM but left some detail for later. Before we can design and implement the editor section of the program, we need to fill in some of this detail.

Each Address object is a collection of fields. The first name, last name, and phone number fields are single-line fields; the address field can contain multiple lines. The Address editor will actually be an editor within an editor: A simple, line-based text editor will be called from within an outer editor that presents the fields one at a time. The user interface can be described by the following rules:

- For each line of each field in the record, the user will be presented with a prompt containing the name of the field being edited (for example "first name") and the current value of the current line of the field. For single-line fields, a "line" means the entire field in these rules.

- If the user types in a new string and presses the Enter (Return) key, the new text replaces the old text for the line.

- If the user presses the Enter key without entering any other text, the line is left unchanged.

- If the user types a single period (.) and presses Enter, the current line is left unchanged, all other changes are committed and the entire editing session ends without advancing to the next field. This is a short-cut for finishing the edit session when the user has finished all his or her edits.

- If the user types !x and presses Enter, all changes in the edit session are discarded and the edit session is terminated. This allows the user to abort after making a mistake.

For multiple-line fields, the following rules also apply:

- When all the lines in the field have been presented, editing continues as though there were blank lines at the end. The user could thus add lines to the field by "editing" these empty lines.

- If the user types !n and presses Enter, the current line is left unchanged and the editor advances to the next field.

- If the user types !i and presses Enter, a blank line is inserted before the current one. The editor then presents this empty line for editing.

- If the user types !d and presses Enter, the current line is deleted and the editor advances to the next line.

The same rules apply for editing both address book records and date book records. As you can see, there is nothing sophisticated here. No windows or dialog boxes. No cursor control and full-screen editing. Our interface is primitive because the C++ Standard Library does not provide facilities for graphical user interfaces. Perhaps part of the reason that the library does not provide any facilities for modern interfaces is that there are already C and C++ bindings for the popular user interface libraries such as X Window, Microsoft Foundation Classes, and the Macintosh Toolkit. Graphical user interface libraries have historically been considered to be the province of operating systems, not portable computer languages, although this is certainly an arguable point today, given languages such as Java and portable windowing systems such as X Window.

Whatever the reason, it is a simple fact that the C++ Standard Library only supports basic text and binary input and output, so I will stick to the C++ input/output library in this book. This is not entirely a bad thing. The C++ I/O streams library is very useful for file input and output and using it as we do in this book will allow us to explore its nooks and crannies.

The Editor Base Class

Now that we have completed a specification for the editor user interface, let's move on to the design. Figure 5.1 shows the piece of the UML class diagram concerning the editors.

Figure 5.1

UML class diagram of editor classes.

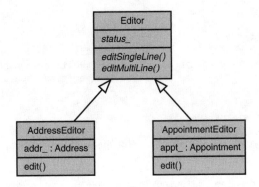

The `Editor` base class implements the inner editor of our editor-within-an-editor design. It provides two functions for single-field editing: one for editing single-line fields such as last name, the other for editing multiple-line fields such as address.

The derived classes implement the outer editor in our design. Each derived class implements an `edit` function that knows about the layout and meaning of fields for a specific record type. `AddressEditor` will call the `Editor` functions for each field in an `Address` record and `AppointmentEditor` will call the `Editor` functions for each field in an `Appointment` record.

Converting our design into code, Listing 5.1 shows the class definition for `Editor`.

 Note   **Code Note**   Listings 5.1–5.6 correspond to files on the companion Web page in the `Chapter 5 Code\Editor` directory. The files in this directory can be compiled and linked together to create an executable program. (See the end of the Introduction for information on accessing this book's companion Web page.)

Listing 5.1   The Editor Base Class

```
1:  // TinyPIM (c) 1999 Pablo Halpern. File Editor.h
2:
3:  #ifndef Editor_dot_h
4:  #define Editor_dot_h 1
5:
```

continues

Listing 5.1   continued

```
 6:   #include <string>
 7:
 8:   // Editor base class.
 9:   // Provides basic functionality for single- and multi-line editing.
10:   class Editor
11:   {
12:   public:
13:     enum editStatus {
14:       normal,    // Edit is proceeding normally
15:       finished,  // User has indicated that editing is complete.
16:       canceled   // User has indicated that editing should be canceled.
17:     };
18:
19:     Editor() : status_(normal) { }
20:
21:     // Edit a single line of text. The prompt and initial value are
22:     // passed in.  This function modifies the value and returns true if
23:     // edit status is normal or false if editing is finished or
24:     // canceled.  The following inputs have special meaning:
25:     //
26:     //    [CR]  Pressing [ENTER] will leave value unchanged.
27:     //    .     A period by itself signals that editing is complete.
28:     //    !x    signals that editing should be canceled.
29:     bool editSingleLine(const std::string& prompt, std::string& value);
30:
31:     // Edit a multi-line string. The prompt for all lines and an
32:     // initial multi-line value are passed in. The edited string is
33:     // stored back in value.  Within the edit session, each line is
34:     // edited separately.  This function modifies the value and returns
35:     // true if edit status is normal or false if editing is finished or
36:     // canceled.  The following inputs have special meaning:
37:     //
38:     //    [CR]  Pressing [ENTER] without entering any text will
39:     //          leave the current line unchanged and advance to the
40:     //          next line.
41:     //    .     A period by itself signals that editing is complete.
42:     //    !x    signals that editing should be canceled.
43:     //    !n    Editing this field is complete. Caller should advance
44:     //          to next field (status remains normal).
45:     //    !i    Insert a new line before the current one.
46:     //    !d    Delete the current line.
47:     bool editMultiLine(const std::string& prompt, std::string& value);
48:
49:     // Return the status of the edit.
50:     editStatus status() const { return status_; }
51:
52:   private:
53:     editStatus status_;
54:   };
55:
56:   #endif // Editor_dot_h
```

Most of the definition is comments. The `editSingleLine` and `editMultiLine` functions, declared at lines 29 and 47 respectively, both take two arguments: a prompt string and a value to edit. Both functions return a Boolean value of true if editing was terminated normally, by pressing Enter in the case of a single line, or by typing `!n` in the case of multiple lines.

If editing was terminated by the user entering either a single period (`.`) or `!x`, the status of the edit becomes `finished` or `canceled`, respectively, as defined in the enumeration at lines 13–17. The `status` function at line 50 returns the status of the last call to one of the edit functions. At line 19 the constructor initializes the status to `normal`. If status is not `normal`, `editSingleLine` and `editMultiLine` will return false.

Displaying a Prompt Using Type-Specific Output

We begin with the implementation of `editSingleLine`. This function must display the prompt to the user, read a line of text from the terminal, and decide what to do with the input. Listing 5.2 shows the code for `editSingleLine`.

Listing 5.2   Implementation of `Editor::editSingleLine`

```
 1:  // TinyPIM (c) 1999 Pablo Halpern. File Editor.cpp
 2:
 3:  #include <iostream>
 4:  #include "Editor.h"
 5:
 6:  bool Editor::editSingleLine(const std::string& prompt,
 7:                                  std::string& value)
 8:  {
 9:    status_ = normal;
10:
11:    std::cout << prompt;
12:    if (! value.empty())
13:      std::cout << " [" << value << ']';
14:    std::cout << ": ";
15:
16:    std::string result;
17:    std::getline(std::cin, result, '\n');
18:
19:    // Clear input state and abort edit if an input error occurred
20:    if (std::cin.fail())
21:    {
22:      status_ = canceled;
23:      return false;
24:    }
25:
26:
27:    // If user pressed return key without entering anything,
28:    // leave value unchanged.
```

continues

Listing 5.2   continued

```
29:    if (result.empty())
30:      return true;
31:
32:    // If user entered a period by itself, then end edit.
33:    if (result == ".")
34:    {
35:      status_ = finished;
36:      return false;
37:    }
38:
39:    // If user entered the abort code, then abort.
40:    if (result == "!x")
41:    {
42:      status_ = canceled;
43:      return false;
44:    }
45:
46:    // Return new string
47:    value = result;
48:    return true;
49:  }
50:
```

The code is surprisingly long but quite straightforward. In lines 11–14, we display a prompt to the user. Line 11 simply sends the prompt string to the standard output device. If the `prompt` string does not end in a newline character, the output will not end in a newline and the cursor on our text-based terminal will stay at the end of the line. If the string being edited is not empty, we want to display it to the user so that he or she can see the old value. In line 13, we format the string being edited within square brackets ([ ]). We end our prompt with a colon and a space in line 14.

The prompt code was implemented using the insertion operator (<<) for output streams. At line 13, the insertion operator enables us to chain together a sequence of formatted output operations; first we outputted the null-terminated character string, " [" (type `const char*`), then the standard string value, (type `std::string`), and finally the single character, ']', (type `char`). The machinery for printing each individual data type is different. In addition, the integer, floating point, and other types each require their own output machinery, although you would still use the same output syntax.

The standard library relies on operator overloading to implement the type-specific output machinery. The `std::cout` object represents the standard output device and is an instance of a class called `std::ostream`. (The `std::cerr` and `std::clog` objects are also instances of `std::ostream`, representing the standard error and standard logging devices, respectively.) When the compiler sees `std::cout << x`, it looks at all the currently visible overloaded versions of `operator<<` and selects the one in which the first argument is of type `std::ostream` and the second argument is the type of `x`. Each overloaded version of `operator<<` works differently, thus giving each type its own machinery for output.

Thus, when the code says

```
std::cout << 5;
```

the compiler invokes the following member function of `ostream`:

```
class ostream
{
public:
  ostream& operator<< (int);
  // ...
}
```

In other words, the use of the `<<` operator translates into the following function call:

```
std::cout.operator<<(5);
```

In contrast, when the code says

```
std::string s("hello");
std::cout << s;
```

the compiler invokes the following global (not member) function:

```
std::ostream& operator<<(std::ostream&, const std::string&);
```

So in the case of `std::string`, the use of the `<<` operator translates into the global function call as follows:

```
operator<<(std::cout, s);
```

The `ostream` class has member functions for `operator<<` overloaded for all the built-in types such as `char`, `int`, `float`, and so on. Other types, such as `std::string`, are handled by versions of `operator<<` that are global.

C++ programmers who come from a C background often continue to use the `printf` function from the C Standard Library for formatted output, even after having switched to C++. The `printf` function uses a formatting string to indicate the type of parameter that comes next—for example, `"%d"` for an integer. If you are a `printf` adherent, consider the following reasons to switch to using ostreams: The operator notation of C++ output streams is efficient because it uses overloading; the choice of which formatting function to use is made at compile time. This also makes it *type safe*, preventing potential crashes that can come as a result of passing one type but telling the library that you are passing a different type (as too often happens in the case of `printf`). The operator notation makes the syntax look like it were built into the language, even though it is actually part of the library. Finally, the mechanism is extensible, as we will see when we implement the date and time classes.

Type safe is a construct in which the compiler prevents the program from believing that an object is of a different type than it actually is, thus preventing it from misinterpreting the data (and causing undefined behavior). The C++ language provides mechanisms (such as certain casts) that allow the programmer to deliberately violate type safety at his or her own risk.

As we proceed, you'll learn that the streams library lets you do everything that `printf` (and its input counterpart, `scanf`) let you do, and more.

EXCURSION

Unformatted Input and Output

The insert and extract operators (<< and >>, respectively) perform *formatted* I/O. This means that they interpret the stream as something that makes sense to humans, not just computers. The formatted I/O functions convert an integer into a sequence of digits or vice versa, break the input into words separated by whitespace, and so on.

Sometimes it is necessary to treat a stream as a sequence of characters without regard to the meaning of the characters. This is called *unformatted input and output*.

The `ostream` class provides the following member functions for unformatted output:

* `put(char c)` writes a single character, `c`.
* write(const char* s, unsigned n) writes n characters starting at s.

The `istream` functions for unformatted input are more extensive:

* `get()` reads and returns a single character from the input stream.
* `get(char& c)` reads a single character, c, from the input stream.
* `get(char* s, unsigned n, char delim = '\n')` reads up to n-1 characters from the input stream and puts them in the buffer pointed to by s, stopping either when n-1 characters have been read or when the `delim` character is encountered, whichever comes first. The `delim` character is not extracted. A null terminator is always appended to the buffer.
* `getline(char* s, unsigned n, char delim = '\n')` works like `get` except that the delimiter is read and discarded. Also, if n-1 characters are read before the delimiter is found, the stream's `failbit` flag is set (which causes `fail()` to return true).
* `read(char* s, unsigned n)` reads n characters and stores them in the buffer pointed to by s. A null terminator is not appended to s.

The `get`, `getline`, and `read` functions set the stream's `eofbit` flag if end of file is encountered before all the requested characters have been read. The `read` function also sets `failbit` in this case.

If the output stream is redirected to a device that permits repositioning the output pointer (random access), the following functions are available:

* `tellp()` returns the current stream position.
* `seekp(position)` moves the output pointer to the specified position.

- `seekp(offset, dir)` moves the output pointer by the specified offset amount. The `dir` parameter can be `ios::beg`, `ios::cur`, or `ios::end`, to specify whether the offset should be counted from the beginning, current position, or end of the stream.

The corresponding `istream` functions are `tellg` and `seekg` (overloaded the same way as `seekp`). In case you're wondering, the "p" in `tellp` and `seekp` means "put" and the "g" in `tellg` and `seekg` means "get."

Accepting User Input and Handling Errors

The type-specific output mechanism has an exact counterpart on the input side, using the >> operator from an `istream` object instead of the << operator to an `ostream` object. Returning to Listing 5.1, then, you might be surprised to see that we don't use the >> operator in line 17. The problem with >> in this case is that on input it only reads one word (that is, the characters up until the next whitespace character). If we rewrite line 17 to use the >> operator, the code would look like this:

```
std::cin >> result;
```

This reads a word from the standard input device, `std::cin`. If the user then types 10 Oak St., `result` would only contain the string 10. The rest of the line would still be waiting to be read. What we want is to read a whole line, even if it might contain spaces. The `getline` function lets us do this.

The `getline` function is defined in <string> as follows:

```
std::istream& getline(std::istream&, std::string&, char delim = '\n');
```

This function reads characters from the input stream into a string, stopping when the `delim` character is read. The delimiter in line 17 is the newline character (`'\n'`); thus we are reading a single line of text from the standard input stream (typically the terminal) into `result`. The delimiter (newline) is read from the input stream but is not appended to the result. We could have left the delimiter out of the argument list because it defaults to newline anyway.

In line 20, we do an error check, in case, for example, we hit an unexpected end-of-file or our connection to the terminal was disrupted. The `fail` member function is one of four member functions that indicate the status of an input or output stream. It returns `true` if the last input operation fails for any reason. A related function, `bad`, returns `true` only for input errors (for example, a device error). The `fail` function always returns `true` if `bad` returns `true`. Another Boolean function, `eof`, returns `true` if an end-of-file condition has been detected. Depending on the type of input stream, `eof` might not be detected until after an attempt to read past the end of the file fails. Thus, it is not generally wise to rely on `eof` unless `fail` is already `true`. One more function, `good`, returns `true` only if all the previous three functions return `false`. If good is `false`, the next input operation is guaranteed to fail. If good is `true`, the next input operation *might* succeed, but there is no guarantee.

 Tip   Use good to test the state of your input stream *before* input. Use `fail` *after* input to check if the last input failed, and then use bad and eof to find out why it failed.

The good, bad, `fail`, and eof functions are actually all defined in a base class of both istream and ostream called ios. Thus these functions work equally well for output as they do for input. However, there is much less need to test for output errors because there is so much less that can go wrong. For example, you can't hit an unexpected end of file, and of course, there is no poorly formed user input to worry about.

EXCURSION

The Gory Details: `basic_ios`

In a truly conforming C++ Standard Library implementation, ostream is actually a typedef for `basic_ostream<char, char_traits<char> >`. The istream and ios types are type-defs for similarly complex template instantiations. Describing the template parameters in detail would be too gory even for this sidebar. Suffice to say that this is intended to allow creation of special streams to handle output to devices where the quantum of I/O is not a single byte. The most common case of this is for wide (16-bit) international character sets. The wostream, wistream, and wios typedefs take care of this situation and make it unnecessary to work with the template parameters directly, even then. There are also standard objects—wcout, wcerr, wclog, and wcin—which are wide-character versions of cout, cerr, clog, and cin, respectively.

You can usually ignore this whole mess except while debugging. As is the case for string, the debugger will probably show you the whole, gory type expansion and you are expected not to panic. This is one area where older, less-conforming libraries have the advantage. Many almost-but-not-quite-conforming libraries don't have a template version of the iostream library. Debugging is a bit easier in those environments because an ostream is really an ostream and not a typedef.

If we detect that the readline call completed unsuccessfully in line 20 (of Listing 5.2), we must take some evasive action. We could raise an exception or try to diagnose the problem, but we'll just be satisfied to end the edit session by setting the edit status to canceled in line 22 and then returning from editSingleLine in line 23. If we had not checked for failure, each successive input call using the same istream (in this case, cin) would fail harmlessly. This can be a useful feature because it enables you to perform a series of input calls and then find out if any of them failed using a single check at the end.

When we get to line 29, we have read a line of text successfully. We now start processing the special cases, starting with the user pressing Enter without entering anything else. In line 29, we check for an empty input string, using the `empty` member function of `std::string`. If it is empty, we return a `true` at line 30, indicating a normal completion of the single-line edit. The input string remains unchanged and the edit status remains normal (as set in line 9).

We check for the premature exit code, ., in line 33. Notice that we are comparing a `std::string` object to a string literal (`const char*`) using the equality operator, `==`. The `<string>` header defines the equality operator (as well as the other relational operators) to compare two `std::string` objects. For efficiency and convenience, the relational operators are also defined to compare a `std::string` to a `const char*`, with either one being on the left. Even if this were not the case, there exists an implicit conversion from `const char*` to `std::string`, so a `const char*` could be used anywhere a `std::string` value is expected.

If the input string is a single period (.), we end the edit with a status of `finished` in lines 35 and 36. A similar construct is used in lines 40–44 to cancel an edit session if the user types `!x`. If none of these special case inputs is detected, we come to line 47, where we replace the value of the string being edited with the value just entered by the user. Finally, in line 48, we return after having modified the input string. This completes our single-line edit. The user's input replaces the string argument unless one of the special input sequences is detected, in which case the argument is left unchanged.

Adding and Replacing Individual Lines in a Multiple-Line String

The general algorithm for implementing `multiLineEdit` is to break up the value argument into separate lines and use `singleLineEdit` to edit each individual line. The result is shown in Listing 5.3.

Listing 5.3   Implementation of `Editor::editMultiLine`

```
51:
52:  bool Editor::editMultiLine(const std::string& prompt,
53:                  std::string& value)
54:  {
55:    status_ = normal;
56:
57:    // Append a newline to value. This makes the rest of the code
58:    // simpler by making every line end with newline. The extra newline
59:    // is stripped off at the end.
60:    value += '\n';
61:
```

continues

Listing 5.3   continued

```
62:   std::string::size_type lineBegin = 0, lineEnd = 0, lineLen = 0;
63:   for (;;)
64:   {
65:     // If at end of string, append a new line
66:     if (lineBegin >= value.length())
67:       value += '\n';
68:
69:     // Extract the next line from value
70:     std::string line;
71:     lineEnd = value.find('\n', lineBegin);   // Should always succeed
72:     lineLen = lineEnd - lineBegin;
73:     line = value.substr(lineBegin, lineLen);
74:
75:     // Edit line
76:     if (! editSingleLine(prompt, line))
77:       break;
78:
79:     // Check for special sequences
80:     if (line == "!n")
81:       break;   // User has signaled end of multi-line input
82:
83:     if (line == "!i")
84:     {
85:       // User wants to insert a line.
86:       value.insert(lineBegin, "\n");    // Insert an empty line
87:       continue;    // Loop around and edit the empty line
88:     }
89:
90:     if (line == "!d")
91:     {
92:       // User wants to delete a line.
93:       // Erase line and the newline after it.
94:       value.erase(lineBegin, lineLen + 1);
95:       continue;    // Loop around and edit the next line
96:     }
97:
98:     // Replace line with new value
99:       value.replace(lineBegin, lineLen, line);
100:
101:    // Advance position past inserted line and past newline
102:    // character.
103:    lineBegin += line.length() + 1;
104:   }
105:
106:   // Editing is done. Strip extra newlines off end of string
107:   std::string::size_type strip = value.find_last_not_of('\n') + 1;
108:   value.erase(strip, std::string::npos);
109:
110:   return (status() == normal);
111: }
```

In line 62, we initialize a number of variables that will contain the position and length of a line within the `value` argument. The type of these variables is the *member type*, `std::string::size_type`, which is an unsigned integral type capable of holding the maximum length of a string. Most of the time, a plain `unsigned int` would suffice; using the formal type insures maximum portability and robustness. The position of the start of the line being edited is stored in `lineBegin`; the end of the line is stored in `lineEnd`; and the length of the line is stored in `lineLen`.

A *member type* is a member of a class that happens to be a typedef or another class. For example, in the case of

```
class string { public: typedef unsigned long size_type };
```

`size_type` is *member type* of `std::string`.

Line 63 begins the loop through the lines in `value`. It is an infinite loop that terminates when we detect certain user actions. At this point, `lineBegin` contains the start of the next line to be edited. At line 71, we look for the end of the line using the `find` function of the `string` class. The `find` function looks for a character or string within another string. There are four overloaded versions of the `find` function, as follows:

```
size_type find(const string& str, size_type pos = 0);
size_type find(const char* p, size_type pos, size_type len);
size_type find(const char* p, size_type pos = 0);
size_type find(char c, size_type pos = 0);
```

All four functions effectively do the same thing: They look for an occurrence of a target string (`str`, `p`, or `c`) within another string and return the position of the first character of the target string within the string being searched. The `pos` argument specifies the place where to start the search within the searched-for string. The `len` argument specifies the length of the string pointed to by `p`. If `len` is not specified, `p` is assumed to be null-terminated.

If any one of the `find` functions fails to locate the target string, it returns `std::string::npos`, a constant equal to the largest value that can be represented in a `std::string::size_type`. The call in line 71 should never return `npos` because in lines 60 and 67 (which we'll get to in a minute) we ensured that we will always find a newline (the search target) at or after `lineBegin`. Thus, `lineBegin` and `lineEnd` define the boundaries of a single line within a multiple-line string and line 72 is a simple computation of the length of the line (excluding the newline character).

In line 73, we extract a single line from the larger, multiple-line string. The `substr` function returns a substring given a starting point and length. The standard library does not have formal notion of a substring as a separate type. Instead, a substring is represented as a trio of arguments comprising a string, starting position, and length. The length can usually be omitted to indicate a substring that extends to the end of the string. We will see this combination of arguments appearing repeatedly in string member function argument lists. If you think of these three arguments as a unit representing a substring, it will make it easier for you to remember how to use the member functions of string. Be aware, however, that the `find` function and a number of other string functions starting with `find` do not follow this convention. In the case of member functions such as `substr`, the string argument is specified to the left of the `.` or `->` operator, rather than in the argument list.

Concept   Many `string` member functions take other strings as arguments. Most of these functions are overloaded to accept the following representation of the other string.

A string:

`string s`

A substring:

`string s, size_type pos, size_type len`

A C-string:

`const char* s`

A char array:

`const char* buf, size_type len`

A char:

`size_type count, char c`

In the last case, `count` is the number of desired repetitions of `c`.

After executing line 73, `line` contains a copy of a single line from the original value. In line 76, we use our own `editSingleLine` to edit the line. If `editSingleLine` returns false, it means that the user terminated the edit session. In this case, we simply return. The following few lines, starting at line 80, check for the special codes that apply to multiple-line input. In line 80, we stop editing this field by breaking out of the loop if the user enters !n.

In line 83, we check for the code, !i, which means that the user wants to insert a line. We insert this line in line 86 using the `insert` function. The first argument to `insert` is the position at which you want to insert. The second argument in this case is a null-terminated character string. There are also overloaded versions of `insert` that insert a single `string`, a trio of arguments representing a substring, or a char pointer and a length. In this case, we are inserting the literal string, "\n", at the start of the current line. This has the effect of creating a new empty line at the position specified by lineBegin. In line 87, we loop back to edit this new empty line.

In line 90, we check for the code !d, which means that the user wants to delete the current line. Deleting the line is accomplished on line 94 using the erase member function of string. The arguments to erase are the position of the substring to be removed and its length. Because lineLen does not include the newline character at the end of the line, we delete one more character so as to remove both the line contents and its newline terminator. After calling erase, the character at the position specified by lineBegin will be the first character of the next line within the value string. In line 95, we loop back to edit the next line.

If the user did not enter any special codes, we replace the old line with the new one specified by the user. For this, we use the replace function in line 99. The first two arguments to replace are the position and length of the substring being replaced; the third argument is the string that will replace it. Like most other string functions, the replace function is also overloaded so that the third argument can be replaced by a substring argument trio, a const char*, or a const char* and a length.

After line 99 executes, the current line in the value string has been modified and lineBegin now specifies the beginning of the line's new value. We are at the end of the loop and need to advance to the beginning of the next line. Line 103 advances lineBegin by the number of characters in the new line plus one for the newline character. Returning to the top of the loop, we check in line 66 if we have reached the end of the string. If so, we append another empty line (in line 67) so that the user can add to the multiple-line field. The += operator is the same as the append member function. (The string class also supplies a + operator that concatenates two strings and returns the result as a third string.) Line 67 will continue to give the user more lines to edit until the user enters !n, !x, or . to exit the edit loop.

Lines 60 and 67 ensure an invariant condition that value will always end in a newline character at the point that we terminate the loop. To keep our string clean, we want to erase all trailing newlines from the value string. Line 107 uses the find_last_not_of function to locate the last character in the string that is not a newline character. The arguments to find_last_not_of are exactly the same as for find. This function searches backward from the end of the string for a character that is not in the set of characters specified by the argument. The complete set of search functions in string are find, find_last, find_first_of, find_last_of, find_first_not_of, and find_last_not_of. All these functions have the same four overloaded versions as find. The find and find_last functions search for a string. The rest search for a character in a set or not in a set. The find_last functions search backward; the rest search forward.

When line 107 completes, `strip` specifies the position one past the last non-newline in `value`. Line 108 erases from that position until the end of the string, thus removing all trailing newline characters. In line 110, we return true if the status (as set by `editSingleLine`) is `normal` and false otherwise.

As you can see, the `string` class provides many functions for modifying and searching strings. The interface is large, but patterns make it easier to remember. Most functions specify string arguments either as a `string` object, a trio of arguments representing a substring, a single character, a pointer to a null-terminated character array, or a pointer to a character array with a specified length. The search functions are a bit different, but they, too, have a pattern that is followed consistently.

Editing an Address Object Using the Editor Framework

We now turn our attention to the `AddressEditor`-derived class. This class implements the outer editor or our two-layer editor design. The purpose of the `AddressEditor` is to take an `Address` object and manage the editing of each individual field of the object. The *client* code simple says "edit the `Address`" and the `AddressEditor` object does the rest.

A *client* is a program or part of a program that uses a modular component. In modular programming, every class or function provides a *service*. Every piece of code that uses this service is called a *client* of that service. The industry buzzword "client/server" describes a specific relationship where the client code and service code exist in separate programs that communicate over a network.

The class definition for `AddressEditor` is shown in Listing 5.4.

Listing 5.4   Class Definition for `AddressEditor`

```
 1:  // TinyPIM (c) 1999 Pablo Halpern
 2:
 3:  #ifndef AddressEditor_dot_h
 4:  #define AddressEditor_dot_h 1
 5:
 6:  #include "Editor.h"
 7:  #include "Address.h"
 8:
 9:  // Class for editing an Address object.
10:  class AddressEditor : public Editor
11:  {
12:  public:
```

```
13:     // Start with an empty Address object
14:     AddressEditor();
15:
16:     // Edit an existing Address object
17:     AddressEditor(const Address& a);
18:
19:     // Use compiler-generated destructor
20:     // ~AddressEditor();
21:
22:     // Main loop returns true if address was successfully edited,
23:     // false if edit was aborted.
24:     bool edit();
25:
26:     // This accessor is used to retrieve the modified address.
27:     Address addr() const { return addr_; }
28:
29:     // This accessor is used to set the Address object to edit:
30:     void addr(const Address& a) { addr_ = a; }
31:
32: private:
33:     // Disable copying
34:     AddressEditor(const AddressEditor&);
35:     const AddressEditor& operator=(const AddressEditor&);
36:
37:     // Member variables
38:     Address    addr_;
39: };
40:
41: #endif // AddressEditor_dot_h
```

The interface is simple. The edit function in line 24 simply indicates whether the editing session completed normally. The Address object to be edited is specified either via the constructor (line 17) or via the addr accessor (line 30). As an alternative, the default constructor in line 14 can be used to edit an empty Address object. Editing an empty object is our way of enabling the user to create a new address record. If editing completes normally (edit returns true), the modified Address object can be retrieved using the addr read-accessor (line 27).

Implementing this interface is relatively easy, thanks to the functionality inherited from the Editor, as shown in Listing 5.5.

Listing 5.5   Implementation of AddressEditor Class

```
1: // TinyPIM (c) 1999 Pablo Halpern
2:
3: #include <iostream>
4:
5: #include "AddressEditor.h"
6:
```

continues

Listing 5.5   continued

```
 7:  // Start with an empty Address object.
 8:  AddressEditor::AddressEditor()
 9:  {
10:  }
11:
12:
13:  // Edit an existing Address object
14:  AddressEditor::AddressEditor(const Address& a)
15:    : addr_(a)
16:  {
17:  }
18:
19:  // Main loop returns true if address was successfully edited,
20:  // false if edit was aborted.
21:  bool AddressEditor::edit()
22:  {
23:    // Unpack the address
24:    std::string lastname(addr_.lastname());
25:    std::string firstname(addr_.firstname());
26:    std::string phone(addr_.phone());
27:    std::string address(addr_.address());
28:
29:    editSingleLine("Last name", lastname) &&
30:    editSingleLine("First name", firstname) &&
31:    editSingleLine("Phone Number", phone) &&
32:    editMultiLine("Address", address);
33:
34:    if (status() == canceled)
35:      return false;
36:
37:    // Commit changes
38:    addr_.lastname(lastname);
39:    addr_.firstname(firstname);
40:    addr_.phone(phone);
41:    addr_.address(address);
42:
43:    return true;
44:  }
```

The core of this class is the edit function. In lines 24–27, we use the Address accessors to extract each of the Address fields into separate strings. In lines 29–31, we edit each single-line field with the editSingleLine function and in line 32 we edit the multiple-line address field with editMultiLine. The calls to the base class edit functions are separated by the logical-AND (&&) operator so that each edit will occur only if the previous one returned true. If, while editing a field, the user terminates the edit session with . or !x, the subsequent fields will not be edited or modified and the status of the most recent field edit will be available via the status function. In lines 34 and 35, we return false if the user canceled the edit by typing !x in any field. Notice that the addr_ member variable has not been modified at this point. We commit changes back to addr_ only if the edit was not canceled, by storing each modified field back into its corresponding addr_ data member in lines 38 to 41. Finally, at line 43, we return a successful status.

To test this program, we will create an AddressEditor object and invoke its edit function repeatedly, printing out the edited Address record after each call. The test program is shown in Listing 5.6.

Listing 5.6   Test Program for AddressEditor Class

```
1:   // TinyPIM (c) 1999 Pablo Halpern. File AddrEditTest.cpp
2:
3:   #include <iostream>
4:
5:   #include "Address.h"
6:   #include "AddressEditor.h"
7:
8:   void dump(const Address& a)
9:   {
10:     std::cout << "Record " << a.recordId() << '\n'
11:       << a.firstname() << ' ' << a.lastname() << '\n'
12:       << a.address() << '\n' << a.phone() << '\n' << std::endl;
13:   }
14:
15:   int main()
16:   {
17:     Address a;
18:
19:     AddressEditor editor(a);
20:     while (a.lastname() != "done")
21:     {
22:       editor.edit();
23:       a = editor.addr();
24:       std::cout << std::endl;
25:       dump(a);
26:     }
27:
28:     return 0;
29:   }
```

Lines 8–13 of our test program is the same dump function we used in Chapter 2, "Implementing the Address Class with Text Strings." Line 19 creates an AddressEditor object, initializing it with an empty Address object. In line 20, we loop until the user enters done in the last name field. In line 22 we call the edit function and then copy the results back into a in line 23. In line 25, we print the results of the edit.

Let's run the program and type some data. The results are shown in Listing 5.7 (your input is shown in *italics*).

Listing 5.7   Results of Running AddrEditTest Program

```
 1:  Last name: Lincoln
 2:  First name: Abe
 3:  Phone Number: (202) 555-9933
 4:  Address: The White House
 5:  Address: Pennsylvania Ave.
 6:  Address: Washington, DC
 7:  Address: .
 8:
 9:  Record 0
10:  Abe Lincoln
11:  The White House
12:  Pennsylvania Ave.
13:  Washington, DC
14:  (202) 555-9933
15:
16:  Last name [Lincoln]: Washington
17:  First name [Abe]: George
18:  Phone Number [(202) 555-9933]: .
19:
20:  Record 0
21:  George Washington
22:  The White House
23:  Pennsylvania Ave.
24:  Washington, DC
25:  (202) 555-9933
26:
27:  Last name [Washington]: Dole
28:  First name [George]: Bob
29:  Phone Number [(202) 555-9933]:
30:  Address [The White House]: !x
31:
32:  Record 0
33:  George Washington
34:  The White House
35:  Pennsylvania Ave.
36:  Washington, DC
37:  (202) 555-9933
38:
39:  Last name [Washington]: Bush
40:  First name [George]:
41:  Phone Number [(202) 555-9933]: 202.555.0011 ext. 1
42:  Address [The White House]: !n
43:
44:  Record 0
45:  George Bush
46:  The White House
47:  Pennsylvania Ave.
```

```
48:   Washington, DC
49:   202.555.0011 ext. 1
50:
51:   Last name [Bush]: Gore
52:   First name [George]: Al
53:   Phone Number [202.555.0011 ext. 1]: 1/202.555-0002
54:   Address [The White House]: !d
55:   Address [Pennsylvania Ave.]: !d
56:   Address [Washington, DC]:
57:   Address: .
58:
59:   Record 0
60:   Al Gore
61:   Washington, DC
62:   1/202.555-0002
63:
64:   Last name [Gore]:
65:   First name [Al]:
66:   Phone Number [1/202.555-0002]:
67:   Address [Washington, DC]: !i
68:   Address: Vice President's Residence
69:   Address [Washington, DC]: .
70:
71:   Record 0
72:   Al Gore
73:   Vice President's Residence
74:   Washington, DC
75:   1/202.555-0002
76:
77:   Last name [Gore]: done
78:   First name [Al]: .
79:
80:   Record 0
81:   Al done
82:   Vice President's Residence
83:   Washington, DC
84:   1/202.555-0002
85:
```

As the program begins, it creates an empty Address object and then invokes the editor. In lines 1–3, the editor prompts for values for each single-line field: last name, first name, and phone number. We entered data and pressed Enter for each field. (Yes, I know that Abe Lincoln didn't have a phone. It's just a toy test program.) In lines 4–6, we enter values for the multiple-line address field. The editor continues prompting us for more lines until we terminate the field entry, in this case by entering a single period (.) in line 7. The period was interpreted by the Editor::editMultiLine function as a desire to terminate the edit session. It set the status to normal but returned a false value to AddressEditor::edit, which stopped editing and saved the results. Lines 9–14 are a dump of the resulting Address record.

In lines 16 and 17, the editor prompts us for last name and first name again, but this time presents us with the current value of those fields. We replace these values by entering new data then, in line 18, terminating the edit session. In line 21, we see that our edit took effect and in lines 22–25 we see that no other fields were affected.

In the next iteration, we test our ability to abort an edit session with no change to the data. In lines 27 and 28, we enter new values for last name and first name but then in line 30, we enter !x, which aborts the edit. As we can see in line 33, the changes were discarded.

In the next iteration we test the ability of the editor to leave a field unchanged if we don't type a new value. In line 40, we press Enter without typing any other text. In line 42, we type !n into a multiple-line field. This advances to the next field, but because there are no more fields, it ends the edit session. In lines 45 and 49 we see that the last name and phone number fields were changed to our new values, but that the first name and address fields were not changed because we did not enter new values.

In the next iteration, we test the delete-line capability of multiple-line editing. After entering new values for the single-line fields, in lines 54 and 55 we delete the first two lines of the address field. In line 56, we leave the last line of the address field alone. The results, in lines 60–62, are what we hoped for: the two deleted lines are gone.

Finally, we test our ability to insert lines into a multiple-line field. In line 67, the editor prompts us with the first line of the address. Instead of entering a new value, we type !i, which instructs the editor to insert a new line. At line 68, the editor prompts us for the new line then, in line 69, it again shows us the old line of text, which is now the second line of the field. We make no more changes and type a single period (.). Line 73 shows the new line inserted into the address field.

We terminate the program by typing done in to the last name field at line 77. The program displays the record one more time in lines 80–85 and then exits.

A New Requirement: Formatted Phone Numbers

As so often happens in software development, some of the requirements are not discovered until well into the implementation. In this case, our customer (or we) might be disappointed with the results of our program so far. We look at the way phone numbers are displayed and discover a new requirement: phone numbers should be formatted according to North American formatting conventions. When a phone

number is entered, regardless of how it is punctuated, it should be reformatted as
follows:

7 digits:	*ddd-dddd*
8 digits starting with 1:	1-*ddd-dddd*
10 digits:	(*ddd*) *ddd-dddd*
11 digits starting with 1:	1 (*ddd*) *ddd-dddd*

Punctuation marks—·, (,), /, and .—or spaces are ignored. If a phone number contains both digits and alphabetic characters, only the part up to first alphabetic character is reformatted and the rest of the number is left unchanged. If the number does not match one of the preceding patterns, the entire number is left unchanged. Using these rules, the number 617/555.6262 ext. 123 would be reformatted to (617) 555-6262 ext. 123. Implementing these rules gives us an opportunity to reinforce and expand our understanding of string manipulations.

Finding Funny Characters

The first task in reformatting a phone number is to find the alphabetic characters in the original phone number. Listing 5.8 shows the editPhone function from AddressEditor.cpp. This function would also need to be declared within the AddressEditor class in AddressEditor.h.

Note

Code Note   Listings 5.8 and 5.9 correspond to files on the companion Web page in the Chapter 5 Code\US Phones directory. The files in this directory can be compiled and linked together to create an executable program.

Listing 5.8   editPhone **Function**

```
1:  bool AddressEditor::editPhone(const std::string& prompt,
2:                               std::string& phone)
3:  {
4:    if (! editSingleLine(prompt, phone))
5:      return false;
6:
7:    // Set the phone number.
8:    // Phone numbers are converted into standard US notation.
9:    // Transformations of input string:
10:   //    7 digits         => ddd-dddd
11:   //    '1' + 7 digits   => 1-ddd-dddd
12:   //    10 digits        => (ddd) ddd-dddd
13:   //    '1' + 10 digits  => 1 (ddd) ddd-dddd
```

continues

Listing 5.8   continued

```
14:     // Identify suffix that contains uncommon phone-number characters
15:     static const std::string digits("0123456789");
16:     std::string::size_type suffix =
17:         phone.find_first_not_of(digits + "-()/. ");
18:     if (suffix == std::string::npos)
19:       suffix = phone.length();
20:
21:     // Extend suffix back to include non-digits after the last digit.
22:     suffix = phone.find_last_of(digits, suffix);
23:     if (suffix == std::string::npos)
24:       return true;    // prefix contains no digits. No reformatting
25:     ++suffix;    // Advance suffix to exclude last digit
26:
27:     // Okay, prefix string contains only digits and normal punctuation
28:     // Copy digits only to new phone number.
29:     std::string newnum;
30:     std::string::size_type p = phone.find_first_of(digits);
31:     while (p < suffix)
32:     {
33:       std::string::size_type q = phone.find_first_not_of(digits, p);
34:       // The range [p, q) contains only digits.
35:       // Append them to new number.
36:       newnum.append(phone, p, q - p);
37:       if (q == std::string::npos)
38:         break;
39:       p = phone.find_first_of(digits, q);
40:     }
41:
42:     // Now we insert just the punctuation we want:
43:     switch (newnum.length())
44:     {
45:     case 7:
46:       newnum.insert(3, 1, '-');
47:       break;
48:
49:     case 8:
50:       if (newnum[0] != '1')
51:         return true;    // 8-digit number not starting with '1'.
52:
53:       newnum.insert(4, 1, '-');
54:       newnum.insert(1, 1, '-');
55:       break;
56:
57:     case 10:
58:       newnum.insert(6, 1, '-');
59:       newnum.insert(3, ") ");
60:       newnum.insert((int) 0, 1, '(');
61:       break;
62:
63:     case 11:
```

```
64:       if (newnum[0] != '1')
65:         return true;    // 11-digit number not starting with '1'.
66:
67:       newnum.insert(7, 1, '-');
68:       newnum.insert(4, ") ");
69:       newnum.insert(1, " (");
70:       break;
71:
72:     default:
73:       return true;    // non-standard number of digits
74:     }
75:
76:     // Number has been punctuated. Append suffix.
77:     phone.replace(0, suffix, newnum);
78:     return true;
79:   }
```

In line 4 we edit the phone number as usual, using `editSingleLine`. Reformatting the results begins at lines 16, where we declare a variable, `suffix`, that will hold the position of the first character that is not part of a standard phone number (typically an alphabetic character). The substring from `suffix` until the end of `phone` will be excluded from reformatting and will be appended to the end of phone number after the standard part is reformatted. In line 17, we set `suffix` by looking for the first character that is not in the string `0123456789-()/`. (Note that the last character in this set is a space). The set of characters to match is constructed by using `operator+` to concatenate the list of characters in `digits` with a string literal. The results of this concatenation are passed to `find_first_not_of`, which locates the start of the non-numeric suffix.

Lines 18 and 19 make it easier to calculate the length of the nonnumeric suffix by making sure that `suffix` does not extend more than one character past the length of the `phone` string. At this point `suffix` either marks the beginning of the alphabetic phone number suffix, or else points one past the end of the phone number.

It is possible that there are punctuation marks and spaces between the last digit and the start of the suffix and indicated by the `suffix` variable. We would like to extend the suffix backward to include these other nonnumeric characters. In line 22, we search backward from the point indicated by `suffix` to the last digit in the `phone` string. The `find_last_of` function returns the index of the last digit before the suffix. Note that if we did not pass `suffix` as the second argument, `find_last_of` would search from the end of the string, incorrectly finding digits that belong in the suffix (for example phone extension). In line 25, we increment our suffix to exclude the digit itself, but first, we need to make sure that `find_last_of` actually found something. Line 23 checks for the condition where `find_last_of` failed to find anything by comparing the result to `string::npos`, the special value returned by all the search functions to indicate failure. If we did not find any digits searching backward from suffix, the phone number does not contain any digits before the first alphabetic character and no reformatting is necessary. In this case, we leave phone exactly as the user typed it and return success in line 24.

Extracting and Counting Digits

In our next step we will separate the digits from the punctuation and whitespace so we can then add our own punctuation and whitespace. We will hold the string of digits in a string called newnum, declared in line 29. In line 30, we set p to the position of the first digit in the phone number. The loop starting at line 31 will continue looking for digits until we hit end of normal portion of the phone number (start of suffix). In line 33, we find the first nonnumeric character after p. Thus, the string between p and q (excluding q) contains a sequence of consecutive digits. At line 36, we append this sequence of digits to newnum. The append function, like many string member functions, accepts a substring in the form of a trio of arguments for string, position, and length. Note that if q is string::npos (meaning that find_first_not_of failed to find any more nonnumeric characters), q - p will be a large number. For all the functions that use the substring idiom, a substring that extends past the end of a string is automatically truncated to the length of the string. In this case (as in most cases), the truncation behavior is just what we want.

Warning   Only the length portion of a substring argument trio can extend past the length of a string. The position of the substring within the string must be a valid index or (in most cases) the value of length(), which is one larger than the largest valid index.

Lines 37 and 38 terminate the loop if we reached the end of the string. At line 39, we reinitialize our loop by finding the start of next cluster of digits (starting our search at the end of the previous cluster). At end of the loop, newnum will contain all the digits prior to suffix.

Inserting Punctuation

Continuing with our analysis of Listing 5.8, having removed the user's punctuation we are now ready to add our own. We select which format to apply based on the number of digits using a switch on the length of our digit string. Line 46 inserts a dash after the third digit if there are exactly seven digits in the number. The second argument (1) to the insert function indicates how many copies of the character to insert.

Note

You might find it surprising that you cannot insert a single character without a repetition count using a call like `newnum.insert(3, '-')`. It is just a quirk of the C++ Standard Library that such an expression is not valid.

At lines 50 and 64 we test if an 8- or 11-digit number starts with "1". If not, the number is nonstandard and we do nothing. Lines 53 and 54 insert dashes after the first and fourth digit of an 8-digit number. Note that we insert the second dash first to avoid shifting digits to right (after inserting the first dash, the fourth digit becomes the fifth character). It is often a good idea to insert from the end of a string toward the beginning to avoid renumbering characters.

Lines 58–60 insert a dash, parentheses, and spaces into a 10-digit number. Line 59 uses the `insert` function with string literal arg. The `insert` function also works with a `string` or substring argument trio. In line 60, we cast the first argument (0) to `int` because some compilers will think it is a null pointer in this context (such compilers are buggy, though not uncommon). Finally, lines 67–69 insert punctuation into an 11-digit number. If the number does not have exactly 7, 8, 10, or 11 digits we execute line 73, which leaves the `phone` string exactly as the user entered it and returns without reformatting.

When we get to line 77, we have a standard-format phone number in `newnum` and the original phone number in `phone`. Any nonstandard suffix from the original number starts at the position indicated by `suffix`. At this point, we replace the portion of `phone` before the suffix with the standard-format phone number. The first two arguments to the `replace` function are the position at which to begin replacing and the length of the substring being replaced. The rest of the arguments designate the string, substring, C-style string, or character array to insert in place of the specified substring.

Now We're Happy

We must make one little change to `AddressEditor::edit` as shown in Listing 5.9.

Listing 5.9   edit Function Changed to Use editPhone

```
1:  // Main loop returns true if address was successfully edited,
2:  // false if edit was aborted.
3:  bool AddressEditor::edit()
4:  {
5:    // Unpack the address
6:    std::string lastname(addr_.lastname());
7:    std::string firstname(addr_.firstname());
```

continues

Listing 5.9   continued

```
 8:    std::string phone(addr_.phone());
 9:    std::string address(addr_.address());
10:
11:    editSingleLine("Last name", lastname) &&
12:    editSingleLine("First name", firstname) &&
13:    editPhone("Phone Number", phone) &&
14:    editMultiLine("Address", address);
15:
16:    if (status() == canceled)
17:      return false;
18:
19:    // Commit changes
20:    addr_.lastname(lastname);
21:    addr_.firstname(firstname);
22:    addr_.phone(phone);
23:    addr_.address(address);
24:
25:    return status() != canceled;
26:  }
```

The only change is line 13, where we now call `editPhone` instead of `editSingleLine`.

The test program is the same one we used before (refer to Listing 5.6). Using the same input, the output now looks like Listing 5.10.

Listing 5.10   Output of Test Program After Changes

```
 1:  Last name: Lincoln
 2:  First name: Abe
 3:  Phone Number: (202) 555-9933
 4:  Address: The White House
 5:  Address: Pennsylvania Ave.
 6:  Address: Washington, DC
 7:  Address: .
 8:
 9:  Record 0
10:  Abe Lincoln
11:  The White House
12:  Pennsylvania Ave.
13:  Washington, DC
14:  (202) 555-9933
15:
16:  Last name [Lincoln]: Washington
17:  First name [Abe]: George
18:  Phone Number [(202) 555-9933]: .
19:
20:  Record 0
21:  George Washington
22:  The White House
23:  Pennsylvania Ave.
```

```
24: Washington, DC
25: (202) 555-9933
26:
27: Last name [Washington]: Dole
28: First name [George]: Bob
29: Phone Number [(202) 555-9933]:
30: Address [The White House]: !x
31:
32: Record 0
33: George Washington
34: The White House
35: Pennsylvania Ave.
36: Washington, DC
37: (202) 555-9933
38:
39: Last name [Washington]: Bush
40: First name [George]:
41: Phone Number [(202) 555-9933]: 202.555.0011 ext. 1
42: Address [The White House]: !n
43:
44: Record 0
45: George Bush
46: The White House
47: Pennsylvania Ave.
48: Washington, DC
49: (202) 555-0011 ext. 1
50:
51: Last name [Bush]: Gore
52: First name [George]: Al
53: Phone Number [(202) 555-0011 ext. 1]: 1/202.555.0002
54: Address [The White House]: !d
55: Address [Pennsylvania Ave.]: !d
56: Address [Washington, DC]:
57: Address: .
58:
59: Record 0
60: Al Gore
61: Washington, DC
62: 1 (202) 555-0002
63:
64: Last name [Gore]:
65: First name [Al]:
66: Phone Number [1 (202) 555-0002]:
67: Address [Washington, DC]: !i
68: Address: Vice President's Residence
69: Address [Washington, DC]: .
70:
71: Record 0
72: Al Gore
73: Vice President's Residence
74: Washington, DC
75: 1 (202) 555-0002
```

continues

Listing 5.10   continued

```
76:
77:  Last name [Gore]: done
78:  First name [Al]: .
79:
80:  Record 0
81:  Al done
82:  Vice President's Residence
83:  Washington, DC
84:  1 (202) 555-0002
85:
```

Line 49 shows a complete case: A 10-digit phone number with an extension was entered in nonstandard form. The editor reformatted the first part of the number into standard form and left the extension number suffix alone. Line 62 shows the case of an 11-digit number starting with 1. We could have tested all the cases, but I'll leave that as an exercise for the reader. It appears that our phone number format now meets our new requirement.

Next Steps

Now we have an editor for creating and modifying addresses. Along the way, we learned to use stream input and output and to handle input error conditions. We used a number of string manipulations to edit multiple-line text and reformat phone numbers. Our next task will be to enhance the AddressBook class in such a way that it supports all the operations needed by the user interface module. This will introduce you to sorted associative containers and to the algorithm library.

Chapter 6

An Enhanced AddressBook Using Algorithms and Sorted Containers

Address Book Requirements from the User Interface

We are almost ready to implement the main part of the user interface for the address book part of TinyPIM. Before we proceed, however, let's make sure that we will be able to implement all the operations identified in our requirements analysis. Looking at our use cases from Chapter 1, "Introducing TinyPIM," we can identify the following core operations that AddressBook does not yet allow us to perform:

1. **Pick from a list of address records**—The user interface is going to need to list the entries in the address book in order for the user to pick one to view, edit, or delete. In order to do this, it needs a function in AddressBook that gives it access to each record in sequence. The print function in AddressBook is intended for debugging only. It does not provide the ability to select a record from the list or to scroll the list in a controlled way.

2. **Detect duplicate records**—The user interface will warn the user before saving a second address record with the same last name and first name as one that already exists. The AddressBook class currently provides no way to detect this condition.

3. **Search for an address record by name**—The user interface will need to call a function that finds the desired name.

4. **Search for a string anywhere in an address record**—Again, the user interface will rely on AddressBook to do the search.

Before we go ahead with the user interface, let's return to the core package and take a couple more steps in the evolution of AddressBook.

An Idiom for Giving Public Access to Private Containers

Let's first add an interface to AddressBook that enables the user interface to access each record in sequence, so that it can be displayed. The Address records are stored in a list container in alphabetical order. Our task then can be translated into finding an appropriate way to give the user interface access to the list of Address records.

The Problem with Normal Accessors

One way to allow the user interface (or any other client of AddressBook) the ability to traverse all the records in the address book is to simply give the client a reference to the list of Address records. We could, for example, define the following accessor within AddressBook:

```
const list<Address>& addresses() const { return addresses_; }
```

The client code could then iterate over all the addresses or do anything else that one can do with a list object. However, this approach seriously undermines modularity. In any program of reasonable complexity, we want to keep the different parts as independent as possible to avoid changes in one part of the program from rippling through to the rest of the program. One thing that keeps a program modular is the creation of clean class interfaces that do not expose the internal representation of a class. When we changed our implementation of AddressBook from using vector to using list, the public part of the class interface did not change one iota. This is a hallmark of successful modular design. If we return a reference or copy to the addresses_ member of AddressBook, future clients would become dependent on the fact that it is a list object. Our opportunity for changing the implementation without affecting the client will be closed.

Giving Our AddressBook Class an STL-Style Interface

What we need, instead, is a mechanism to provide the client with each Address object in turn, without exposing the container containing the sequence. In other words, we want to provide our AddressBook class with iterators. Listing 6.1 shows an enhanced AddressBook class using this concept. In addition to the iterators, this listing shows declarations for the other functions that will be discussed in this chapter.

Note

Code Note   Listings 6.1–6.7 correspond to files on the companion Web page in the Chapter 6 Code\Searches directory. The files in this directory can be compiled and linked together to create an executable program. See the end of the Introduction for information on accessing this book's companion Web page.

Listing 6.1   The AddressBook Class with the Missing Functions Added

```
 1:  // TinyPIM (c) 1999 Pablo Halpern. File AddressBook.h
 2:
 3:  #ifndef AddressBook_dot_h
 4:  #define AddressBook_dot_h
 5:
 6:  #include <list>
 7:  #include "Address.h"
 8:
 9:  class AddressBook
10:  {
11:    // Shorthand name for list type
12:    typedef std::list<Address> addrlist;
13:
14:  public:
15:    AddressBook();
16:    ~AddressBook();
17:
18:    // Exception classes
19:    class AddressNotFound { };
20:    class DuplicateId { };
21:
22:    int insertAddress(const Address& addr, int recordId = 0)
23:      throw (DuplicateId);
24:    void eraseAddress(int recordId) throw (AddressNotFound);
25:    void replaceAddress(const Address& addr, int recordId = 0)
26:      throw (AddressNotFound);
27:    const Address& getAddress(int recordId) const
28:      throw (AddressNotFound);
29:
30:    // Return number of records found with specified name.
31:    int countName(const std::string& lastname,
32:                  const std::string& firstname) const;
33:
34:    // Iterator to traverse address records
35:    typedef addrlist::const_iterator const_iterator;
36:
37:    // Functions to traverse all address records
38:    const_iterator begin() const { return addresses_.begin(); }
39:    const_iterator end()   const { return addresses_.end();   }
40:
```

6

continues

Listing 6.1   continued

```
41:     // Find first Address with name greater-than-or-equal to specified
42:     // name. Usually, this will be a name that starts with the
43:     // specified strings.
44:     const_iterator findNameStartsWith(const std::string& lastname,
45:                            const std::string& firstname="") const;
46:
47:     // Find next Address in which any field contains the specified
48:     // string. Indicate starting point for search with start parameter.
49:     const_iterator findNextContains(const std::string& searchStr,
50:                            const_iterator start) const;
51:
52:     // Return iterator to specified records ID.
53:     const_iterator findRecordId(int recordId) const
54:       throw (AddressNotFound);
55:
56:   private:
57:     // Disable copying
58:     AddressBook(const AddressBook&);
59:     AddressBook& operator=(const AddressBook&);
60:
61:     static int nextId_;
62:
63:     addrlist addresses_;
64:
65:     // Get the index of the record with the specified ID.
66:     // Returns NULL if not found.
67:     addrlist::iterator       getById(int recordId)
68:       throw (AddressNotFound);
69:     addrlist::const_iterator getById(int recordId) const
70:       throw (AddressNotFound);
71:   };
72:
73:   #endif // AddressBook_dot_h
```

The AddressBook iterator is defined in line 35 as a synonym for
list<Address>::const_iterator. (We moved the abbreviation for our list type up to
line 12 because we need to refer to it in line 35.) The begin function on line 38 is a
simple inline function that returns an iterator to the first record in the address book.
Similarly, the end function on line 39 returns an iterator to one past the last record.
We can use the address book iterator in the user interface to display a list of
addresses by traversing the whole address book, starting with the iterator returned by
begin() and incrementing it until it equals end(), exactly as if we were traversing a
vector or list. Only a const iterator is defined because the iterator will only be used
to provide a client with read-only access to the sequence of Address records. In order
to modify the set of records, the client needs to use the insertAddress,
eraseAddress, or replaceAddress functions. With this traversal mechanism in place,

we can eliminate our print debug function, and instead add a printAddressBook function to our test program, as shown in Listing 6.2.

Listing 6.2   A printAddressBook Function Added to the Test Program

```
1:  // TinyPIM (c) 1999 Pablo Halpern. File AddressBookTest.cpp
2:
3:  #ifdef _MSC_VER
4:  #pragma warning(disable : 4786)
5:  #endif
6:
7:  #include <iostream>
8:  #include "AddressBook.h"
9:
10: void printAddressBook(const AddressBook& book)
11: {
12:     for (AddressBook::const_iterator i = book.begin();
13:          i != book.end(); ++i)
14:     {
15:       const Address& a = *i;
16:       std::cout << "Record Id: " << a.recordId() << '\n'
17:                 << a.firstname() << ' ' << a.lastname() << '\n'
18:                 << a.address() << '\n' << a.phone() << '\n'
19:             << std::endl;
20:     }
21: }
22: // ... Rest of AddressBookTest.cpp unchanged ...
```

This code is almost identical to the print function that was part of AddressBook. Lines 12 and 13 define the key loop that treats the book object as an ordinary container.

 Tip

When creating your own container-like classes, give them interfaces that resemble the standard container types. This will make it easier for other programmers to understand how to use them (assuming the other programmers are familiar with the STL).

Because the client uses AddressBook::const_iterator instead of list<Address>::const_iterator, we could substitute a different data structure (for example, a vector) for the list and the client code would still work. If the data structure that we choose does not support a straightforward iterator that is usable by the client code, we could write our own. In any event, the client code would be independent of our choice. This method of decoupling a class from its clients is facilitated by the uniform interface shared by all iterator types. The client code can increment, compare, and dereference an iterator without regard to the type of container it belongs to.

Checking for Duplicates with the count Algorithm

Let's turn our attention to detecting records with duplicate names. The requirement is that we be able to tell the user before saving a record with the same name as one that already exists. In Listing 6.1 line 31, we provide a function countName that can be used to accomplish this goal. The countName function returns the number of records in the address book that have the specified last name and first name. If the number of records returned is zero, we can add a record with that name without fear of duplicates. Otherwise, the user interface needs to warn the user.

It turns out that counting the number of items with a specific value in a collection is a common enough task that facilities were included in the C++ Standard Library to make this job simpler.

Looking for an Exact Match

Listing 6.3 shows an implementation of countName using the count *algorithm* from the standard library. Be aware that this implementation does not quite do what we want, but we'll correct that in a minute.

Listing 6.3   The countName Function Using the count Algorithm

```
 1:  #include <algorithm>
 2:
 3:  // Return number of records found with specified name.
 4:  int AddressBook::countName(const std::string& lastname,
 5:                        const std::string& firstname) const
 6:  {
 7:    Address srchAddr;
 8:    srchAddr.lastname(lastname);
 9:    srchAddr.firstname(firstname);
10:
11:    // Return number of matching addresses
12:    return std::count(addresses_.begin(), addresses_.end(), srchAddr);
13:  }
```

We can read line 12 as follows: Count the number of values in the range, begin() to end(), which match the value in srchAddr. Let's back up and discuss each concept separately.

What Is an Algorithm?

According to Webster's New Universal Unabridged Dictionary (Dorset & Baber, 1983), an *algorithm* is "…any special method of solving a certain kind of problem." Most algorithms do not solve a single problem, but a whole class of problems. For example, we can specify a general algorithm for sorting a collection of objects by size, regardless of whether the items we are sorting are apples, coins, or integers in a computer program. In the C++ Standard Library, the term *algorithm* refers to a template function that can be applied to a wide variety of data types and containers.

The count algorithm used in Listing 6.3 counts the number of elements in a container that match a specified value. The type of container and type of value can be almost anything. The code in line 12 causes the count function is *instantiated* at compile time. (See the Excursion titled "A Quick Review of Templates," in Chapter 3, "Creating the AddressBook Using Container Classes.") Thus, a custom version of count is created for our specific need. Using the count algorithm makes the code easier to read than it would be if we used an explicit loop.

Concept   Using an algorithm from the standard library often has the effect of reducing the number of loops in your program.

The C++ Standard Library supplies about 60 standard algorithms, defined in the header <algorithm> (see line 1 of Listing 6.3). In this chapter we will begin to explore the concepts that are common to most algorithms in the library.

What Is an Iterator Range?

Most of the algorithms in the standard library don't operate on a container directly. Instead, they operate on a contiguous subset of the elements in a container specified by an *iterator range*. Algorithms that operate on iterator ranges take two parameters for each range: an iterator to the first element in the range and an iterator pointing one past the last element in the subset. Thus, in line 12 of Listing 6.3, we pass count the iterator range starting at addresses_.begin() and ending at addresses_.end(), which contains all the elements in addresses_.

Concept   A function or algorithm that takes two iterator arguments of the same type with names such as start and finish or begin and end expects the arguments to comprise an *iterator range*.

In books such as this one, an iterator range is often specified using the mathematical notation of a *half-open interval*. The half-open interval, [X, Y), is a concise way to describe the range of values from X up to, but not including, Y. The square bracket before the X indicates that X is included in the range. The round parenthesis after the Y indicates that Y is not included in the range. In Figure 6.1 the shaded items represent container elements present in the iterator range [start, finish).

Figure 6.1

*Elements selected by the iterator range [*start*, *finish*).*

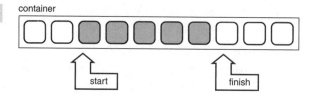

 A *half-open interval* is a set of values in a range, [*begin, end*), where *begin* is included in the set and *end* is excluded from the set. For example: [0.0, 100.0) specifies the set of nonnegative real numbers less than one hundred.

Matching a Value

Looking again at line 12 of Listing 6.3, we can begin to understand what is happening. The count algorithm is declared roughly as follows (but see "The Gory Details: Traits Classes" later in this chapter):

```
template <class Iterator, class T>
long count(Iterator start, Iterator finish, const T& value);
```

For a given set of types Iterator and T, it returns a count of the number of items in [start, finish) that compare equal to value. The T type must be compatible with the Iterator type (that is, *start == value must be a valid expression). Our use of count instantiates it with Iterator type list<Address>::const_iterator and T type Address. In order to search for a last name and first name, we must construct an Address object containing those names. We do this in lines 7 to 9 by declaring a dummy Address object which we pass to count in line 12.

Compiler Note   Some versions of the standard library, most notably the one that comes with the SunPro 5.0 compiler, have an older (prestandard) version of count that doesn't return a value but instead puts the result into a third, pass-by-reference parameter. A workaround for this situation is to redefine count as follows:

```
#ifdef __SUNPRO_CC
// Bug in SunPro library: old definition of count().
// Overload with correct definition.
namespace std
{
  template <class FwdIt, class T>
  inline long count(FwdIt start, FwdIt end, const T& t)
  {
    unsigned ret = 0;
    count(start, end, t, ret);
    return ret;
  }
}
#endif // __SUNPRO_CC
```

The same workaround is needed for count_if, distance, and a few other algorithms.

Unfortunately, if we left the code this way, we would almost always return a count of zero, even if the name is in fact present in the address book. The problem is that two Address objects with the same first name and the same last name don't necessarily compare equal. Our dummy Address object has empty phone number and address strings. The equality operator for Address looks at all the fields and returns false if the phone number or address differ. This was, and still is, a reasonable definition for equality, but it doesn't serve our needs in this instance.

Succeeding with count_if and Function Objects

How do we make count look only at the name portion of an Address? The trick is to make it use a different notion of equality. In other words, we need to supply it with an equality comparison function different from operator==.

Introducing Function Objects

A function object (sometimes called a *functor*) is an object that defines operator() (the function call operator) so that it acts like a function. For example, the standard library defines a function object class equal<T> which simply invokes the equality operator on its arguments. Thus, an object of type equal<int> acts like a function that compares its arguments for equality. The program fragment

```
std::equal<int> intequals;
int x, y;
if (intequals(x, y))
  // do something
```

is equivalent to

```
int x, y;
if (x == y)
  // do something
```

The usefulness of equal<int> lies in the ability to use it as a type to parameterize algorithms. Thus, an algorithm instantiated with equal<int> will behave differently from an algorithm instantiated with not_equal<int>. What algorithms use this concept and how does it help us? There exists an algorithm in the standard library called count_if, which is a variant of count. The count_if algorithm lets you supply your own matching operation in the form of a function object, instead of relying on the comparison operator. Let's look at how to do this.

Creating Our Own Function Object

Listing 6.4 shows a new version of `countName` using our own function object class and the `count_if` algorithm. (Line numbers are relative to the start of the `AddressBook.cpp` file.)

Listing 6.4   The `countName` Function Using a Function Object and `count_if`

```
 1:  // TinyPIM (c) 1999 Pablo Halpern. File AddressBook.cpp
 2:
 3:  #ifndef _MSC_VER
 4:  #pragma warning(disable : 4786)
 5:  #endif
 6:
 7:  #include <algorithm>
 8:  #include <functional>

...  // Rest of code unchanged from Chapter 4

 98: // Function object to compare the name fields of two Address objects
 99: struct AddressNameEqual :
100:   public std::binary_function<Address, Address, bool>
101: {
102:   bool operator()(const Address& a1, const Address& a2) const
103:   {
104:     // Return true if names match
105:     return (a1.lastname() == a2.lastname() &&
106:             a1.firstname() == a2.firstname());
107:   }
108: };
109:
110: // Return number of records found with specified name.
111: int AddressBook::countName(const std::string& lastname,
112:                            const std::string& firstname) const
113: {
114:   Address searchAddr;
115:   searchAddr.lastname(lastname);
116:   searchAddr.firstname(firstname);
117:
118:   // Return number of matching addresses
119:   return std::count_if(addresses_.begin(), addresses_.end(),
120:                        std::bind2nd(AddressNameEqual(), searchAddr));
121: }
122:
```

In line 99, we define a class, `AddressNameEqual` which will be a *binary function* object class. A binary function is one that takes two arguments, whereas a *unary function* is one that takes only one argument. We derive our class from the standard binary_function template and specify the two argument types and the return type, respectively of our binary function. The binary_function template (and corresponding unary_function template) defines some typedefs that become important when we use our function object with *negators* and *binders*, in the next section of this chapter.

 The phrase *define a function object* is often used as a sloppy way to say "define a function object *class*." In truth, defining the class and creating an object of that class are two different things and mixing them up is a common source of confusion for beginning function object users. Nevertheless, we are not always precise in our speech or writing and this particular shortcut is here to stay.

In lines 102–107, we define the function call operator, operator(), which will be called when an AddressNameEqual object is used as a function. It simply compares the last name and first name fields of its two arguments and returns true if they compare equal. AddressNameEqual, like most function object classes, has no data members and only the one, public, member function. The compiler will automatically generate a do-nothing default constructor, copy constructor, assignment operator, and destructor.

To use AddressNameEqual as a function, we must actually create an object of that type, as shown in the following code fragment:

```
AddressNameEqual aneq;      // Create function object
Address a, b;
if (aneq(a, b))     // Compare the names of a and b
  // etc.
```

Because aneq is an empty object (it contains no data members) and because its constructor doesn't do anything, we could replace aneq with the expression AddressNameEqual(), which constructs the function object on the spot. Thus our code fragment becomes

```
Address a, b;
if (AddressNameEqual()(a, b))     // Compare the names of a and b
  // etc.
```

The extra set of parentheses after AddressNameEqual looks strange. What we see is a two-step expression. First, we construct a (temporary) AddressNameEqual object using the default constructor (the empty parentheses). Then we use this function object as a function, passing it the arguments a and b. You won't see this idiom very often, though it does show up from time to time. However, you *will* often see empty parentheses used to create function objects from function object classes.

EXCURSION

Function Objects Versus Pointers to Functions

A function object has a purpose similar to a pointer to function; both are used as ways of passing little bits of client code to a function or algorithm. So why introduce the concept of function objects instead of using plain old pointers to functions?

The answer is versatility. A function object can hold state information in its data members. This state information can be used as additional parameters affecting the result. In addition, only function objects can be used with binders and negators (discussed in the next section). Function objects are bound at compile time, making them eligible for inlining. Pointers to functions are bound at runtime and can almost never be inlined.

The last point is a double-edged sword. Sometimes it is desirable to select a function at runtime. For this reason, the standard library provides the following set of adapter functions that convert pointers to functions into function objects:

`ptr_fun` converts a static or global function pointer into a function object. If the function takes one argument, it returns a unary function object. If the function takes two arguments, it returns a binary function object.

`mem_fun` converts a pointer to a class member function into a function object. If the member function takes no arguments, it returns a unary function object whose argument is a pointer to an object of the class. If the member function takes one argument, it returns a binary function object where the first argument is a pointer to an object of the class and the second argument is the argument to the member function.

`mem_fun_ref` works like `mem_fun` except that the first argument of the resulting function object is a reference, rather than a pointer, to the class object.

For example, the following will find the first element in v for which `isValid` returns true:

```
class myclass { public: bool isValid(); };
std::vector<myclass> v;
std::vector<myclass>::iterator vi =
  std::find_if(v.begin(), v.end(),
               std::mem_fun_ref(&myclass::isValid));
```

Note that some older implementations of these adapters have names like `mem_fun1` and `mem_fun2` instead of overloading `mem_fun` for both unary and binary function objects. This is a workaround for older compilers with less-capable overload resolution. The library that comes with the Microsoft 6.0 compiler has a bug that makes `mem_fun` and `mem_fun_ref` fail to compile with **const** member functions.

Using Binders and Negators

Now that we have a way of comparing only the name portion of `Address` objects, we need to adapt it to a form used by `count_if`. The `count_if` algorithm looks a lot like `count`:

```
template <class Iterator, class Predicate>
long count_if(Iterator start, Iterator finish, Predicate pred);
```

The third argument to count_if should be a *unary predicate* function object. It takes one argument and returns true if that object should be included in the count and false if it should not. The count_if function will pass each object in the range [start, finish) to the pred function object and count the number of times pred returns true.

A *predicate* is a function that answers a yes/no question. A predicate is used as a test to determine whether or not to take an action.

A *unary predicate* is a predicate function or function object that takes one argument. Example isupper returns true if its argument is an uppercase letter.

A *binary predicate* is a predicate function or function object that takes two arguments. Example less<int> returns true if its two integer arguments compare equal.

We seem to have a problem here. The count_if algorithm expects a *unary* predicate but AddressNameEqual is a *binary* predicate. To understand what is really needed here, we need to ask ourselves, Given an Address X, when should X be included in the count? The answer is that X should be included in the count if the last name and first name of X are equal to searchAddr. Because we want to compare every element to the same value, searchAddr in effect becomes a constant for the duration of the count_if algorithm. We want to call AddressNameEqual with one argument being the element being tested and the other argument being *bound* to a constant value.

This situation comes up more frequently than you might expect. We often want to call algorithms with questions such as, Is X greater than 5? The library provides special functions for this purpose called *binders*. A binder takes a binary function object, Func, as an argument and returns a unary function object as a result. The bind1st function binds the first argument of Func to a specified value. The bind2nd function does the same for the second argument. To see binders in action, look at line 120 of Listing 6.4. The first argument to bind2nd is an anonymous AddressNameEqual object constructed by putting parenthesis after the class name. The second argument is searchAddr, which is then bound to the second argument of AddressNameEqual. The result of calling bind2nd is a unary predicate, which is then passed as the third argument to count_if.

The syntax for using binders is a bit peculiar. The binder affects one of the arguments of its own argument. When trying to remember how to use bind2nd, you might get confused and try to pass it as an argument to the function object, instead of the other way around. Remember that a binder *transforms* a function object, producing another function object as a result.

A close relative of the binders are the *negators*, not1 and not2. Like binders, negators are functions that take a function object as an argument and return another function object as a result. The `not1` function expects a unary predicate and returns another unary predicate. The `not2` function expects a binary predicate and returns a binary predicate. The predicate returned by `not1` and `not2` works just like the original predicate except that calling it produces the logical negation of calling the original. For example, `not2(equal<int>())` will return a binary predicate that returns true if its arguments are not equal. In other words, it converts `equal<int>` into `not_equal<int>`.

We don't have any need to, but if we wanted, we could modify `countName` to count the number of address records that *do not* have the specified last name and first name by changing lines 119 and 120 to the following.

```
119:    return std::count_if(addresses_.begin(), addresses_.end(),
120:            std::not1(std::bind2nd(AddressNameEqual(), searchAddr)));
```

It is interesting to note that this is exactly equivalent to the following:

```
119:    return std::count_if(addresses_.begin(), addresses_.end(),
120:            std::bind2nd(std::not2(AddressNameEqual()), searchAddr));
```

Before you get too excited about the idea that you can express complex algebra using binders and negators, I should tell you that this is about as far as it goes. They're useful, but they don't constitute a whole new programming language.

The Gory Details: Traits Classes

The actual declaration of `count` does not return a `long`; instead, it returns the type `iterator_traits<Iterator>::difference_type`, which happens to be a `long` in most cases. The `iterator_traits` class is one of a number of *traits* classes in the standard library; classes that allow templates to "discover" certain properties about their parameters. Traits classes are one of the more arcane parts of the standard library and beyond the scope of this book. They work with the help of an advanced template feature called *partial specialization*, which is not yet supported by many compilers. For compilers that don't support partial specialization, it is usually possible to create transparent workarounds for most of the cases where traits classes are needed. In some cases, however, the workarounds are not transparent and require changes in the code that uses the library. See also the compiler note for SunPro compiler, earlier in this chapter.

Searching with `lower_bound` and `find_if`

One of the most common operations on collections of objects is searching for an element or set of elements based on different search criteria. In the case of the `AddressBook` class, we will need to search for a record with a particular name or that contains a particular string. We will need to combine several facilities in the C++ Standard Library to accomplish these searches.

Lookup by Name

The next function we want to implement is a name lookup. In the user interface, we will make it easier for the user by only requiring that she type the first few letters of the name she wants. TinyPIM will then show a screenful of names, starting with the first address record with a name greater than or equal to the one the user asked for. The core function that makes this possible is findNameStartsWith (see Listing 6.1). This function finds the first record greater than or equal to the one specified. For example, if there is no entry with the name *Car*, then *Car* will match *Carter*, because *Carter* is greater than *Car*. This matching of the first few letters is the reason we call our function findNameStartsWith.

The interesting thing about this function is that it doesn't look for an exact match. The fact that our list of addresses is kept in sorted order is critical because we can search it efficiently using a *binary search*. This means that if we have 1000 addresses, we can find the one we're looking for using a maximum of 10 comparisons.

A *binary search* is a common method for efficiently locating a value in a sorted sequence. You first look at the middle of the sequence. If the value is smaller than the middle value, you look at the middle of the lower half. In each iteration, you divide the remaining part of the sequence in half until you have located the desired value. In an N-element sequence, the search takes a maximum $\log_2(N)$ comparisons (20 comparisons for a million items).

A *linear search* is a brute-force searching method of looking at every element in a container sequentially until the search value is found. In an N-element sequence, the search takes a maximum of N comparisons ($N/2$ on average). Linear search is used when the sequence is not in sorted order or when the programmer is too lazy to implement a binary search.

A binary search is one of those funny things in computer science. Many people understand the theory, but if asked to implement it, they either need to look it up in a book or else do it from memory and spend an hour debugging it. The final code looks so simple, but the boundary conditions are tricky. Fortunately, the C++ Standard Library has made it unnecessary to ever again implement a binary search yourself. Listing 6.5 shows an implementation of findNameStartsWith using a version of the binary search algorithm called lower_bound.

Listing 6.5   The findNameStartsWith Function Using the lower_bound Algorithm

```
123: // Find first Address with name greater-than-or-equal to specified
124: // name. Usually, this will be a name that starts with the specified
125: // strings.
126: AddressBook::const_iterator
```

continues

Listing 6.5   continued

```
127: AddressBook::findNameStartsWith(const std::string& lastname,
128:                                  const std::string& firstname) const
129: {
130:   Address searchAddr;
131:   searchAddr.lastname(lastname);
132:   searchAddr.firstname(firstname);
133:
134:   return std::lower_bound(addresses_.begin(), addresses_.end(),
135:                           searchAddr);
136: }
137:
```

The `lower_bound` function takes three arguments. The first two arguments represent an iterator range over which it will search. The third argument is the search object. The return value of `lower_bound` is an iterator to the first object in the range that is greater than or equal to the search object. If the search object is larger than any object in the range, the end iterator of the range is returned. This algorithm only works on ranges of sorted elements. The return value is actually the first point at which you could insert the search object while maintaining the sort order.

In lines 130–132, we create a dummy search object, just as we did in `countName`. In lines 134 and 135, we call `lower_bound` and pass it the iterator range for the entire `addresses_` container and the dummy search object. If the binary search finds a record whose name exactly matches the search object, `lower_bound` will return an iterator to that record. Otherwise, it will return an iterator to the record with the next larger name. Thanks to the `lower_bound` function, our search function turned out to be quite simple and we didn't have to debug the binary search.

Note

Concept   Algorithms in the standard library can improve the robustness of your code by providing debugged implementations of common operations. Because efficient algorithms are already implemented for you, they discourage inefficient, quick-and-dirty implementations—for example, linear search.

One more note on the efficiency of `lower_bound`. This algorithm works most efficiently with sequences that give random access to elements (`vector` and `deque`). Although it works with `list`, the need to traverse the list sequentially can cause a substantial performance penalty. We will address this and other inefficiencies later in this chapter.

Searching for a String

The last requirement we need to address at this point is searching for a string anywhere in an Address record. Because the string does not necessarily appear in some "sort key," sorting and binary search will not help us. A straight linear search is all that will work.

The interface to this operation in AddressBook is the findNextContains function (see Listing 6.1). We pass it the search string and a starting point, and it returns an iterator to the next record containing the string (or end() if no more records are found). By incrementing the resulting iterator and passing it back to findNextContains, we can traverse the entire set of matching records.

An implementation of findNextContains using the find_if algorithm is shown in Listing 6.6.

Listing 6.6   Implementation of findNextContains Using find_if

```
138: // Function object class to search for a string within an Address.
139: class AddressContainsStr : public std::unary_function<Address, bool>
140: {
141: public:
142:   AddressContainsStr(const std::string& str) : str_(str) { }
143:
144:   bool operator()(const Address& a)
145:   {
146:     using std::string;
147:
148:     // Return true if any Address field contains str_
149:     return (a.lastname().find(str_) != string::npos ||
150:             a.firstname().find(str_) != string::npos ||
151:             a.phone().find(str_) != string::npos ||
152:             a.address().find(str_) != string::npos);
153:   }
154:
155: private:
156:   std::string str_;
157: };
158:
159: // Find next Address in which any field contains the specified
160: // string. Indicate starting point for search with start parameter.
161: AddressBook::const_iterator
162: AddressBook::findNextContains(const std::string& searchStr,
163:                               const_iterator start) const
164: {
165:   return std::find_if(start, addresses_.end(),
166:                       AddressContainsStr(searchStr));
167: }
168:
```

Starting at line 139, we once again define a function object. This time we do it a little differently. The `AddressContainsStr` is a unary function object class and has a constructor (line 142) which stores the search string within the function object itself. This is one thing that distinguishes function objects from pointers to functions. A function object can carry a data "payload" in addition to code. Also, function objects can often be in-lined during template instantiation.

In the function-call operator, at line 146, we bring `string` into the local scope, so that we don't need to use the `std::` prefix all the time. In lines 149–152, our function object searches every field in the `Address` object to find the search string. The `find` function of `string` will return `string::npos` if it fails to find the search string. If any of the calls to `find` do not return `string::npos`, the function returns true. The result is a function object that can be called with an `Address` argument and will return true if the search string is found within the address. The search string itself is specified once, when the function object is created.

In lines 165 and 166, we use our function object with the `find_if` algorithm. There are three arguments to `find_if`. The first two arguments are the iterator range that will be searched. The third argument is a unary predicate. `find_if` will return an iterator to the first object within the range for which the predicate evaluates true. The iterator range we pass to `find_if` is interesting. For the first time we are passing a range that represents less than a complete container. This call will only search the range from `start` to the end of `addresses_`. It will return an iterator to the first `Address` for which `AddressContainsStr` returns true. Note that we don't have an empty pair of parenthesis after `AddressContainsStr` like we did for `AddressNameEqual`. Instead, we specify a constructor argument, `searchStr`, which is stored within the function object. It is important not to confuse *constructing* a function object with *calling* a function object. What we see in line 166 is construction. The `find_if` algorithm is responsible for calling the function object's function-call operator.

Finding a Record by ID

There is one more function that we added to the `AddressBook` class. The `findRecordId` function works like `getAddress` except it returns an iterator to the `Address` object instead of the object itself. This will be used by the user interface to get a starting point for traversals and string searches. It is implemented as shown in Listing 6.7.

Listing 6.7   Implementation of `findRecordId`

```
169: // Return iterator to specified records ID.
170: AddressBook::const_iterator
171: AddressBook::findRecordId(int recordId) const throw (AddressNotFound)
```

```
172: {
173:     return getById(recordId);
174: }
```

As you can see, it is just a call-through to getById. As you recall, getById is implemented using a linear search, so findRecordId will have the same performance characteristics.

Keeping Our Addresses Sorted More Efficiently with the Set Container

Let's look at where we stand in our implementation of AddressBook. We have managed to implement all the need functions using the list container template. We chose list over vector because the ability to insert efficiently in the middle allowed us to keep the list sorted by name. However, most of the operations on AddressBook do not involve inserting records. They involve searching by name, string, or record ID, all of which are slowed down by the linear nature of list access. Most operations rely on the getById private function, which has linear performance characteristics.

It's time to go back to the standard library to find containers that are better suited for the type of data and manipulations we have in AddressBook. You might consider changing containers again to be overkill for such a small project, but our task here is to learn about the C++ Standard Library, which you will use for projects much larger than this one, with much tougher performance requirements.

A multiset of Address Objects

The main attribute of the data we store in AddressBook is that it has a natural sort order: alphabetical by name. In the real world, keeping things sorted alphabetically helps us find what we're looking for quickly. So it is in the computer world, as well, as evidenced by the binary search algorithms. The problem with the list class is that access to the elements is linear. Finding something in a list is like finding a name in the phone book by flipping one page at a time.

A better choice of data structures would be one of the standard library's *sorted associative containers*. These are containers that automatically keep their contents sorted and are optimized for inserting, removing, and searching for elements by value.

 An *associative container* is a container that organizes its elements based on their *values* instead of on order in which they were inserted. Compare with *sequence container*.

 A *sequence container* is a container that organizes its elements in a linear order determined by the order and position of insertion. (See Chapter 3.)

The simplest sorted associative containers are set and multiset. The difference between them is that a set never contains more than one of any value, whereas multiset allows duplicates. Because AddressBook allows duplicates based on name, let's try modifying the AddressBook class definition to use multiset instead of list, as shown in Listing 6.8.

> **Code Note**   Listings 6.8–6.10 correspond to files on the companion Web page in the Chapter 6 Code\Set Version directory. The files in this directory can be compiled and linked together to create an executable program.

Listing 6.8   A New Definition of AddressBook Using multiset Instead of List

```
 1:  // TinyPIM (c) 1999 Pablo Halpern. File AddressBook.h
 2:
 3:  #ifndef AddressBook_dot_h
 4:  #define AddressBook_dot_h
 5:
 6:  #include <set>
 7:  #include "Address.h"
 8:
 9:  class AddressBook
10:  {
11:    // Data structure abbreviations
12:    typedef std::multiset<Address>          addrByName_t;
13:
14:  public:
15:    AddressBook();
16:    ~AddressBook();
17:
18:    // Exception classes
19:    class AddressNotFound { };
20:    class DuplicateId { };
21:
22:    int insertAddress(const Address& addr, int recordId = 0)
23:      throw (DuplicateId);
24:    void eraseAddress(int recordId) throw (AddressNotFound);
25:    void replaceAddress(const Address& addr, int recordId = 0)
26:      throw (AddressNotFound);
27:    const Address& getAddress(int recordId) const
28:      throw (AddressNotFound);
29:
30:    // Return number of records found with specified name.
31:    int countName(const std::string& lastname,
32:                  const std::string& firstname) const;
33:
34:    // Iterator to traverse address records
35:    typedef addrByName_t::const_iterator const_iterator;
```

```
36:
37:     // Functions to traverse all address records
38:     const_iterator begin() const { return addresses_.begin(); }
39:     const_iterator end()   const { return addresses_.end();   }
40:
41:     // Find first Address with name greater-than-or-equal to specified
42:     // name. Usually, this will be a name that starts with the
43:     // specified strings.
44:     const_iterator findNameStartsWith(const std::string& lastname,
45:                           const std::string& firstname="") const;
46:
47:     // Find next Address in which any field contains the specified
48:     // string. Indicate starting point for search with start parameter.
49:     const_iterator findNextContains(const std::string& searchStr,
50:                           const_iterator start) const;
51:
52:     // Return iterator to specified records ID.
53:     const_iterator findRecordId(int recordId) const
54:       throw (AddressNotFound);
55:
56:  private:
57:     // Disable copying
58:     AddressBook(const AddressBook&);
59:     AddressBook& operator=(const AddressBook&);
60:
61:     static int nextId_;
62:
63:     addrByName_t addresses_;
64:
65:     // Get the index of the record with the specified ID.
66:     addrByName_t::iterator getById(int recordId)
67:       throw (AddressNotFound);
68:     addrByName_t::const_iterator getById(int recordId) const
69:       throw (AddressNotFound);
70:  };
71:
72:  #endif // AddressBook_dot_h
```

The changes are very modest and don't affect the public interface at all. In line 6, we
include the <set> header, which includes definitions for both set and multiset.
Then in line 12 we changed the main data type from list<Address> to
multiset<Address> and also changed its name from addrlist to addrByName_t.
Although the iterators' types have changed, they work exactly the same as they did in
the list version.

Inserting, Erasing, and Retrieving Address Records

Internally, set and multiset use a tree structure to keep their elements in sorted
order. This makes insertion, removal, and retrieval of elements very efficient. (For
more information on tree structures check out any good book on data structures.) To

take advantage of this efficient data structure, many of the search algorithms we used with list can be performed with member functions in set and multiset. The transition is remarkably simple. In fact, of the main insert, retrieve, erase, and replace functions, only insertAddress requires any changes at all, as seen in Listing 6.9.

Listing 6.9   First Part of Implementation of AddressBook Using multiset

```
 1:  // TinyPIM (c) 1999 Pablo Halpern. File AddressBook.cpp
 2:
 3:  #ifdef _MSC_VER
 4:  #pragma warning(disable : 4786)
 5:  #endif
 6:
 7:  #include <algorithm>
 8:
 9:  #include "AddressBook.h"
10:
11:  int AddressBook::nextId_ = 1;
12:
13:  AddressBook::AddressBook()
14:  {
15:  }
16:
17:  AddressBook::~AddressBook()
18:  {
19:  }
20:
21:  int AddressBook::insertAddress(const Address& addr,
22:                                 int recordId) throw (DuplicateId)
23:  {
24:    if (recordId == 0)
25:      // If recordId is not specified, create a new record id.
26:      recordId = nextId_++;
27:    else if (recordId >= nextId_)
28:      // Make sure nextId is always higher than any known record id.
29:      nextId_ = recordId + 1;
30:    else
31:    {
32:      for (addrByName_t::iterator i = addresses_.begin();
33:           i != addresses_.end(); ++i)
34:        if (i->recordId() == recordId)
35:          throw DuplicateId();
36:    }
37:
38:    // Assign recordId to copy of Address
39:    Address addrCopy(addr);
40:    addrCopy.recordId(recordId);
41:
42:    // Insert record into set
43:    addresses_.insert(addrCopy);
44:
```

```
45:     return recordId;
46:   }
47:
48:   AddressBook::addrByName_t::iterator
49:   AddressBook::getById(int recordId) throw (AddressNotFound)
50:   {
51:     for (addrByName_t::iterator i = addresses_.begin();
52:          i != addresses_.end(); ++i)
53:       if (i->recordId() == recordId)
54:         return i;
55:
56:     throw AddressNotFound();
57:   }
58:
59:   AddressBook::addrByName_t::const_iterator
60:   AddressBook::getById(int recordId) const throw (AddressNotFound)
61:   {
62:     for (addrByName_t::const_iterator i = addresses_.begin();
63:          i != addresses_.end(); ++i)
64:       if (i->recordId() == recordId)
65:         return i;
66:
67:     throw AddressNotFound();
68:   }
69:
70:   void AddressBook::eraseAddress(int recordId)
71:     throw (AddressNotFound)
72:   {
73:     addrByName_t::iterator i = getById(recordId);
74:     addresses_.erase(i);
75:   }
76:
77:   void AddressBook::replaceAddress(const Address& addr, int recordId)
78:     throw (AddressNotFound)
79:   {
80:     if (recordId == 0)
81:       recordId = addr.recordId();
82:
83:     eraseAddress(recordId);
84:     insertAddress(addr, recordId);
85:   }
86:
87:   const Address& AddressBook::getAddress(int recordId) const
88:     throw (AddressNotFound)
89:   {
90:     return *getById(recordId);
91:   }
92:
```

Line 37 is an empty line, which is notable because of what is missing: There is no linear search for the insertion point. Instead, at line 43, we simply insert a copy of the `Address` into the `multiset`, which then takes care of putting it in sorted order. The `insert` function is fast, taking place in *logarithmic time*.

Logarithmic time is the performance classification of an operation that gets slightly slower as the number of elements in the container grows. The relationship between the time needed and the current size of the container is proportional to the log of *n*, where *n* is the number of elements in the container. Computational mathematicians refer to this as "Order log N" or "O(log(n))." Logarithmic time is much faster (for large collections) than linear time, though not as fast as constant time. (See Chapters 1, "Introducing TinyPIM," and 4, "An Alternative Implementation Using a List Container," for definitions of *constant time* and *linear time*, respectively).

In lines 39 and 40, we make a copy of the `Address` and then set its record ID prior to inserting it in to the `multiset`, in line 43. The extra copy was not needed in the `list` implementation, so why do we need it here? In the list implementation, the `insert` function returned an iterator to the new element in the list. We used this iterator to set the record ID of the new element after it was inserted in the list. Although the `insert` function for `multiset` also returns an iterator to the newly inserted element, that iterator cannot be used to modify the element. The reason for this is that modifying an element in an associative container could change its position in the sort order, causing an inconsistency in the internal state of the container. The container guards against this by never returning modifiable references to its elements.

EXCURSION

Defects in the Standard

In most standard library implementations today, a `set` or `multiset` iterator is virtually indistinguishable from its corresponding `const_iterator`. Depending on the implementation, they might even be of the exact same type.

Unfortunately, the official standard document is vague and contradictory when it comes to the const nature of the `set` and `multiset` iterators. The standards committee is currently (as of Oct 1999) reviewing a defect report that seeks to resolve these discrepancies. Some implementations, including the one that comes with the popular Microsoft 6.0 compiler, do allow modifying a `set` element through a nonconst iterator. This is a valid interpretation of the standard and corresponds to one proposed resolution of the defect.

Even if the eventual resolution of the defect in the standard allows modification of `set` and `multiset` elements, you should never modify an element in such a way that it would change the position of the element in the sort order. Such a change would result in undefined behavior. For maximum portability until the issue is resolved and compilers implement the updated standard, you should assume that `set` and `multiset` iterators do not provide write access to the container elements.

So far, then, we have improved performance a bit by removing one linear search (for finding the insertion point) and replacing it with a logarithmic operation. The getById function is still implemented using a linear search because the multiset is sorted by name, not by ID, so the sort order does not make ID lookups any easier. Let's look now at search operations.

Searching the multiset

Associative containers are designed for efficient searching, so it stands to reason that there should be improved ways of implementing these operations. Listing 6.10 shows these improvements. It is worth noting, however, that the old list-based implementations would have worked as well, although they would not have gained any in performance.

Listing 6.10   Search Functions in AddressBook Using multiset

```
 93:   // Return number of records found with specified name.
 94:   int AddressBook::countName(const std::string& lastname,
 95:                              const std::string& firstname) const
 96:   {
 97:     Address searchAddr;
 98:     searchAddr.lastname(lastname);
 99:     searchAddr.firstname(firstname);
100:
101:     // Return a count of the number of matching records
102:     return addresses_.count(searchAddr);
103:   }
104:
105:   // Find first Address with name greater-than-or-equal to specified
106:   // name. Usually, this will be a name that starts with the
107:   // specified strings.
108:   AddressBook::const_iterator
109:   AddressBook::findNameStartsWith(const std::string& lastname,
110:                                   const std::string& firstname) const
111:   {
112:     Address searchAddr;
113:     searchAddr.lastname(lastname);
114:     searchAddr.firstname(firstname);
115:
116:     return addresses_.lower_bound(searchAddr);
117:   }
118:
119:   // Function object class to search for a string within an Address.
120:   class AddressContainsStr : public std::unary_function<Address, bool>
121:   {
122:   public:
123:     AddressContainsStr(const std::string& str) : str_(str) { }
124:
125:     bool operator()(const Address& a)
```

continues

Listing 6.10   continued

```
126:    {
127:      using std::string;
128:
129:      // Return true if any Address field contains str_
130:      return (a.lastname().find(str_) != string::npos ||
131:              a.firstname().find(str_) != string::npos ||
132:              a.phone().find(str_) != string::npos ||
133:              a.address().find(str_) != string::npos);
134:    }
135:
136: private:
137:   std::string str_;
138: };
139:
140: // Find next Address in which any field contains the specified
141: // string. Indicate starting point for search with start parameter.
142: AddressBook::const_iterator
143: AddressBook::findNextContains(const std::string& searchStr,
144:                               const_iterator start) const
145: {
146:   return std::find_if(start, addresses_.end(),
147:                       AddressContainsStr(searchStr));
148: }
149:
150: // Return iterator to specified records ID.
151: AddressBook::const_iterator
152: AddressBook::findRecordId(int recordId) const throw (AddressNotFound)
153: {
154:   return getById(recordId);
155: }
```

Let's look first at the simple change we made to findNameStartsWith. In line 116, we replaced the std::lower_bound algorithm function with the lower_bound member function of multiset. The basic concept is the same, but the member function takes advantage of the internal tree structure of the multiset, making it much more efficient.

In countName, we eliminated the use of the count_if algorithm in favor of the count member function of multiset. For all associative containers, count will return the number of elements with a given value. The count function is efficient because it uses a tree search instead of a linear search to find the values. But wait! What happened to our AddressNameEqual class? Won't count use the wrong equality test?

The answer might surprise you: Neither count nor any other operation on a sorted associative container uses the equality operator (==) at all. Two objects, *x* and *y*, are considered *equivalent* if neither *x<y* nor *y<x* is true, even if they don't compare equal using the == operator. Because our < operator is defined to only look at the names portion of an Address, the equivalence relationship is exactly what we need.

When sorting and searching, two objects are considered *equivalent* if they have the same rank in the sort order, even if they do not compare equal. For example, two AddressRecords with the same first and last names are *equivalent* but not *equal*.

Two objects are *equal* if the result of comparing them with == is true.

The findNextContains and findRecordId functions remain unchanged. Certainly, the change to multiset has made insertAddress, countName, and findNameStartsWith more efficient and simpler. But the other functions still rely on the same old getById function, which must do a linear search in order to find a record. Should we have sorted our multiset by record ID instead? That would make some things faster, but we would lose the alphabetical order in our iterators. Next, we'll look at a way to sort on *both* name and record ID.

Double Indexing with a Map Container

We would like AddressBook to look up records by name or by ID with equal efficiency. To accomplish this goal, we need to maintain two containers, one sorted on name, the other sorted on ID. Both to save memory and to reduce the chance that they will get out of sync, there should only be one copy of each record. Thus, the second container should *point* to the records in the first container, rather than contain a whole copy.

Creating a Second Index Using a Map

Our current implementation stores the Address records in a multiset container (addresses_) sorted by name. Our second container should therefore be sorted by record ID and should associate each record ID with an object in the multiset. In database parlance, this is called a second *index* (the first index is the multiset itself). Figure 6.2 shows the desired relationship.

Figure 6.2

Adding a second index to AddressBook.

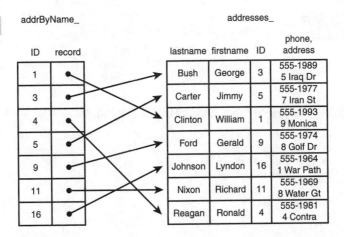

For each record ID in the `addrById_` container, we can quickly get the corresponding record in the `Addresses_` container. The `addrById_` container establishes a mapping from an ID to a record. The standard library container that will help us implement this mapping is appropriately called a `map`.

The `map` template class is instantiated with at least two template parameters. The first template parameter is the type of *key* that will be kept in sorted order, just as in the case of `set`. The second template parameter is the type of *content* that will be associated with each key. There is also a `multimap` template that works like `map` except that `map` rejects any attempt to store a duplicate key, whereas `multimap` allows duplicate keys. (This is the same relationship as between `set` and `multiset`). Although we allow `Address` records to have duplicate name fields, they must not have duplicate record IDs, so we choose a `map` rather than a `multimap` for our second index.

 A *key* is an attribute of a data record used to identify that record and distinguish it from other data records.

 A *value*, in this context, is the data record associated with a key. Unfortunately, the standard library uses *value* to mean the entire key-value combination, so I will try to avoid confusion by using the term *content*, instead, to refer the record associated with a key.

Clearly, the key to `addrById_` should be an integer representing a record ID. What should the content be? It cannot be an `Address` object because then it would duplicate the `Address` object already in the `addresses_` set. It could be a pointer to an address, but there is a better choice. We will make the content an *iterator* to the `Address` in the `addresses_` set. As we move though the implementation, you'll see that this gives us quite an advantage. For now, just remember that iterators are *pointer-like*. Listing 6.11 shows the new class definition with the second index, `addrById_` added.

 Note   **Code Note**   Listings 6.11 and 6.12 correspond to files on the companion Web page in the `Chapter 6 Code\Double Index` directory. The files in this directory can be compiled and linked together to create an executable program.

Listing 6.11   `AddressBook` Enhanced with a Second Index

```
1:  // TinyPIM (c) 1999 Pablo Halpern. File AddressBook.h
2:
3:  #ifndef AddressBook_dot_h
4:  #define AddressBook_dot_h
5:
6:  #include <set>
```

```
 7:  #include <map>
 8:  #include "Address.h"
 9:
10:  class AddressBook
11:  {
12:    // Data structure abbreviations
13:    typedef std::multiset<Address>                   addrByName_t;
14:    typedef std::map<int, addrByName_t::iterator> addrById_t;
15:
16:  public:
17:    AddressBook();
18:    ~AddressBook();
19:
20:    // Exception classes
21:    class AddressNotFound { };
22:    class DuplicateId { };
23:
24:    int insertAddress(const Address& addr, int recordId = 0)
25:      throw (DuplicateId);
26:    void eraseAddress(int recordId) throw (AddressNotFound);
27:    void replaceAddress(const Address& addr, int recordId = 0)
28:      throw (AddressNotFound);
29:    const Address& getAddress(int recordId) const
30:      throw (AddressNotFound);
31:
32:    // Return number of records found with specified name.
33:    int countName(const std::string& lastname,
34:                  const std::string& firstname) const;
35:
36:    // Iterator to traverse address records
37:    typedef addrByName_t::const_iterator const_iterator;
38:
39:    // Functions to traverse all address records
40:    const_iterator begin() const { return addresses_.begin(); }
41:    const_iterator end()   const { return addresses_.end();   }
42:
43:    // Find first Address with name greater-than-or-equal to specified
44:    // name. Usually, this will be a name that starts with the
45:    // specified strings.
46:    const_iterator findNameStartsWith(const std::string& lastname,
47:                              const std::string& firstname="") const;
48:
49:    // Find next Address in which any field contains the specified
50:    // string. Indicate starting point for search with start parameter.
51:    const_iterator findNextContains(const std::string& searchStr,
52:                                    const_iterator start) const;
53:
54:    // Return iterator to specified records ID.
55:    const_iterator findRecordId(int recordId) const
56:      throw (AddressNotFound);
57:
```

continues

Listing 6.11   continued

```
58:  private:
59:    // Disable copying
60:    AddressBook(const AddressBook&);
61:    AddressBook& operator=(const AddressBook&);
62:
63:    static int nextId_;
64:
65:    addrByName_t addresses_;
66:    addrById_t   addrById_;
67:
68:    // Get the index of the record with the specified ID.
69:    addrByName_t::iterator getById(int recordId)
70:      throw (AddressNotFound);
71:    addrByName_t::const_iterator getById(int recordId) const
72:      throw (AddressNotFound);
73:  };
74:
75:  #endif // AddressBook_dot_h
```

The only changes to the header file are in lines 7, 14, and 66. In line 14, we create a typedef abbreviation, addrById_, for the map class, using the map template included in line 7. The two template parameters are int for the key type and addrByName_t::iterator for the content type. Line 66 declares the addrById_ map container as a member of AddressBook.

Keeping the Two Containers in Sync

Every time we insert or erase a record in the AddressBook we will need to update both address_ and addrById_. Listing 6.12 shows the changes we need to make in the insertAddress, eraseAddress, and getById functions. The remaining functions are unchanged. In particular, the search functions did not change because they worked entirely with the name and content of the records, not with their IDs.

Listing 6.12   Keeping Two Containers in Sync in the Insert and Erase Functions

```
 1:  // TinyPIM (c) 1999 Pablo Halpern. File AddressBook.cpp
 2:
 3:  #ifdef _MSC_VER
 4:  #pragma warning(disable : 4786)
 5:  #endif
 6:
 7:  #include <algorithm>
 8:
 9:  #include "AddressBook.h"
10:
11:  int AddressBook::nextId_ = 1;
12:
13:  AddressBook::AddressBook()
```

```
14:  {
15:  }
16:
17:  AddressBook::~AddressBook()
18:  {
19:  }
20:
21:  int AddressBook::insertAddress(const Address& addr,
22:                                 int recordId) throw (DuplicateId)
23:  {
24:    if (recordId == 0)
25:      // If recordId is not specified, create a new record id.
26:      recordId = nextId_++;
27:    else if (recordId >= nextId_)
28:      // Make sure nextId is always higher than any known record id.
29:      nextId_ = recordId + 1;
30:    else if (addrById_.count(recordId))
31:      // recordId is already in map
32:      throw DuplicateId();
33:
34:    // Assign recordId to copy of Address
35:    Address addrCopy(addr);
36:    addrCopy.recordId(recordId);
37:
38:    // Insert record into set
39:    addrByName_t::iterator i = addresses_.insert(addrCopy);
40:
41:    // Insert Address iterator into id-based map
42:    // addrById_.insert(std::make_pair(recordId, i));
43:    addrById_[recordId] = i;
44:
45:    return recordId;
46:  }
47:
48:  AddressBook::addrByName_t::iterator
49:  AddressBook::getById(int recordId) throw (AddressNotFound)
50:  {
51:    // Find record by Id.
52:    addrById_t::iterator idIter = addrById_.find(recordId);
53:    if (idIter == addrById_.end())
54:      throw AddressNotFound();
55:
56:    return idIter->second;
57:  }
58:
59:  AddressBook::addrByName_t::const_iterator
60:  AddressBook::getById(int recordId) const throw (AddressNotFound)
61:  {
62:    // Find record by Id.
63:    addrById_t::const_iterator idIter = addrById_.find(recordId);
64:    if (idIter == addrById_.end())
```

continues

Listing 6.12   continued

```
65:        throw AddressNotFound();
66:
67:     return idIter->second;
68:   }
69:
70:   void AddressBook::eraseAddress(int recordId)
71:     throw (AddressNotFound)
72:   {
73:     addrByName_t::iterator i = getById(recordId);
74:
75:     // Remove entry from both containers
76:     addresses_.erase(i);
77:     addrById_.erase(recordId);
78:   }
```

In line 30, we replaced our linear search loop with a single call to map member function, count. This works the same way that count works for set and multiset—it returns the number of times the specified key appears in the map. Because map does not permit duplicate keys, the value returned from count will be either 0 (the key does not appear) or 1 (the key does appear). If count returns true (1), we throw the duplicate ID exception.

A Map as an Associative Array

When we have established that this is not a duplicate, we insert the record in to the multiset in line 39 as before, but this time we save the return value of insert. The insert member of set returns an iterator to the newly inserted value. This is exactly the iterator we want to store in our ID map. Line 43 shows one way to insert a record into a map. The map class template provides an index operator (operator[]) which lets you treat a map as an *associative array* or a *sparse array*.

An *associative array* is a data structure that can be used with array-like indexing, but where the indexes are not necessarily nonnegative integers. Example: An associative array of grades indexed by student name.

A *sparse array* is an array having many unused elements (that is, they have null or empty values). A sparse array data structure is designed to avoid wasting space on these unused elements.

There are actually two operations going on in line 43. The first is the indexing operation, addrById_[recordId], and the second is the assignment to i. The indexing operator looks up the specified key in the map and returns a reference to the content associated with the key. If the key is not found, it inserts the key into the map using the default constructor for the content object. Because recordId is a new key, the index operator inserts it into the map and associates it with a default iterator value. Then it returns a reference to this (useless) iterator, which is subsequently assigned the value, i. Note that this method of accessing a map does not work with `multimap` because there is no way to resolve the index to a unique element in the container.

The Pair Class

An alternative way to insert a value into the `map` object is shown in the comment on line 42. Here, we bundle the key-content pair into a single object and pass them as a unit to the `insert` function. The result of calling `make_pair` is an object of class `pair`, which is defined in the standard as shown in Listing 6.13.

Listing 6.13   The Standard Pair `struct` Template in the `<utility>` Header

```
 1:   template <class T1, class T2>
 2:   struct pair
 3:   {
 4:     typedef T1 first_type;
 5:     typedef T2 second_type;
 6:
 7:     T1 first;
 8:     T2 second;
 9:
10:     pair();
11:     pair(const T1& x, const T2& y);
12:     template <class U, class V> pair(const pair<U, V>& p);
13:   };
```

All the members of `pair` are public, including the data members. A pair is simply a structure template that can be instantiated to hold two values of arbitrary type. The most important members of `pair` are `first` and `second`, defined on lines 7 and 8. The `pair` template is defined in the header `<utility>` and, of course, it is in namespace `std`. The `make_pair` function is a simple convenience template that takes any two values and returns a `pair` instantiated on the right types and containing the specified values.

Note

Compiler Note   The `make_pair` function is very literal in its recognition of the type of its arguments. For example, `make_pair(5, "hello")` will return a value of type `pair<int, const char[6]>`, not `pair<int, const char*>`, as you might expect. This is usually invisible to you because the conversion operators built into `pair` (line 12 of Listing 6.13) make this a nonissue. However, many compilers do not yet support member templates, which are needed to implement the conversion operators. As a result, these compilers will complain of a type mismatch if you pass one type of pair and it expects a different type of pair. The simplest workaround is not to use `make_pair` at all, but rather to explicitly specify the types by using the `pair` constructor directly, as in `pair<int, const char*>(5, "hello")`. In the case of the `map` template, it is simpler and better to use the `value_type` typedef from `map` as in `addrById_t::value_type(recordId, i)`.

Pair is used in several places in the standard library. In addition to being the type passed to insert for maps and multimaps, it is also used the type returned from dereferencing an iterator. If you are only interested in iterating over the key or the content of the map, you need to explicitly refer to the first or second data members. For example, if you wanted to print out all the keys in addrById, you would write:

```
for (addrById_t::iterator i = addrById.begin(); i != addrById.end(); ++i)
  std::cout << i->first << std::endl;
```

Compiler Note   On some older compilers, notably the SunPro 4.2 compiler, the -> operator is not implemented for iterators. This is a particular handicap for map iterators where we almost always want to use it. The workaround is to use (*i).first instead of i->first.

One piece of esoterica that you absolutely must know: The result of dereferencing a map or multimap iterator is not pair<key, content>& but pair<**const** key, content>&. In other words, you can modify the content part of the pair (the second member) but not the key part (the first member). This prevents you from changing the position of the key in the sort order. If you want to change the key associated with a value, you must erase and then reinsert the value.

Finally, a pair is also returned as the result of an insert operation on a map or set. The insert function for multimap and multiset containers return an iterator to the newly inserted element. However, a map or set container permits only one instance of a key and rejects attempts to insert a duplicate key. What would be returned if a duplicate insertion is attempted? The answer is that these containers return a object of type pair<iterator,bool>. The second member of the returned pair is set to true if the insertion succeeded or false if the key already exists in the container. The first member of the returned pair is an iterator to the inserted element if the insertion succeeded and to the existing element with the same key if the insertion failed. If you are only interested in one part of the pair, you can explicitly refer to the first or second member. For example:

```
if (! myset.insert(x).second)
  std::cout << "Duplicate item, " << x << std::endl;
```

Finishing Up or Implementation

Returning to Listing 6.12, let's look at the getById function in lines 48–57. Remember that this is the function that is used in several places to look up a record by ID. The previous implementation used a linear search. Our new implementation uses the find function on line 52 to obtain an iterator into the addrById_ map. If the key wasn't found, it will return addrById_.end(), which we test for in line 53. On line 56, we return at the second part of the pair pointed to by idIter. This is the content object that was associated with the specified recordId and is an iterator into the addresses_ set. Confusing? Refer back to Figure 6.2. If we are looking up the record with an ID of 9, the find function will return an iterator pointing to the pair containing record ID 9. Dereferencing the iterator and looking at the second member of the pair will yield a different iterator pointing to the record for Gerald Ford in the addresses_ set.

A shortcut implementation of getById could be reduced to one line:

```
return addrById[recordId].second;
```

Unfortunately, this would not detect invalid record IDs. If a record ID was specified that was not found in the map, it would be added and associated with an invalid set iterator. The return value of getById would be invalid and cause undefined behavior. This form of ad-hoc insertion into a map is best saved for situations where the content type has a meaningful default constructor. One final note on this shortcut: Because the index operator returns a reference to a pair instead of an iterator to a pair, we must use the dot (.) operator instead of the arrow (->) operator to refer to its members.

Finally, let's look at eraseAddress, which starts on line 70 of Listing 6.12. After we remove the record from the addresses_ multiset in line 76, we also remove it from the addrById_ map in line 77. All associative containers have overloaded versions of erase. The version we see in line 77 identifies the element to remove by its key. The version in line 76 identifies the element using an iterator.

6

EXCURSION

Hashed Associative Containers

Many people were disappointed that the C++ Standard Library was completed without including hashed containers, due to the fact that proposals for hashed containers were received too late in the standardization process. A hashed container is one that allows elements to be found in about constant time. You can learn about hashes in any data structure book. Hashed containers are associative—that is, elements are stored and retrieved by value, rather than position. Unlike sorted containers, the elements in a hashed container appear to be in random order. However, for situations where the order of elements is unimportant, hashed containers provide the performance improvement of constant-time versus logarithmic-time lookups.

Although it didn't make it into the standard, most implementations of the standard library come with a collection of hashed containers. The interface for these containers is remarkably consistent across different vendors. Each hashed must be instantiated with two function objects: one for the hash function and one for the equality function. Most implementations provide default hash functions for the built-in types, pointers, and standard strings. There is a hashed associative container template corresponding to each sorted associative container template as follows:

```
hash_set<T, H = hash<T>, EQ = equal<T> >
hash_multiset<T, H = hash<T>, EQ = equal<T> >
hash_map<Key, T, H = hash<Key>, EQ = equal<Key> >
hash_multimap<Key, T, H = hash<Key>, EQ = equal<Key> >
```

Note that some implementations use different names—for example, `hashset` instead of `hash_set`. Also, some vendors put these names in namespace `std`, although this is not technically allowed by the standard. See your vendor's documentation for more details.

Next Steps

We have made a lot of changes to our `AddressBook` in this chapter. First, we added search functions to find records by name or to find records using a string within the records. We used several parts of the algorithms and function objects library to accomplish this. We became concerned about efficiency and reimplemented `AddressBook` using sorted associative containers, first using a `multiset`, and then adding a `map`.

Our new implementation should be very efficient for inserting, removing, accessing, and finding records, but we haven't even tested whether it works. The new search features were added to meet the requirements of our user interface. In our next chapter, we will implement that user interface and exercise both the new and old features of our address book quite thoroughly. The user interface code will introduce more features of the stream I/O library as well as new container types and algorithms.

In this chapter

- *Specification of the Display List*
- *Design of the Display List*
- *The* `DisplayList` *Class*
- *Implementing the Scrolling List*
- *Reading Numeric Input and Handling Errors*
- *Defining the* `AddressDisplayList`

Chapter 7

Scrolling Display Lists Using deques and I/O streams

In the previous chapter, we added functions to the `AddressBook` that will allow us to visit each record or search for specific records. These features will let us implement the next part of our project: a display list. The purpose of the display list class is to display a list of records to the user and allow the user to choose one to view, edit, or delete. Because there could be more records than can fit on the terminal screen, the display list must be able to "scroll" back and forth over the records, presenting the user with one screenful at a time.

Specification of the Display List

To be more precise, we'll specify our display list as follows:

1. For each record, the display list will show a one-line summary. In the case of the address book, the summary includes the last name, first name, and phone number. (The phone number is included so that the user can see it in display mode without viewing the whole record).

2. The display list shows one screenful of summaries at a time. For our purposes, a screenful will be considered 15 lines. Each summary line is preceded by a line number in the range from 1 to 15. When first entering a list view, the first screenful of summaries is displayed.

3. If the user enters the command to scroll forward, the next screenful of summaries is displayed. If the user enters the command to scroll backward, the previous screenful of summaries is displayed.

4. If the summary for the last record is displayed, a message to that effect is displayed at the end of the list and forward scrolling is disabled. If the summary for the first record is displayed, a message is displayed at the top of the list and backward scrolling is disabled. If there are no records to display at all, a message indicating that is displayed.

5. If the user chooses a record to view, edit, or delete, the display list will validate that the user's choice is a number in the allowable range (1–15). If not, the user is prompted to enter another choice.

Design of the Display List

As I described in Chapter 1, "Introducing TinyPIM," our overall design is divided into a core package, a user interface package, and (eventually) a persistence package. Remember that someday we might want to have the user interface package and the core package separated by a network connection. To avoid taxing this connection, we want the display list not to retrieve all the records at once, but a few at a time as needed to fill the screen. We also don't want the display list to retrieve records more often than necessary. So, for example, if the user searches for a name in the middle of the alphabet, the display list should retrieve a screenful of records from the middle of the address book and not retrieve all the records starting at the beginning. When retrieved, however, it should hold on to them so that if the user scrolls backward and then forward again, it is unnecessary to retrieve the original screenful again. This means that we should *cache* records that we have seen before.

 A *cache* is a container that holds recently-used items so that they do not need to be recomputed or retrieved if needed again. As a verb, *cache* means to manage data using a cache.

A simple cache structure that will meet our needs is a sequence that holds the records currently visible on the screen, as well as the records before and after it. As the user scrolls forward and backward, more screenfuls of records are added to the cache. The design of this cache is illustrated in Figure 7.1.

The cache holds a contiguous subset of the whole address book. The screen displays a subset of the cache. If the user scrolls forward past the end of the cache, more records are retrieved from the address book and appended to the cache. If the user scrolls backward past the beginning of the cache, more records are retrieved and inserted at the front of the cache. To display record summaries, the display list must show records from the middle of the cache.

Thus we need a data structure that efficiently allows us to insert elements at both the beginning or end and that gives us *random access* to the elements in the middle.

Figure 7.1

Design of the display list cache.

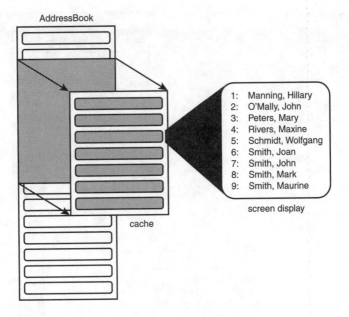

1: Manning, Hillary
2: O'Mally, John
3: Peters, Mary
4: Rivers, Maxine
5: Schmidt, Wolfgang
6: Smith, Joan
7: Smith, John
8: Smith, Mark
9: Smith, Maurine

screen display

Random access is the ability to efficiently access elements of a container at random—that is, at neither the beginning nor end of the container.

A list lets us insert at both ends and a vector gives us random access to elements, but neither of them meet both requirements. These requirements are met by another container type called a deque. The operations defined in the deque class template are the same as in the vector class template and have the same performance characteristics, except that deque also provides the functions push_front and pop_front, which insert and remove elements from the front of a deque in constant time. As in the case of vector, inserting into the middle of a deque is a linear-time operation. A deque seems to have the right qualities for our list cache. We'll see a deque in action as we start coding in the next section.

how too
pro nouns' it   **deque**   /dek/ as in a *deck* of cards.

Even with the help of the deque class template, there is still quite a bit of work to do to manage the class and print the display list. Because the address book and date book both need display lists, it would be a good idea to share the display list machinery between them. We do this by creating a DisplayList base class, with subclasses AddressDisplayList and AppointmentDisplayList. Figure 7.2 shows the UML class diagram for the display lists from Chapter 1.

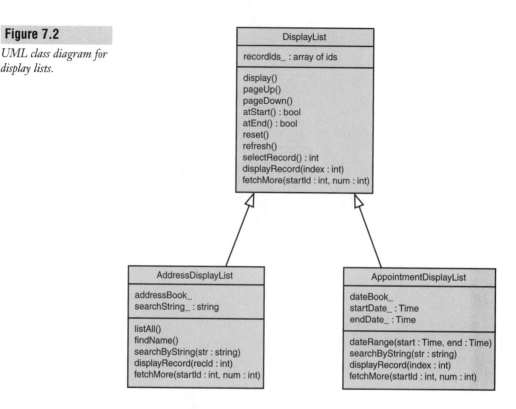

Figure 7.2
UML class diagram for display lists.

Because the cache management is in the base class, it needs to work for both Address records and Appointment records. Because both Address and Appointment objects contain an integer record ID, we will use our cache to hold record IDs. Actually retrieving records and displaying records is left up to the derived class. The base class delegates these tasks to the derived classes by calling the virtual functions fetchMore to retrieve records and displayRecord to actually display the summary. The base class provides the functions for scrolling and picking a record from the list.

The DisplayList Class

Listing 7.1 shows the class definition for DisplayList.

Code Note   Except where otherwise noted, the listings in this chapter correspond to files on the companion Web page in the Chapter 7 Code\Display List directory. The files in this directory do not comprise an executable program. However, this code is reused in the Chapter 8 Code\Menus directory, which contains additional pieces of code for compiling and linking an executable program. (See the end of the Introduction for information on accessing this book's companion Web page.)

Listing 7.1   Class Definition for `DisplayList`

```
1:  // TinyPIM (c) 1999 Pablo Halpern. File DisplayList.h
2:
3:  #ifndef DisplayList_dot_h
4:  #define DisplayList_dot_h 1
5:
6:  #include <deque>
7:  #include <vector>
8:
9:  // This abstract class is used to display a list of records
10: // where the specific record type being displayed is
11: // determined by the derived classes.
12: // If there are more records in the list than can fit on
13: // a screen, a partial list is displayed and functions
14: // are provided for scrolling up and down in the list.
15: class DisplayList
16: {
17: public:
18:   DisplayList(int linesPerScreen = 15);
19:   virtual ~DisplayList();
20:
21:   void display();    // Display the list
22:   void pageDown();   // Scroll down one screenful
23:   void pageUp();     // Scroll up one screenful
24:   void toStart();    // Scroll to the first screenful
25:   bool atStart();    // True if displaying first screenful
26:   bool atEnd();      // True if displaying last screenful
27:   void reset();      // Reinitialize (discard cached records)
28:   int screenRecord(int n) const; // Return ID of nth record on screen
29:
30:   // Scroll so that specified record is at the top of the screen.
31:   void scrollToTop(int recordId);
32:
33:   // Ask the user for a record number and return selected recordId
34:   // Returns 0 if no record selected (e.g. user aborted).
35:   int selectRecord();
36:
37: protected:
38:   // Derived classes define displayRecord to display a
39:   // particular record type.
40:   virtual void displayRecord(int recordId) = 0;
41:
42:   // Derived classes define fetchMore to get numRecords more records
43:   // starting at, but not including startId. result is vector of
44:   // record IDs. If numRecords is negative, then retrieve -numRecords
45:   // records BEFORE startId. If startId is zero, then return the
46:   // first (or last) records. Result may have more records than
47:   // requested. Returns true if the last (or first) record is in
48:   // result.
49:   virtual bool fetchMore(int startId, int numRecords,
```

continues

Listing 7.1   continued

```
50:                                 std::vector<int>& result) = 0;
51:
52:   private:
53:
54:     typedef std::deque<int> cache_t;     // Type of record Id cache
55:
56:     int     linesPerScreen_;   // Number of lines per screenful
57:     cache_t cache_;            // Cache of known record IDs.
58:     bool    cachedFirst_;      // true if cache_ contains first record
59:     bool    cachedLast_;       // true if cache_ contains last record
60:     int     firstVisibleIdx_;  // Deque index of first visible record
61:
62:     // Fill cache in the forward direction.
63:     // Specify start index and number of desired records. If not
64:     // enough records are available, will set cachedLast_.
65:     void fillCacheFwd(int start, int numNeeded);
66:
67:     // Fill cache in the backward direction.
68:     // Specify start index and number of desired records. If not
69:     // enough records are available, will set cachedLast_.
70:     void fillCacheBkwd(int start, int numNeeded);
71:   };
72:
73:   #endif // DisplayList_dot_h
```

In line 6, we include the header for deque. In line 54 we define an abbreviation for a deque of integers and use it to declare our cache in line 57. We also define a number of variables to keep track of the state of the display list. The linesPerScreen_ variable (line 56) is set in the constructor and doesn't change for the life of the DisplayList object. The cachedFirst_ and cachedLast_ variables (lines 58 and 59) indicate whether the first and last record are in the cache and thus whether it is possible to scroll backward or forward. The firstVisibleIdx_ variable is the index in the cache that contains the first record to be displayed in the current screenful.

Lines 21–31 declare the main functions used both by the client code and by the derived display list classes, as described in the comments for each function. In line 35, we declare the selectRecord function which interacts with the user. The user is expected to enter a number from 1 to linesPerScreen and selectRecord will return the recordId associated with that row on the screen. If the user enters 0, the function returns 0 to indicate that the user wants to cancel. If the user enters any other value, it displays an error message and prompts the user again until a valid value is entered.

The function displayRecord on line 40 is used by DisplayList to print out a summary of the specified record. This function is *pure virtual* (see Chapter 1 for a definition of pure virtual), so it must be overridden in each derived class. The specific derived class knows what kind of record is being displayed (for example, an AddressDisplayList displays Address records) and decides how it will be displayed (for example, last name, first name, phone number).

The fetchMore function declared in lines 49 and 50 is another pure virtual function which is called to retrieve records to fill the cache. When the caching logic determines that it needs more records, it calls fetchMore and asks for a certain number of additional records starting at startId. The fetchMore function (which is implemented in the derived class) will retrieve the specified number of additional records and put their record IDs in the result vector. If the DisplayList is filling the cache in backward (that is, if the user is scrolling up), it passes the ID of the last record instead of the first and requests a negative number of records. The vector returned by fetchMore will then contain record IDs ending at startId. In both the forward and reverse cases, startId itself is not put into the results vector. If fetchMore can go no farther (for example, it has reached the end or beginning of the available records), it returns true. As we will see, fetchMore function will be the trickiest of the functions defined in the derived classes.

In lines 65 and 70, we declare two functions used to fill the cache. These are private internal functions that make sure that the cache contains the actual records to display before attempting to display them. They contain the core of the caching logic.

Implementing the Scrolling List

Let's take a closer look at the caching logic, starting with the initial state of the cache and then stepping though the process of filling it up. Listing 7.2 shows the first part of the DisplayList implementation.

Listing 7.2   Initialization and Cache Filling Logic of DisplayList

```
 1:  // TinyPIM (c) 1999, Pablo Halpern. File DisplayList.cpp
 2:
 3:  #ifdef _MSC_VER
 4:  #pragma warning(disable : 4786)
 5:  #endif
 6:
 7:  #include <cassert>
 8:  #include <iostream>
 9:  #include <iomanip>
10:  #include <algorithm>
11:  #include <iterator>
12:
13:  #ifdef _MSC_VER
14:  #define min _cpp_min
```

continues

Listing 7.2   continued

```
15:   #define max _cpp_max
16:   #endif
17:
18:   #include "DisplayList.h"
19:
20:   // Constructor sets screen size.
21:   DisplayList::DisplayList(int linesPerScreen)
22:      : linesPerScreen_(linesPerScreen)
23:   {
24:     reset();
25:   }
26:
27:   // Destructor doesn't have to do much.
28:   DisplayList::~DisplayList() { }
29:
30:   // Clear all data
31:   void DisplayList::reset()
32:   {
33:     cache_.clear();
34:     cachedFirst_ = false;
35:     cachedLast_ = false;
36:     firstVisibleIdx_ = 0;
37:   }
38:
39:   // Fill cache in the forward direction.
40:   // Specify start index and number of desired records. If not
41:   // enough records are available, will set cachedLast_.
42:   void DisplayList::fillCacheFwd(int start, int numNeeded)
43:   {
44:     int startId = 0;
45:     if (cache_.empty())
46:       // Start caching from beginning of list
47:       cachedFirst_ = true;
48:     else
49:     {
50:       // Start retrieving from last item in cache
51:       assert(start < cache_.size());
52:       startId = cache_.back();
53:     }
54:
55:     int recordsTillEnd = cache_.size() - start;
56:     if (! cachedLast_ && recordsTillEnd < numNeeded)
57:     {
58:       // Too few entries in cache to fill screen. Need to fetch more.
59:
60:       std::vector<int> moreRecords;
61:       cachedLast_ = fetchMore(startId, numNeeded - recordsTillEnd,
62:                               moreRecords);
63:
64:       std::copy(moreRecords.begin(), moreRecords.end(),
```

```
65:                    std::back_inserter(cache_));
66:     }
67:   }
68:
```

The constructor, destructor, and reset functions are pretty straightforward. When the display list is in an initial state, the cache is empty and, therefore, neither the first nor the last available record is in the cache.

The fillCacheFwd function, beginning at line 42, takes two arguments. The first argument is the position in the cache where we want to see records. The second argument is the number of records we want to see. If the number of records in the cache is less than what we want, we go out and get more. If we are filling an empty cache, we will start filling from the first available record, so we set cachedFirst to true in line 47.

Catching Bugs Early Using the assert Macro

At line 51, we use the assert macro to make sure that our start index is not larger than the largest index in the deque. The assert macro is used as a debugging aid to ensure that a condition that must always be true is in fact true. It takes one argument and will abort the program if its argument evaluates to false at run time. This condition is known as a *failed assertion* and means that some bug in the program is causing a required condition not to hold true. In line 51 we assert that the index is within range. If a bug causes it to be out of range, I'd rather see a controlled abort than have to track down undefined behavior caused by an indexing error.

Note that assert is a macro, not a function. That is why you cannot use the std:: qualification in front of it. The assert macro is usually defined conditionally so that it evaluates to an empty expression if debugging is disabled at compile time. This means you can use assert liberally, knowing that when you are ready to release production code, you can speed up the code by turning off all the assert tests. Even with assertions turned off, the presence of an assert in the code nicely documents invariant conditions.

Because the assert macro might be compiled out of the code, it is essential that the condition being asserted does not have any side effects, or else the code will behave differently depending on whether debugging is enabled. For example, you should never write assert(i++) because i would only be incremented when debugging was enabled.

The assert macro is inherited from the C language and is defined in the <cassert> standard header (included in line 7).

Filling the deque with the copy Algorithm and back inserters

As we continue through Listing 7.2, in line 56 we check whether there are fewer than numNeeded records between start and the end of the deque. If so, we call fetchMore in line 61, asking for the number of additional records we will need. In line 64, we copy record IDs into the cache from the moreRecords vector returned from fetchMore. The copy algorithm takes three iterator arguments. The first two iterators form an iterator range, specifying the elements to be copied. The third argument specifies the beginning of an iterator range for the destination of the copy. Let's forget about back_inserter for a moment and imagine that lines 64 and 65 were written as follows, instead:

```
64:     std::copy(moreRecords.begin(), moreRecords.end(),
65:             cache_.begin());
```

The first two arguments specify an iterator range comprising all of moreRecords. The third argument specifies the iterator range beginning at cache_.begin(). The copy algorithm is good for copying between different types of containers because the target iterator does not need to be of the same type as the two other arguments. Although we normally need two iterators to specify an iterator range, in this case and similar cases, the second target iterator is implied by the number of elements in the input range. So if moreRecords contains 12 elements, the previous code will copy those elements into the first 12 positions of cache_, overwriting the previous value of those elements in cache_.

Wait a minute. Did I just say *overwrite*? Yes, the target of the copy is a range of existing elements that will be overwritten by the copy algorithm. But that's not what we want. We want to *append* the elements from moreRecords to cache_. Our next attempt, then, is to specify the *end* of the cache as the target:

```
64:     std::copy(moreRecords.begin(), moreRecords.end(),
65:             cache_.end());
```

This is a common beginner's mistake. This code wants to overwrite elements of cache_ starting at cache_.end(). Because there are no elements after cache_.end(), we get undefined behavior. As far as the copy algorithm is concerned, cache_.end() is just another iterator and it does not know that it is at the end of a container. This brings us back to the original code in Listing 7.2. On line 65 we call the function back_inserter and pass cache_ as an argument. The back_inserter function returns a special kind of iterator that *appends* rather than *overwrites* elements. The following two lines are equivalent to each other:

```
cache_.push_back(x);
```

```
*std::back_inserter(cache_) = x;
```

The act of dereferencing and assigning through a back_inserter causes it to call push_back on its container. When we pass a back_inserter to the copy algorithm, the result is to append the whole range of elements (one at a time) to the specified container. You should form an association in your mind between copy and back_inserter because they are so often used together.

When the newly inserted record IDs have been appended to the cache, the fillCacheFwd function is finished. When it exits, either the cache_ container will contain numNeeded elements starting at start, or else cachedLast_ will be set true, indicating that there are no more records to fetch.

EXCURSION

Copying Containers

The standard library provides several ways to make a copy of a container. The simplest is to use copy initialization or assignment. For example, given containers, x and y, of type std::set<Address>, you can make a copy of x using copy initialization,

```
std::set<Address> z(x);
```

or using assignment,

```
y = x;
```

After executing these statements, z and y contain copies of all of the elements of x. The elements previously held in y are destroyed.

Another way to copy containers is using the copy algorithm as we have just seen in Listing 7.2, lines 64 and 65. Copy can be used to overwrite a set of elements or (with back_inserter) to append elements to a container. This type of copying is useful when we only want to copy a range of elements rather than the whole container, when we want to append to rather than replace the contents of the target of the copy, or when the source container is not of the same type as the target container (for example, copying elements from a vector to a deque).

Whatever method of copying you use, you must take extra care when the container you are copying contains pointers. Be aware that only the pointers are copied, not the objects being pointed to. After the copy, both containers will point to the same (shared) objects.

Filling the Cache Backward with Reverse Iterators

The counterpart to fillCacheFwd is fillCacheBkwd, which ensures that the front of the cache contains enough records to scroll backward. The logic is very much like fillCacheFwd but inserting elements at the front of the cache without reversing their order poses an interesting challenge. To understand this challenge, imagine a deck of numbered index cards, stacked in ascending numerical order from the bottom of the deck to the top. (I am told that the term *deque* was inspired by the concept of a deck of cards.) Adding additional cards in ascending order, one at a time, to the top of the deck preserves the order of the whole deck. However, adding cards in ascending order, one at a time, to the bottom of the deck causes the newly added cards to appear in reverse order (that is, largest at the bottom). Let's examine the solution to this problem in Listing 7.3.

Listing 7.3   Implementation of `fillCacheBkwd`

```
69:  // Fill cache in the backward direction.
70:  // Specify start index and number of desired records. If not
71:  // enough records are available, will set cachedLast_.
72:  void DisplayList::fillCacheBkwd(int start, int numNeeded)
73:  {
74:    int startId = 0;
75:    if (cache_.empty())
76:      // Start caching from end of list
77:      cachedLast_ = true;
78:    else
79:    {
80:      // Start retrieving from first item in cache
81:      assert(start < cache_.size());
82:      startId = cache_.front();
83:    }
84:
85:    int recordsTillStart = start;
86:    if (! cachedFirst_ && recordsTillStart < numNeeded)
87:    {
88:      // Too few entries in cache to fill screen. Need to fetch more.
89:
90:      std::vector<int> moreRecords;
91:      cachedFirst_ = fetchMore(startId,
92:                               -(numNeeded - recordsTillStart),
93:                               moreRecords);
94:
95:      std::copy(moreRecords.rbegin(), moreRecords.rend(),
96:                std::front_inserter(cache_));
97:
98:      // We inserted records before the first visible one.
99:      // We must update firstVisibleIdx_ to reflect its new position.
100:     firstVisibleIdx_ += moreRecords.size();
101:   }
102: }
103:
```

The `fillCacheBkwd` function starts out the same as `fillCacheFwd` except for the reversal of `cachedFirst_`/`cachedLast_` and `back()`/`front()` in lines 77, 82, and 86. In lines 91–93, we call `fetchMore`, this time with a negative record count, indicating that we want a new set of records *before* `startId`, not after it. When we get to line 95, the `moreRecords` vector contains some number of record IDs, in the desired order of presentation. We want to copy these record IDs to the front of the `cache_` deque. You can see in line 96 that there is a `front_inserter` function that, as you might guess, works like `back_inserter` except that it uses `push_front` to insert elements at the front of the container.

The `back_inserter` and `front_inserter` functions belong to a family of three functions which also includes `inserter`. The `inserter` function takes two arguments: a container and an iterator to the insertion point. When dereferenced, it inserts elements at the specified insertion point. All three functions are defined in the `<iterator>` header, which we included in line 11 of Listing 7.2. The `back_inserter` function can be used with any container that supports `push_back`—that is, `vector`, `list`, and `deque`. The `front_inserter` function can be used with any container that supports `push_front`—that is, `list` and `deque` but not `vector`. The `inserter` function can be used with any container, including the associative containers. Because it doesn't really make sense to specify an insertion point to a container that maintains its own ordering criteria, the associative containers only use the insertion point specification as a hint that sometimes makes insertion faster.

If we copied the `moreRecords` vector to the `cache_` deque using `front_inserter` alone, the `copy` algorithm would insert each element into the `cache_` one at a time, causing the problem of reversing the elements that I illustrated with the card deck. What we would like to do is to start from the end of the vector and move toward the front, thus inserting the first element last. This can be accomplished using *reverse iterators*.

A reverse iterator is a variant on an iterator that traverses a container in the reverse order. When you increment a reverse iterator, the iterator advances toward the front of the container. Each container supplies the type `reverse_iterator` and the functions `rbegin` and `rend`, which return reverse iterators to the last element and one-before-the-first element of the container, respectively. Figure 7.3 shows the relationship between normal iterators and reverse iterators.

7

Figure 7.3

The relationship between forward and reverse iterators.

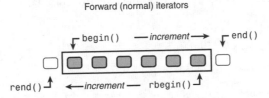

A forward iterator can be converted into a reverse iterator using a cast. Such a conversion produces an iterator that points to one item *before* the original iterator, thus the following two expressions are equivalent:

```
mylist.rbegin()
```

```
std::list<int>::reverse_iterator(mylist.end())
```

The reason for this displacement is so that there is a one-to-one mapping between forward iterators and reverse iterators, including the iterators returned by end() and rend(). Also, for any two iterators, a and b, the iterator range [a, b) is equivalent to the range [reverse_iterator(b), reverse_iterator(a)). A reverse iterator can be converted back to its corresponding forward iterator using the base member function. Thus the following two expressions are equivalent:

```
mylist.begin()
```

```
mylist.rend().base()
```

Finally, I should mention that a reverse iterator can also be a const iterator. This is declared as a type in each container called const_reverse_iterator.

Returning to Listing 7.3, we see reverse iterators in use at line 95. By copying the vector from back to front using rbegin and rend, we undo the reversing effects of using front_inserter. From the standpoint of copy or any other algorithm, the reverse iterators are no different from forward iterators. The power of reverse iterators, then, is that almost any algorithm can be used to process a container in reverse order.

One effect of inserting at the front of the deque is that the element indexes will change. If our first visible item was at index 5 and we inserted another 10 elements at the front of the deque, our first visible item will now be at index 15. In line 100, we make this correction, advancing firstVisibleIdx_ by the number of elements just inserted.

Formatting Using I/O Manipulators

We are now ready to display a screenful of record summaries. The code to do this is in Listing 7.4.

Listing 7.4   The display Function

```
104: void DisplayList::display()
105: {
106:     // Make sure cache contains a screenful of records
107:     fillCacheFwd(firstVisibleIdx_, linesPerScreen_);
108:
109:     // If after attempting to fill cache, it is still empty, then
110:     // there are no records to display.
111:     if (cache_.empty())
112:     {
```

```
113:        // Display empty-list marker.
114:        std::cout << "============== No records selected ==============="
115:                  << std::endl;
116:        return;
117:    }
118:
119:    // Calculate the number of records to display.
120:    // It is the smaller of the number of lines in a screenful or the
121:    // number of records left at the end of the cache.
122:    int recsToShow = std::min(linesPerScreen_,
123:                              int(cache_.size() - firstVisibleIdx_));
124:
125:    if (atStart())
126:        // Display start-of-list marker.
127:        std::cout << "=============== Start of list ===============\n";
128:
129:    std::deque<int>::iterator start = cache_.begin()+ firstVisibleIdx_;
130:    std::deque<int>::iterator finish = start + recsToShow;
131:    for (std::deque<int>::iterator i = start; i != finish; ++i)
132:    {
133:        // Display line number
134:        int lineNum = i - start + 1;   // Start counting at 1
135:        std::cout << std::setw(2) << std::setfill(' ')
136:                  << std::right << std::dec << lineNum << ": ";
137:        displayRecord(*i);
138:        std::cout << std::endl;
139:    }
140:
141:    if (atEnd())
142:        // Display end-of-list marker.
143:        std::cout << "=============== End of list ===============";
144:
145:    std::cout << std::endl;
146: }
147:
```

At line 107 we begin by calling fillCacheFwd to ensure that there are enough records in the cache, starting at firstVisibleIdx_, to display a screenful. If after doing that the cache is still empty, it means that no records are available and we print a message at line 114 and return at line 116.

At lines 122 and 123 we compute the number of lines that will be displayed. Normally, this would be the value linesPerScreen_. However, it is possible that fillCacheFwd reached the end of the available records before retrieving enough records for a whole screenful. In this case we just want to display the remaining records through the end of the cache. The number of records to display is thus the smaller of the number of records left in the cache and linesPerScreen_. The min function (defined in <algorithm> returns this value.

Note

Compiler Note   The library that ships with the Microsoft VC 6.0 Compiler uses the names _cpp_min instead of min, and _cpp_max instead of max in order to avoid a conflict with the Windows header file, windef.h. Because we are not using windef.h, we can make our code look more standard by redefining these values, as shown in Listing 7.2, lines 13–16. To make your Windows-specific code compile correctly, include windef.h after these #defines and also add the statements, "using std::min; using std::max;".

Unfortunately, because of the way templates work, it is very important that the types of the two arguments to min be exactly the same (that is, don't mix int and long). Otherwise, the compiler cannot figure out which type to use for instantiating min and will give you a rather cryptic error message. This is why we cast the second argument to int in line 123.

At lines 129 and 130 we create an iterator range containing the records to be printed. We compute the value for the start iterator by adding our first-visible index to the beginning of the cache and we compute the value for finish by adding recsToShow to the start iterator. This kind of arithmetic with iterators works just like pointer arithmetic. But beware: This only works with containers that provide random access to elements. (See "Excursion: Iterator Categories," following). In line 131, we have the head of a typical iterator for loop, but this time only iterating over the portion of the deque in the range [start, finish). In line 134 we calculate the line number for the record pointed to by i. Line numbers start at 1 and are counted from the first visible record on the screen. Thus, we can calculate the line number by subtracting start from i and adding 1 (to avoid counting from 0). This subtraction of iterators to find the number of elements between them also works like pointer subtraction and is also limited to random-access containers.

EXCURSION

Iterator Categories

Not all iterators are created equal. In fact, the standard defines five different categories of iterators. Each category supports more operations than the previous one and can be used wherever a less-capable iterator is permitted. The relationship between a more-powerful iterator category and a less-powerful iterator category is similar to inheritance, but it is not typically implemented that way.

The least-powerful categories of iterators are *input* and *output* iterators. Input iterators let you access elements in a sequence in a read-only, one-pass fashion. When you read an object, the iterator or container state change such that you cannot necessarily read it again (hence *one-pass*). Input iterators cannot be decremented or compared. We have not yet seen any iterators limited to the input iterator category; input iterators exist that, for example, read data from an input stream.

Output iterators are the converse of input iterators. They provide write-only, single-pass access to a sequence of elements. When written, you might not be able to read the element back. The result of calling one of the inserter functions produces an output iterator; an insert iterator inserts elements into a container, but the same iterator cannot be used to read them back.

Forward iterators begin to perform more like pointers into a container. Although forward iterators cannot be decremented, it is possible to copy one and reuse it to revisit an element a second or third time. Elements can be both read and written using forward iterators, so forward iterators can be used wherever either input or output iterators are allowed. Although it is possible to create a container class that supports only forward iterators, all the standard container classes support more powerful iterators.

Bidirectional iterators support all the operations of forward iterators but can also be decremented using the `--` operator. The `iterator` type in all the standard container classes except `vector` and `deque` is a bidirectional iterator type.

The most-powerful category of iterators are *random-access* iterators. Random-access iterators most closely resemble pointers into arrays. In addition to all the operations supported for bidirectional iterators, random-access iterators support arithmetic operations with integers (`+`, `-`, `+=`, and `-=`), can be subtracted from one another, and can be compared against one another using `<`, `>`, `<=`, and `>=` to see which comes first in a container. Random-access iterators can also be indexed using the `[]` operator. Given an iterator `i`, the expression `i[n]` is equivalent to `*(i+n)`. The only standard containers with random access iterators are `vector` and `deque`. Native pointers also fit the description of random-access iterators.

Because you cannot add an integer to most iterators to create a big jump, the standard `<iterator>` header defines a function, `advance(i,n)`, which will increment iterator `i` by `n`. For non–random-access iterators, this operation is performed using `n` increment operations. For bidirectional iterators, `n` can be negative, causing the iterator to be decremented. Another common function not supported by most iterators is subtraction of two iterators to find the number of elements between them. The `<iterator>` header also defines `distance(i1,i2)`, which returns the number of times `i1` must be incremented to equal `i2`. In order to avoid undefined behavior, `i2` must come after `i1` in the same container.

In line 135 we begin to actually display the records. We want to print a line number in front of each record so that the user can refer to the record by number. To make it easy to read, we want all the line numbers to line up, so we allocate two spaces for each line number and pad unused space on the left with blanks. Thus, the number 3 will be printed with a blank in front but the number 11 will have no blanks in front of it. This formatting is done with the help of special functions called *I/O manipulators*. The `setw` manipulator sets the desired width of the next field; the `setfill` manipulator sets the character that will be used to pad the field to the desired width; the `right` manipulator indicates that the padding should go to the left of the field value (the field is right-justified); and the `dec` manipulator indicates that we want to display numbers in decimal (as opposed to hex or octal) notation. These four I/O manipulators are equivalent to the following four separate function calls:

```
std::cout.width(2);
std::cout.fill(' ');
std::setf(std::ios::right, std::ios::adjustfield);
std::setf(std::ios::dec, std::ios::basefield);
```

The `fill` and `width` functions return the previous value of the fill character and field width, respectively. The manipulators are usually easier to use because they appear as part of the output sequence, and can be chained together, as shown. The manipulators that take arguments (`setfill` and `setw`) require the inclusion of the `<iomanip>` header. With the exception of the `width` function and corresponding `setw` manipulator, the format settings specified by the format functions and I/O manipulators apply to all subsequent output operations on this stream.

The field width set by `width` or `setw` is a *minimum* width for the next output field. If the field being output would require fewer than the specified number of characters, the output is padded with the fill character (default space). But if the field being output would require more than the specified number of characters, it is not truncated to the specified width. The `width` function and `setw` manipulator affect only the next field being output. In lines 135 and 136, only the formatting of `lineNum` is affected by the width setting. After the `lineNum` field is formatted, `width(0)` is called automatically, causing the next field to be output without padding. The string ": " just happens to be two characters long, but is not affected by the prior call to `setw(2)`. (Finding documentation of the temporary nature of `width` in the standard document is like finding a needle in a haystack.)

Compiler Note   The library that comes with the egcs 1.1.2 compiler has a bug in class `string` that causes strings to ignore the width specifier. Given a string, s, and a stream, `strm`, the workaround is to is to use

```
strm << std::setw(n) << s.c_str();
```

instead of

```
strm << std::setw(n) << s;
```

Alternatively, you can modify the `<string>` and submit your fix to the egcs development team.

If you are from a C background and are used to formatting output with `printf`, you will find this mechanism for specifying field widths and formats to be somewhat less compact. However, certain `printf` errors can be avoided due to the type-based nature of output streams. For example, it is impossible to inadvertently format a string as if it were a number or vice versa. (Either of these errors using `printf` could cause a program to crash in a way that is very difficult to trace.)

After we have printed out a line number, we call `displayRecord` in line 137 to format a summary of the record. Remember that `displayRecord` is not implemented in the `DisplayList` class but rather is implemented differently in each derived class of `DisplayList`. When our loop terminates, we determine if we are at the end of the list of available records and, if so, print a message for the user (lines 141–143). We add a final newline at line 145. Note that `endl` is itself a output manipulator, equivalent to the following two lines of code:

```
std::cout.put('\n');
std::cout.flush();
```

The `put` function sends a character to the output stream with no additional formatting. Because the output stream usually *buffers* some amount of output in memory, the `flush` function is used to send any remaining characters in the buffer to the actual output device. The `endl` manipulator is a convenient way to end an output line and flush the buffer at the same time. It is not usually necessary to explicitly flush the buffer, but some output will not show up on the display until the buffer is flushed, which could be a nuisance when debugging. The `cout` stream is automatically flushed before any input operation involving `cin`, so you don't have to worry about prompts showing up.

A *buffer* is a chunk of memory used as a temporary location for some characters or objects. *To buffer* means to temporarily put characters or objects into a buffer on their way to some other location, often for efficiency reasons (for example, it is more efficient to send a whole buffer full of characters at once than to send the same data one character at a time).

Now we have a way to fill the cache forward or backward and display one screenful of record summaries from the cache. We can now move forward to implement the other functions of the `DisplayList` class.

Implementing the Other Functions

The implementation for the rest of `DisplayList` except the `selectRecord` function is shown in Listing 7.5.

Listing 7.5 `DisplayList` **Functions That Don't Require User Input**

```
148: void DisplayList::pageDown()
149: {
150:    // Scroll current bottom-of-screen line to top of screen
151:    if (atEnd())
```

continues

Listing 7.5   continued

```
152:    return;
153:
154:    // Cache current screenful and next screenful
155:    fillCacheFwd(firstVisibleIdx_, 2 * linesPerScreen_);
156:
157:    // Advance visible index one screenful, but only if there exists
158:    // at least one screenful past the current firstVisibleIdx_.
159:    if (! atEnd())
160:      firstVisibleIdx_ += linesPerScreen_;
161: }
162:
163: void DisplayList::pageUp()
164: {
165:    // Scroll current top-of-screen line to bottom of screen
166:    if (atStart())
167:      return;
168:
169:    // Cache previous screenful
170:    fillCacheBkwd(firstVisibleIdx_, linesPerScreen_);
171:
172:    // Advance visible index backward one screenful, but not past
173:    // start of cache.
174:    firstVisibleIdx_ = std::max(firstVisibleIdx_ - linesPerScreen_, 0);
175: }
176:
177: void DisplayList::toStart()
178: {
179:    if (cachedFirst_)
180:      firstVisibleIdx_ = 0;
181:    else
182:      // Cached records do not include top of cache.
183:      reset();
184: }
185:
186: bool DisplayList::atStart()
187: {
188:    return cachedFirst_ && (firstVisibleIdx_ == 0);
189: }
190:
191: bool DisplayList::atEnd()
192: {
193:    return (cachedLast_ &&
194:            (cache_.size() - firstVisibleIdx_ <= linesPerScreen_));
195: }
196:
197: // Scroll so that specified record is at the top of the screen.
198: void DisplayList::scrollToTop(int recordId)
199: {
200:    assert(recordId != 0);
201:
```

```
202:    // Find specified record in cache:
203:    cache_t::iterator found = std::find(cache_.begin(), cache_.end(),
204:                                        recordId);
205:
206:    // If didn't find record in cache, flush cache and start reloading.
207:    if (found == cache_.end())
208:    {
209:       reset();
210:       cache_.push_back(recordId);
211:       firstVisibleIdx_ = 0;
212:    }
213:    else
214:       firstVisibleIdx_ = found - cache_.begin();
215:
216:    fillCacheFwd(firstVisibleIdx_, linesPerScreen_);
217: }
218:
219: // Return ID of nth record on screen
220: int DisplayList::screenRecord(int n) const
221: {
222:    if (firstVisibleIdx_ + n >= cache_.size())
223:       return 0;
224:    else
225:       return cache_[firstVisibleIdx_ + n];
226: }
227:
```

The pageDown function in lines 148–161 makes sure that there are at least two screenfuls of records (one for the current screen and one for the next screen) in the cache by calling fillCacheFwd, in line 155. Line 160 advances firstVisibleIdx by one screenful unless we are already at the last screenful. (It is possible for atEnd to return true after the call to fillCacheFwd even if it had previously returned false.) The pageUp function in lines 163–175 calls fillCacheBkwd in line 170 to make sure that there is a screenful of records before the current position. In line 174, we adjust the firstVisibleIdx variable back one screenful. The min function is used to prevent firstVisibleIdx from going below 0 in the case where there is less than one screenful worth of records before the current position.

The toStart function in lines 177–184 checks whether the first available record is already cached (if cachedFirst_ is true). If so, it sets firstVisibleIdx to the first record in the cache, which must also be the first record available. Otherwise, it resets the cache, emptying all the records out and causing the next display attempt to fetch records starting from the first available record. The atStart function in lines 186–189 returns true if the first available record is in the current screenful. The condition being tested in line 188 is that the first available record is in the cache and that the first record in the cache is visible. The atEnd function in lines 191–195 returns true if the last available record is in the current screenful. It does this by testing that the last record is in the cache and that there is no more than one screen-ful of records between the first visible record and the end of the cache.

The `scrollToTop` function in lines 198–217 is a bit more complex. Its job is to scroll the display list so that the specified record is at the top of the display. At line 200, we assert that the caller has not asked for the illegal record number 0 to be scrolled to the top. In line 203, we use the `find` algorithm to check whether the desired record is already in the cache. The call to `find` returns an iterator to the first value in the cache that matches `recordId`. In line 207, if `find` returned `cache_.end()`, it means that the record ID was not found in the cache. In this case, we don't know whether to scroll forward or backward, so we just reset the cache and artificially set the desired record as the first (and only) record in the cache. If the record ID was found in the `cache_`, we set it as the first visible record (in line 214) by calculating the offset (index) from the start of the cache. In either case, the call to `fillCacheFwd` at line 216 will retrieve a screenful of records starting at `recordId`.

EXCURSION

Algorithm Naming Conventions

We have seen the related algorithms `count` and `count_if` as well as `find` and `find_if`. These algorithms follow a common naming convention that makes it easier to keep track of the 60 or so algorithms in the C++ Standard Library. Algorithms with names that end in `_if` apply a user-specified unary predicate to each element rather than comparing it against a specific value, as its non-if counterpart does. For example, `count` counts the number of occurrences of a specific value within an iterator range, whereas `count_if` counts the number of elements for which the specified predict returns true. If you understand this convention and you know how `count` works, then you automatically also know how `count_if` works.

Some algorithms modify the elements in an iterator range. Many of these *mutating* algorithms have variants that end in `_copy`. These variants do not modify the input range but rather copy their results into a separate location. For example, the `replace` algorithm takes an iterator range and two values as arguments. Wherever it finds the first value within the range, it replaces it with the second value. The `replace_copy` algorithm takes an iterator range and an output iterator as arguments, as well as the two values. It copies the elements from the range to the output iterator, replacing values as it goes. Remember to use inserters with `_copy` algorithms to avoid overwriting values at the target. On occasion, these two naming conventions are used together, as in the case of `replace_copy_if`.

Another part of the algorithm naming convention is not related to the name of the algorithm itself, but to the types of arguments it expects. Most algorithms take iterator ranges or predicate function objects as template parameters. Documentation for these algorithms describes the type of parameters expected by giving the parameters a descriptive name that looks something like this:

`InIter`: Input iterator or better

`OutIter`: Output iterator or better

FwdIter: Forward iterator or better

BidirIter: Bidirectional iterator or better

RandIter: Random access iterator or better

Comp: A binary predicate that behaves like a less-than comparison

Eq: A binary predicate that behaves like an equality comparison

BinPred: A binary predicate

UniPred: A unary predicate

BinFunc: A binary function object (not necessarily a predicate)

UniFunc: A unary function object (not necessarily a predicate)

T: An element type

For example, a reference book might document replace_if as follows:

```
template <class FwdIter, class UniPred, class T>
OutIter replace_if(FwdIter start, FwdIter finish,
                   UniPred pred, const T& new_value);
```

Note that the actual parameter naming convention is not part of the standard and varies from one reference book to the next. The ISO standard document itself uses longer names such as ForwardIterator instead of FwdIter and uses Pred for both unary and binary predicates.

The screenRecord function in lines 220–226 returns the record ID of the record displayed on the nth line of the current screenful (n is counted from 0, not 1). Line 222 tests that n falls within the cache. If not, it returns 0 in line 223. Otherwise, it indexes the cache_ and returns the value at the nth location after firstVisibleIdx_.

Avoiding Iterator Invalidation

You might have noticed that the implementation of DisplayList relies a lot on integer indexes into the deque and much less on iterators than previous code that uses containers. Even when iterators are used, they are often computed from the index rather than just being stored as member variables. The reason for this has to do with *iterator invalidation*. When the container into which an iterator points is modified, the iterator can become invalid. Using an invalid iterator produces undefined behavior. The reason for this has to do with the way the internal data structures are rearranged when inserting or removing elements. In general, if an iterator becomes invalid, any pointer to the same element also becomes invalid. If you understand the following three rules, you can avoid situations where you might use an invalid iterator.

1. The erase function always invalidates iterators that point to the actual elements being erased.

2. Any operation that inserts or removes an element in a vector or deque usually invalidates all iterators into the container. The other container types have more robust iterators that are not invalidated by these changes.

7

3. The `pop_back` operation is an exception to rule 2. It only invalidates iterators to the actual element being removed.

In the `DisplayList` class, we don't want to store iterators into the deque because they would become invalid every time the cache was updated. Integer indexes, however, do not become invalid and can be used to quickly compute an iterator when necessary.

Reading Numeric Input and Handling Errors

The last function in the `DisplayList` class is `selectRecord`, which interacts with the user and lets the user choose a record from those currently displayed on the screen. The implementation of `selectRecord` is shown in Listing 7.6.

Listing 7.6   The `selectRecord` Function

```
228: // Ask the user for a record number and convert to a recordId
229: int DisplayList::selectRecord()
230: {
231:   while (std::cin.good())
232:   {
233:     int maxSelection = std::min(int(cache_.size()- firstVisibleIdx_),
234:                                 linesPerScreen_);
235:
236:     if (maxSelection <= 0)
237:     {
238:       std::cout << "No records to select\n";
239:       return 0;
240:     }
241:
242:     // Prompt for record number in visible range
243:     std::cout << "Choose a record number between "
244:             << 1 << " and " << maxSelection
245:             << "\nRecord number (0 to cancel)? ";
246:
247:     unsigned selection = 0;
248:
249:     std::cin >> selection;
250:     if (std::cin.fail())
251:     {
252:       if (std::cin.bad() || std::cin.eof())
253:         break;
254:
255:       // Recoverable input error. (User typed a non-numeric input).
256:       // Clear error condition and throw away rest of input line
257:       // then continue loop.
258:       std::cin.clear();
259:       std::cin.ignore(10000, '\n');
260:       std::cout << "Invalid selection, please try again.\n\n";
```

```
261:      continue;
262:    } // end else
263:
264:    // Throw away rest of input line
265:    std::cin.ignore(10000, '\n');
266:
267:    if (selection == 0)
268:      return 0;
269:
270:    // Make sure user chose one of the visible records.
271:    if (1 <= selection && selection <= maxSelection)
272:      return cache_[firstVisibleIdx_ + selection - 1];
273:    else
274:      std::cout << "Invalid selection, please try again.\n\n";
275:
276:  } // end while
277:
278:  return 0;
279: }
```

In line 231 we start an input loop that continues so long as the input stream is in a good state (good() returns true). In lines 233 and 234 we compute actual number of lines visible on this screenful as the minimum of the screen size or the number of records remaining in the cache. In lines 236–240, we return if the selection list is empty. In lines 243–245, we prompt the user to enter a selection in the range 1 to maxSelection. The user's selection will be put into the selection variable, declared on line 247.

In line 249, we read an (unsigned) integer from the standard input stream. With this kind of input, any preceding whitespace characters (including newline) are discarded. This means that if the user presses Enter, the input will not be complete, and the system will continue waiting for a non-whitespace character. After the input is complete, we make sure it was successful with a fail check in line 250. If in case of error, we must take some sort of error handling action. A device error or end-of-file is unrecoverable, so in lines 252 and 253, we break out of the loop if either of these conditions is true. If some other error occurred, we clear the failbit flag by calling clear in line 258 and then discard the rest of the line using ignore in line 259. The ignore function discards input either until a certain number of characters is consumed or until a specified delimiter (default EOF) is consumed. By supplying a large number (10000) for the character count, and newline for the delimiter, we effectively discard the rest of the current input line. After the clear and ignore calls the input stream is once again in a good state. We inform the user of a problem in line 260 and go back to the top of the loop in line 261.

If the input was a valid integer, we will get to line 265. There is always the chance that the user typed superfluous characters after the integer, so we make sure to discard the rest of the line using `ignore`, so that any superfluous characters will not be picked up on the next input operation. Lines 267 and 268 return immediately if the user entered 0, which is the cancellation code. On line 271, we check that the input was in the valid range. If so, we return the record ID at the selected location (line 272), making sure to subtract one from the selection to make it zero-based instead of one-based. If the selection was out of bounds, we print a message in line 274 and the loop is allowed to return to the top.

Defining the `AddressDisplayList`

As you can see, a lot of machinery is built into the `DisplayList` base class. The idea is to make the derived classes, such as `AddressDisplayList`, relatively easy to write. The derived classes need to know about how to retrieve and display a specific record type, but not how to display it in a scrollable list. The class definition for `AddressDisplayList` is shown in Listing 7.7.

Listing 7.7   Class Definition for `AddressDisplayList`

```
 1:  // TinyPIM (c) 1999 Pablo Halpern. File AddressDisplayList.h
 2:
 3:  #ifndef AddressDisplayList_dot_h
 4:  #define AddressDisplayList_dot_h 1
 5:
 6:  #include "DisplayList.h"
 7:
 8:  class AddressBook;
 9:
10:  // Specialized DisplayList for Address records.
11:  class AddressDisplayList : public DisplayList
12:  {
13:  public:
14:     // Construct with a reference to the address book
15:     AddressDisplayList(AddressBook& addrBook);
16:
17:     // Scroll to first Address with name greater-than-or-equal to
18:     // specified name. Usually, this will be a name that starts with
19:     // the specified strings. Returns false if no match found.
20:     bool findNameStartsWith(const std::string& lastname,
21:                             const std::string& firstname = "");
22:
23:     // List only those records that contain the specified string
24:     void listContainsString(const std::string&);
25:
26:     // List all records (use after a listContainsString)
27:     void listAll();
28:
29:  protected:
30:     // Display the specified address record in one-line format.
```

```
31:     // Implements pure virtual base-class function.
32:     virtual void displayRecord(int recordId);
33:
34:     // Override base-class function to retrieve more records.
35:     virtual bool fetchMore(int startId, int numRecords,
36:                            std::vector<int>& result);
37:
38:  private:
39:     AddressBook&       addressBook_;
40:
41:     // String to use for listContainsString mode.
42:     std::string        containsString_;
43:  };
44:
45:  #endif // AddressDisplayList_dot_h
```

The public interface has a few functions not inherited from `DisplayList`. The constructor on line 15 takes an `AddressBook` argument. A reference to that `AddressBook` object is stored in the `addressBook_` member declared on line 39. The `findNameStartsWith` function on line 20 performs a name search as specified in the comments in lines 17–19. This function changes the state of the display list so that the first matching record scrolls to the top of the screen. The `listContainsString` function declared on line 24 also performs a search, but instead of scrolling the display, it actually filters the records so that only those records that contain the search string are displayed. We can undo the effects of a `listContainsString` function by calling `listAll`, declared on line 27.

On lines 32 and 35, we declare the functions that perform the record-specific operations required by the base class logic. The `displayRecord` function displays an address record in a one-line format consisting of last name, first name, and phone number. The `fetchMore` function retrieves address records from the address book.

Let's look at the implementation of the `displayRecord` function in Listing 7.8.

Listing 7.8   **Implementation of `AddressDisplayList` Functions**

```
1:  // TinyPIM (c) 1999 Pablo Halpern. File AddressDisplayList.cpp
2:
3:  #ifdef _MSC_VER
4:  #pragma warning(disable : 4786)
5:  #endif
6:
7:  #include <iostream>
8:  #include <iomanip>
9:  #include <algorithm>
10: #include "AddressDisplayList.h"
11: #include "Address.h"
```

continues

Listing 7.8   continued

```
12:  #include "AddressBook.h"
13:
14:  // Construct with a reference to the address book
15:  AddressDisplayList::AddressDisplayList(AddressBook& addrBook)
16:    : addressBook_(addrBook)
17:  {
18:  }
19:
20:  // Display the specified address record in one-line format
21:  void AddressDisplayList::displayRecord(int recordId)
22:  {
23:    Address record = addressBook_.getAddress(recordId);
24:
25:    // Create a name string in "lastname, firstname" format.
26:    std::string name = record.lastname();
27:    if (! record.firstname().empty())
28:      name.append(", ").append(record.firstname());
29:
30:    // Output name and phone number on one line (two columns).
31:    std::cout << std::setfill('.') << std::setw(40)
32:              << std::left << name << record.phone();
33:  }
34:
```

This `displayRecord` function is called from the base class `display` function, which passes in a record ID. In line 23 we retrieve the `Address` record with the specified ID. (We made this a fast operation in Chapter 6, "An Enhanced `AddressBook` Using Algorithms and Sorted Containers.") In line 26 we extract the last name from the record. In line 28 we append the first name if it is not empty. Notice how we use the `append` function to first attach a comma and space and then append the first name. The `append` function returns a reference to the original string so that it can be chained like this. In lines 31 and 32, we print out the name and phone number in two columns. Using the `setfill`, `setw`, and `left` manipulators cause the name to take up to 40 columns, right-padded with dots (periods). The phone numbers will thus all line up in a single column and can easily be matched up with the names they belong to.

The next major function is `fetchMore`, which is shown in Listing 7.9. This function is rather long because of the various cases it must handle. We'll just touch on the highlights.

Listing 7.9   Implementation of `fetchMore` Function

```
35:  // Fetch more records from AddressBook
36:  bool AddressDisplayList::fetchMore(int startId, int numRecords,
37:                                     std::vector<int>& result)
38:  {
```

```
39:    // Remove old contents of result
40:    result.clear();
41:
42:    if (numRecords == 0)
43:      return false;
44:
45:    bool forwards = true;
46:    if (numRecords < 0)
47:    {
48:      forwards = false;
49:      numRecords = -numRecords;
50:    }
51:
52:    // Check for empty list
53:    if (addressBook_.begin() == addressBook_.end())
54:      return true;
55:
56:    // Declare an iterator
57:    AddressBook::const_iterator iter;
58:
59:    // Get iterator to record specified by startId.
60:    // When fetching forward, increment iterator past matching record
61:    // to avoid a duplicate insertion into the display list.
62:    if (startId == 0)
63:      iter = (forwards ? addressBook_.begin() : addressBook_.end());
64:    else
65:    {
66:      iter = addressBook_.findRecordId(startId);
67:      if (forwards)
68:        ++iter;
69:    }
70:
71:    if (containsString_.empty())
72:    {
73:      // "List all" mode
74:
75:      if (forwards)
76:      {
77:        // retrieve records starting at iter
78:        while (iter != addressBook_.end() && numRecords-- > 0)
79:          result.push_back((iter++)->recordId());
80:
81:        // Return true if reached end of the list
82:        return iter == addressBook_.end();
83:      }
84:      else
85:      {
86:        // retrieve records starting at one before iter
87:        while (iter != addressBook_.begin() && numRecords-- > 0)
88:          result.push_back((--iter)->recordId());
89:
```

continues

Listing 7.9   continued

```
90:            // Records were pushed backwards, reverse them here:
91:            std::reverse(result.begin(), result.end());
92:
93:            // Return true if reached front of the list
94:            return iter == addressBook_.begin();
95:        }
96:    }
97:    else
98:    {
99:      // "Contains string" mode
100:
101:      if (forwards)
102:      {
103:        // Retrieve records AFTER startId
104:
105:        // Find matching record starting at iter
106:        iter = addressBook_.findNextContains(containsString_, iter);
107:        while (iter != addressBook_.end() && numRecords-- > 0)
108:        {
109:          result.push_back(iter->recordId());
110:
111:          // Find next matching record
112:          iter = addressBook_.findNextContains(containsString_,++iter);
113:        }
114:
115:        // Return true if we reached the end
116:        return iter == addressBook_.end();
117:      }
118:      else
119:      {
120:        // retrieve records BEFORE startId
121:
122:        // AddressBook does not a function to search backwards.
123:        // Instead, we retrieve ALL records before iter
124:        AddressBook::const_iterator endIter = iter;
125:        iter = addressBook_.findNextContains(containsString_,
126:                                      addressBook_.begin());
127:        while (iter != endIter)
128:        {
129:          result.push_back(iter->recordId());
130:          iter = addressBook_.findNextContains(containsString_,++iter);
131:        }
132:
133:        return true;  // Yes, we reached the start of the list.
134:      }
135:    }
136: }
137:
```

Lines 40–50 are straightforward tests of input conditions. At line 53, we check to see if the address book is empty. Because AddressBook doesn't supply an empty or size function, we determine whether it is empty by checking if the begin() and end() iterators are the same.

In line 57 we declare an iterator that we will set to the first record we want to retrieve. Because the DisplayList base class does not know about the AddressBook or AddressBook::const_iterator, it passes fetchMore a record ID that we must then convert to an iterator. If startId is 0, we set iter to begin(), in line 63, if we are fetching forward, or end(), if we are fetching backward. Otherwise, if startId contains a nonzero record ID, we get an iterator to the corresponding record in line 66. If we are fetching forward, we increment the iterator to the first record *after* the one specified in startId.

In line 71 we check to see if we are in "contains string" mode, which causes the list to be filtered to contain only those records containing the specified string. If containsString_ is empty, we are in normal ("list all") mode and must iterate over the records in the address book until we have retrieved numRecords records or reached the end (or beginning) of the address book. If we are fetching forward, the loop in lines 78 and 79 will append record IDs to the result vector until either we reach the end of the address book or numRecords decrements to 0.

If we are fetching backward, the loop in lines 87 and 88 appends record IDs to the result as we iterate backward through the address book. Notice that when iterating backward, we pre-decrement the iterator. This is because we always start one element ahead (for example, end() is beyond the last element) and the initial value of iter set in line 66 is the element we *don't* want included in the result. A reverse iterator would make this less confusing, but we didn't bother providing one in AddressBook. Also note that as we append elements to result they are going in *reverse order* of appearance in the address book. We correct this situation using the reverse algorithm in line 91. Just to be complete, I'll mention that the reverse algorithm has a reverse_copy counterpart which does not modify its input range. (See "Excursion: Algorithm Naming Conventions," earlier in this chapter.)

Lines 82 and 94 return true to the caller if we have scrolled as far as we can go in the forward or reverse direction, respectively.

If the display list is in "contains string" mode, we arrive at line 101. Again, we branch depending on whether we are fetching forward or backward. If fetching in the forward direction, we get to line 106 where we search for the next record containing containsString_. Lines 107–113 define a loop where we add each found record ID to the result and search again until we either run out of records or fill the result.

7

If we are in "contains string" mode fetching backward, we come to line 124. Because we did not provide a function such as findNextContains that searches backward, we must start from the beginning and search forward instead, stopping when we get to the current record. We might end up finding more records than was asked for, but that's okay—they'll just end up in the cache. In line 125, we find the first record that contains the matching string. The loop in lines 127–131 is much like the loop in lines 107–113 except that the termination condition is simpler: We stop looping when we reach our original starting point. Because we filled the result in forward order, there is no need to call reverse the way we did in line 91. Also, because we started searching from the beginning of the address book, line 133 always returns true, to indicate that the first record in the list is present in the result.

Now that we have the core functions of AddressDisplayList down, let's look at Listing 7.10, which contains the functions that implement the public interface.

Listing 7.10   Implementation of the Public Functions in AddressDisplayList

```
138: // Scroll to first Address with name greater-than-or-equal to
139: // specified name. Usually, this will be a name that starts with
140: // the specified strings. Returns false if no match found.
141: bool
142: AddressDisplayList::findNameStartsWith(const std::string& lastname,
143:                                        const std::string& firstname)
144: {
145:    containsString_ = ""; // Turn off "contains string" mode
146:
147:    reset();
148:    AddressBook::const_iterator iter
149:      = addressBook_.findNameStartsWith(lastname, firstname);
150:
151:    if (iter == addressBook_.end())
152:      return false;
153:
154:    // Scroll found record to top
155:    scrollToTop(iter->recordId());
156:    return true;
157: }
158:
159: // List only those records that contain the specified string
160: void AddressDisplayList::listContainsString(const std::string& s)
161: {
162:    if (containsString_ == s)
163:      return;
164:
165:    reset();
166:    containsString_ = s;
167:
168:    // Next call to display() will cause search
169: }
```

```
170:
171: // List all records (use after a listContainsString)
172: void AddressDisplayList::listAll()
173: {
174:   listContainsString("");
175:   toStart();
176: }
```

In lines 148 and 149, the findNameStartsWith function in AddressDisplayList calls the function with the same name in AddressBook. If it finds a matching record, it scrolls it to the top of the screen in line 155.

In line 165, the listContainsString function resets the display list because the set of records that should be displayed will be changed by the filtering action of fetchMore. In line 166, it sets a new value for containsString_, which will be used by fetchMore to retrieve selected records. The fetchMore function will be automatically called the next time the list is displayed. The listAll function simply sets the containsString value to empty, in line 174 and then scrolls the list to the beginning in line 175.

Next Steps

Our AddressDisplayList is complete. In implementing it, we took advantage of the deque container class and its support for inserting on both ends as well as random access indexing. We also used reverse iterators and the several algorithms including reverse and find. We used I/O manipulators such as setw and endl to help us format the records for easy viewing. We also learned some tricks for error recovery on input.

Our next step is to use the display list in the context of a complete menu-based user interface. In the process, we will learn about the stack container adapter and we will use more stream input and output.

7

Chapter 8

A Simple Menu System

We continue now to develop our user interface. By the end of this chapter, we will be able to enter addresses, see a list of address records, edit address records, and look up address records by name. We will have completed the basic framework for TinyPIM. We'll use a special stream type called a `stringstream` and a special `stack` container. We'll also learn how to extend the STL with custom components.

Specification of the Menu System

Let's return to the analysis phase and complete a specification for the menu portion of our text-based user interface. The `AddressBook` class supplies functions to insert, delete, remove, replace (modify), and (eventually) search for address records. All these operations must be available through the user interface. The logical top-level interface to access these functions is a menu. The user would select the desired operation from a menu and then complete the operation using a dialog box specific to the chosen operation. For some choices, the dialog box involves additional menus. The following is the general behavior of our text-based menus:

- A menu prompt is printed to the standard output device. The prompt presents a list of menu choices to the user, formatted to fit on a standard 25×80 terminal.
- After the prompt is printed, the user enters a single-character choice through the standard input device.
- If the user's choice matches a legal menu selection, the system takes the action associated with that item. Menu choice matching is not case sensitive.

- If the user's choice does not match a legal menu selection, the program displays `Invalid selection, please try again` and waits for the user to enter an alternative selection.

- After each action, the menu is redisplayed (unless the action involves exiting the menu).

- A menu choice may lead to the display of a submenu. When the submenu interaction is complete, the preceding menu is displayed again.

The main menu in TinyPIM presents the following choices (the letter in parentheses is the letter the user must type to select that choice):

- (A)ddress Book—Brings up the address book submenu
- (D)ate Book—Brings up the date book submenu
- (Q)uit—Saves all data and exits TinyPIM

Many operations in the address book require that the user select a record from a list. The list of available records (the "display list") is displayed above the menu on the screen. The user is then given the following choices:

- (V)iew—Prompts the user to choose a specific address record and then displays it.

- (C)reate—Creates a new address record.

- (D)elete—Prompts the user to choose a specific address record and then deletes it from the address book.

- (E)dit—Prompts the user to choose a specific address record and then enables the user to edit it.

- List (A)ll—Sets the display list to display all records. Used after a search operation to turn off search mode.

- (L)ookup—Prompts the user for a last name and (optional) first name to look up. Scrolls the display list so that the first matching name is at the top of the screen.

- (S)earch—Prompts the user for a search string. Narrows the display list to include only those records containing the search string.

- (R)edisplay—Redisplays the display list and menu.

- (Q)uit—Exits the address book (and returns to the main menu).

The mechanics of displaying the a list of records and choosing a record from the list are covered in Chapter 7, "Scrolling Display Lists Using `deques` and `I/O streams`."

Design of the Menu System

The high-level design of the menu system is described in Chapter 1, "Introducing TinyPIM." Figure 8.1 shows the UML class diagram of the menu system, which also appears in Figure 1.3.

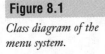

Figure 8.1

Class diagram of the menu system.

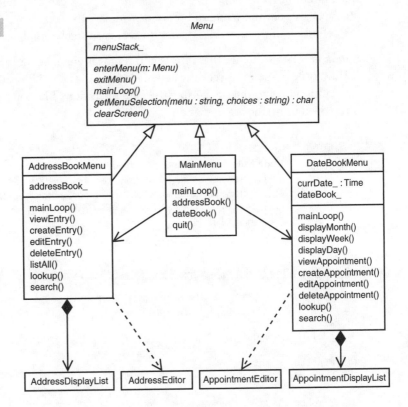

`Menu` is a base class that implements user interaction and error-handling functions common to all menus. It also provides public functions for starting submenus and returning to the preceding menu when done. `MainMenu`, `AddressBookMenu`, and `DateBookMenu` are subclasses of `Menu` that implement the specific menus implied by their names. Each subclass contains private functions corresponding to the choices presented by the menu.

Each derived class must override the `mainLoop` function inherited from `Menu`. The `mainLoop` function uses the `clearScreen` and `getMenuSelection` functions of the base class to display and process a menu. When `getMenuSelection` returns the user's choice, `mainLoop` calls the appropriate function to handle the choice. The client code calls `mainLoop` on the active menu or submenu.

Creating a Menu Hierarchy Using the Stack Template

The semantics of starting a submenu and then returning to the preceding menu when done is best implemented using a *stack*. A stack can be implemented using a vector or list, but the standard library provides a more direct way. Listing 8.1 shows the definition of the Menu class using the standard stack template.

 A *stack* is a data structure that inserts and removes elements in last-in-first-out (LIFO) order. The most recently added element in the stack is called the *top*. A new element is added to the stack using the *push* operation. The top element of the stack is removed using the *pop* operation.

 Code Note   Unless otherwise noted, Listings 8.1–8.13 correspond to files on the companion Web page in the Chapter 8 Code\Menus directory. The files in this directory can be compiled and linked together to create an executable program. (See the end of the Introduction for information on accessing this book's companion Web page.)

Listing 8.1   Definition of the Menu Class Using the Stack Template

```
 1:  // TinyPIM (c) 1999 Pablo Halpern. File Menu.h
 2:
 3:  #ifndef Menu_dot_h
 4:  #define Menu_dot_h 1
 5:
 6:  #include <string>
 7:  #include <stack>
 8:
 9:  // Base class for menus
10:  class Menu
11:  {
12:  public:
13:    Menu() { }
14:
15:    virtual ~Menu() { }
16:
17:    // Execute the menu's main loop
18:    virtual void mainLoop() = 0;
19:
20:    // Return the (global) currently active menu.
21:    static Menu* activeMenu() { return menuStack_.top(); }
22:
23:    // Enter a menu or submenu
24:    static void enterMenu(Menu* m) { menuStack_.push(m); }
```

```
25:
26:     // Exit submenu back to previous-level menu.
27:     static void exitMenu() { menuStack_.pop(); }
28:
29:     // Return true if there is an active menu
30:     static bool isActive() { return ! menuStack_.empty(); }
31:
32:   protected:
33:     // Utilities for use by derived classes:
34:
35:     // Display a menu string and then allow user to enter
36:     // a character from within a string of choices. If user enters
37:     // a character not in the choices string, an error is printed and
38:     // the user is prompted to try again. After a valid character is
39:     // entered, the selected character is returned. In case of an
40:     // I/O error, '\0' is returned. Comparisons are not case sensitive,
41:     // and returned letters are always uppercase.
42:     static char getMenuSelection(const std::string& menu,
43:                                  const std::string& choices);
44:
45:     // Clears the screen
46:     static void clearScreen();
47:
48:   private:
49:     // Stack of menus and submenus.
50:     static std::stack<Menu*> menuStack_;
51:   };
52:
53:   #endif // Menu_dot_h
```

In line 50, we declare the menu stack using the `stack` template (included in line 7). The `menuStack_` variable will contain pointers to the `Menu` objects in our menu/submenu hierarchy. The top of the stack is the active menu. Although the use of `stack` is straightforward, it is worth taking a closer look at its definition, most of which appears in Listing 8.2. (Listing 8.2 is excerpted from the <stack> header. It is not part of the project, nor do you need to type it into your program editor.)

Listing 8.2　The Stack Template as Defined in the ISO C++ Standard

```
 1:   namespace std {
 2:
 3:     template<class T, class Container = deque<T> >
 4:     class stack {
 5:     public:
 6:       typedef Container::value_type value_type;
 7:       typedef Container::size_type size_type;
 8:       typedef Container container_type;
 9:
10:     public:
```

continues

Listing 8.2   continued

```
11:       explicit stack(const Container&  = Container());
12:
13:       bool empty() const             { return (c.empty()); }
14:       size_type size() const         { return (c.size()); }
15:       value_type& top()              { return (c.back()); }
16:       const value_type& top() const  { return (c.back()); }
17:       void push(const value_type& x) { c.push_back(x); }
18:       void pop()                     { c.pop_back(); }
19:
20:     protected:
21:       Container c;
22:     };
23:   }
```

Lines 6–8 declare some typedefs to make it easier to refer to template parameters. In lines 13 and 14, empty and size are defined simply to call the corresponding function in Container. The push function in line 17 adds an element to the end of the sequence. The top function in line 16 returns the last element, which is the element added by the last call to push. The pop function (line 18) removes the last element. If you're familiar with stacks, you might be surprised that pop does not return the element being removed. If you're interested in knowing why this is so, see the sidebar "The Gory Details: Why pop Doesn't Return a Value."

Stack is an example of an *adaptor*: a class template that provides an alternative interface to another class. As you can see, all the operations of stack are implemented as simple inline functions that call the equivalent function in the class Container. The class Container is the second template parameter to stack and specifies the type of sequence container that will hold stack contents. If only one template parameter, T, is specified, the stack will hold its contents in a deque<T>. Any sequence container that supports size, back, push_back, and pop_back can be used in a stack. Thus, we could create a vector-based menu stack by declaring menuStack as follows:

```
stack<Menu*, vector<Menu*> > menuStack;
```

We could also have defined menuStack directly as a vector, list or deque and used push_back instead of push, and so on. However, the stack interface is more direct and prevents code from performing nonstack operations such as inserting in the middle or iterating through the elements. The other container adaptors defined in the standard are queue, in which elements are pushed and popped in first-in-first-out (FIFO) order, and priority_queue, in which top returns the largest element in the queue and pop removes the largest element. You can find out more about these adaptors by consulting the quick reference on the Web page that accompanies this book.

EXCURSION

The Gory Details: Why pop Doesn't Return a Value

One important aspect of containers is that they are *exception safe*. This means that if a well-behaved contained object raises an exception, it doesn't cause resource leaks in the container. If `stack` were defined so that `pop` returned a value, you would use it like this:

```
stack<someclass> mystack;
mystack.push(x);              // push object x on stack
someclass y = mystack.pop();  // Hypothetical pop operation
```

If the copy constructor for y failed with exception `after` pop removed the object from stack, the former top of the stack would be lost forever. Instead, you are forced to rewrite the last statement as two separate operations:

```
Someclass y = mystack.top();
mystack.pop();
```

If the copy constructor for y fails with an exception, the top of the stack remains unchanged. We call `top` to remove the element only after the copy operation succeeds. The same logic applies to the `pop_back` and `pop_front` operations of sequence containers.

Returning to Listing 8.1, `enterMenu` on line 24 uses `push` to add a new menu pointer to the top of the stack. On line 21, `activeMenu` returns the most recently pushed menu pointer. When we call `exitMenu` (line 27), it removes the pointer from the top of the stack and the previously pushed menu becomes active again. To see whether a menu is currently active, we call `isActive`, defined on line 30, which checks whether the stack is empty. When in doubt, it's a good idea to check for an empty stack because calling `pop` or `top` on an empty stack produces undefined behavior. All the functions in `Menu` that manipulate the menu stack are `static` because the menu stack is shared by all menu instances.

Implementing User Interaction Semantics

Lines 42 and 43 of Listing 8.1 declare the `getMenuSelection` function, which is used by classes derived from `Menu` to handle the core interaction between a menu and the user. The menu string contains the list of menu choices and prompt exactly as it will be presented to the user (with imbedded newlines, if necessary). The `choices` string contains the set of characters the user can type to select from the menu. The implementation of this function (as well as `clearScreen`) appears in Listing 8.3.

8

Listing 8.3   Implementation of `getUserSelection` and `clearScreen`

```
 1:  // TinyPIM (c) 1999 Pablo Halpern. File Menu.cpp
 2:
 3:  #include <cctype>
 4:  #include <iostream>
 5:
 6:  #if ! (_MSC_VER ¦¦ __GCC__)
 7:  using std::tolower;
 8:  using std::toupper;
 9:  #endif
10:
11:  #include "Menu.h"
12:
13:  // Display a menu string and then allow user to enter
14:  // a character from within a string of choices. If user enters
15:  // a character not in the choices string, an error is printed and
16:  // the user is prompted to try again. After a valid character is
17:  // entered, the selected character is returned. In case of an
18:  // I/O error, '\0' is returned. Comparisons are not case sensitive.
19:  char Menu::getMenuSelection(const std::string& menu,
20:                              const std::string& choices)
21:  {
22:    while (std::cin.good())
23:    {
24:      std::cout << menu;
25:
26:      char selection = '\0';
27:      std::cin >> selection;
28:      if (std::cin.fail())
29:        break;
30:
31:        // Throw away rest of input line
32:      std::cin.ignore(10000, '\n');
33:
34:      // Search for selection in either uppercase or lowercase
35:      if (choices.find(toupper(selection)) != std::string::npos ¦¦
36:          choices.find(tolower(selection)) != std::string::npos)
37:        return toupper(selection);        // Valid entry
38:      else
39:        std::cout << "Invalid selection, please try again.\n\n";
40:    } // end while
41:
42:    return '\0';
43:  }
44:
45:  // Clear the screen
46:  void Menu::clearScreen()
47:  {
48:    // Because not all terminals respond to the formfeed character to
49:    // clear the screen, we also output 25 newlines:
```

```
50:    std::cout << "\f\n\n\n\n\n\n\n\n\n\n\n\n\n\n\n\n\n\n\n\n\n\n\n\n"
51:            << std::flush;
52:  }
53:
54:  // Define menuStack_ static member variable
55:  std::stack<Menu*> Menu::menuStack_;
```

Reading User Input

We use a while loop in lines 22–40 to prompt the user and wait for input. The loop exits when the user selects a valid input or when an input error occurs. When used in a Boolean context (for example, a loop condition), std::cin can be used as a short-hand for std::cin.good(), but I consider the latter to be easier to read. Line 24 simply displays the menu prompt.

In line 27, we read a single character from the standard input stream. With this kind of input, any whitespace (including newline characters) is discarded. This means that if the user presses Enter, the input will not be complete, and the system will continue waiting for a nonwhitespace character. After the input is complete, we make sure that it was successful with a fail check in line 28. In the case of error, we exit the loop.

If there was no error, we have a character in selection. It is possible that the user typed additional characters after the selection. These spurious characters would be read during the next input operation and produce unexpected results, so we discard the rest of the line using ignore in line 32. The ignore function discards input until either a certain number of characters is consumed or a specified delimiter (default EOF) is consumed. By supplying a large number (10,000) for the character count and newline for the delimiter, we cause it to discard everything up to and including the next newline character.

In lines 35 and 36, we search through the choices string to see whether the character typed by the user can be found within it. As you recall, the find function will return npos if a match is not found. Thus, we know that we have a match if find doesn't return npos. We achieve a non–case-sensitive match by searching for both the uppercase and lowercase versions of selection. The toupper and tolower functions inherited from the C Standard Library do the case conversion we need. These functions are declared in the header <cctype>, included in line 3. The <cctype> header contains many other useful character utilities, including isdigit, to test whether a character is a digit; isspace, to test for whitespace; isupper, and so on. These functions are all in the std namespace, but we bring them into the file namespace with using declarations (in lines 7 and 8) to work around the Microsoft bug discussed in Chapter 2, "Implementing the Address Class with Text Strings."

8

Compiler Note   The egcs compiler, version 1.1.2, has a flaw: All the functions in `<cctype>` are defined as macros and are thus not within the `std` namespace. The workaround is exactly the same as for the Microsoft compiler (see line 6 of Listing 8.3) but applies only to the names in `<cctype>` (whereas the Microsoft workaround applies to all names inherited from C).

If we get to line 37, the user's selection has been found in `choices`. We return the selection to the caller, converting it to uppercase first. If no match was found, the user typed an invalid choice. On line 39, we print an error message and then loop back for another try.

The `Menu` class provides a utility function, `clearScreen`, which (you guessed it) clears the screen. Most terminals clear the screen upon receiving a formfeed character (`'\f'`). However, some terminals (such as the Windows terminal emulator) do not recognize formfeed or print a funny glyph instead of clearing the screen. In line 50, we hedge our bets, first printing the formfeed character and then printing 25 newline characters. For a typical 25-line terminal display, this should be enough to clear the screen.

The `AddressBookMenu` Class

The `AddressBookMenu` class is derived from the `Menu` class. It supplies the set of choices available in the address book mode of TinyPIM, and it implements the actual functions to be called when the user makes a selection. The `AddressBookMenu` class is defined in Listing 8.4.

Listing 8.4   The `AddressBookMenu` Class

```
 1:  // TinyPIM (c) 1999 Pablo Halpern. File AddressBookMenu.h
 2:
 3:  #ifndef AddressBookMenu_dot_h
 4:  #define AddressBookMenu_dot_h 1
 5:
 6:  #include "Menu.h"
 7:  #include "AddressDisplayList.h"
 8:
 9:  class AddressBookMenu : public Menu
10:  {
11:  public:
12:    AddressBookMenu(AddressBook& addrBook)
13:      : addressBook_(addrBook), displayList_(addrBook) { }
14:
15:    void mainLoop();
16:
17:  private:
```

```
18:    void viewEntry();
19:    void createEntry();
20:    void editEntry();
21:    void deleteEntry();
22:    void listAll();
23:    void lookup();
24:    void search();
25:
26:    AddressBook&        addressBook_;
27:    AddressDisplayList  displayList_;
28: };
29:
30: #endif // AddressBookMenu_dot_h
```

On line 26, we declare a member variable that is a reference to an `AddressBook`, and on line 27, we declare a member variable that is an `AddressDisplayList`. These members will be used to service the user's menu choices. On lines 12 and 13, the constructor initializes these two members with the `AddressBook` object passed by the caller. Line 15 declares the main loop, which will be called to display the menu and process the user's choice. Lines 18–24 each declare a function that will be called to service a user's menu selection.

The `mainLoop` Function

The main user interaction is handled by the `mainLoop` function. Let's look at how it is implemented in Listing 8.5.

Listing 8.5   The `mainLoop` Function in `AddressBookMenu`

```
1:  // TinyPIM (c) 1999 Pablo Halpern. File AddressBookMenu.cpp
2:
3:  #ifdef _MSC_VER
4:  #pragma warning(disable : 4786)
5:  #endif
6:
7:  #include <iostream>
8:  #include <iomanip>
9:  #include <climits>
10: #include "AddressBookMenu.h"
11: #include "Address.h"
12: #include "AddressBook.h"
13: #include "AddressEditor.h"
14:
15: void AddressBookMenu::mainLoop()
16: {
17:   clearScreen();
18:   std::cout << "*** Address Book ***\n\n";
19:
20:   displayList_.display();
```

continues

8

Listing 8.5   continued

```
21:    std::cout << '\n';
22:
23:    static const char menu[] =
24:      "(P)revious, (N)ext, (V)iew, (C)reate, (D)elete, (E)dit, \n"
25:      "list (A)ll, (L)ookup, (S)earch  (R)edisplay  (Q)uit ? ";
26:
27:    static const char choices[] = "PNVCDEALSRQ";
28:
29:    switch (getMenuSelection(menu, choices))
30:    {
31:    case 'P': displayList_.pageUp();    break;
32:    case 'N': displayList_.pageDown();  break;
33:    case 'V': viewEntry();              break;
34:    case 'C': createEntry();            break;
35:    case 'D': deleteEntry();            break;
36:    case 'E': editEntry();              break;
37:    case 'A': listAll();                break;
38:    case 'L': lookup();                 break;
39:    case 'S': search();                 break;
40:    case 'R': /* do nothing, just loop */ break;
41:    case 'Q': exitMenu();               break;
42:    default:  exitMenu();               break;
43:    }
44: }
45:
```

The first thing that `mainLoop` does, in lines 17 and 18, is to clear the screen and print the words `Address Book` on the display. Then, in line 20, we ask the display list to display a screenful of record summaries. The `displayList_` member variable initially starts out in a clear state. The first time we call `display` it will retrieve and display the first 15 records in the address book.

The display list lets the user see the records in the address book. Now we want to give the user a choice of actions to perform on one of these records. We design our menu to fit on two lines underneath the display list output. The menu text is defined in a static, null-terminated character string in lines 23–25. Notice that the text of the menu is divided into two string literals with no punctuation between them. Many people don't know that C and C++ let you divide up a string literal like that. The two strings are compiled into one string literal. This is useful when a string doesn't fit on one line. The menu prompt defined in lines 23–25 has a newline imbedded in the middle.

The user's menu choices are highlighted in parentheses. In line 27, we aggregate the choices into a single string of initials. At line 29, we pass both the menu prompt and the string of choices to the `getMenuSelection` function inherited from the `Menu` base class. The `getMenuSelection` function will return one of the letters in the choices string (in uppercase) or the null character indicating an I/O error. We switch on the results, and in lines 31–42, we dispatch the appropriate function to handle the user's selection.

The Next and Previous choices are handled in lines 31 and 32, respectively, by the display list's pageDown and pageUp functions. The Quit and error choices are handled on lines 41 and 42 by calling the base class exitMenu function, which pops the current menu off the menu stack, making it no longer active and causing the preceding active menu (if any) to become active again. The rest of the choices are handled by the member functions of AddressBookMenu. When the action is complete, the mainLoop function ends. The "loop" part of mainLoop is just the loop in getMenuSelection that prompts the user and handles invalid inputs.

The viewEntry Function

If the user enters the V option, the main loop calls the viewEntry function, which appears in Listing 8.6.

Listing 8.6 Implementation of the viewEntry Function

```
46:  void AddressBookMenu::viewEntry()
47:  {
48:    int recordId = displayList_.selectRecord();
49:    if (recordId == 0)
50:      return;
51:
52:    Address addr = addressBook_.getAddress(recordId);
53:    std::cout << "\nName:   " << addr.lastname();
54:    if (! addr.firstname().empty())
55:      std::cout << ", " << addr.firstname();
56:    std::cout << "\nPhone: " << addr.phone();
57:    std::cout << "\nAddress:\n" << addr.address();
58:
59:    std::cout << "\n\nPress [RETURN] when ready.";
60:    std::cin.ignore(INT_MAX, '\n');
61:  }
62:
```

In line 48, we ask the display list for a record selection. The display list will prompt the user for the number of a record on the screen and will return the record ID of the user's selection. It will return 0 if the user cancels the operation. In lines 52–57, we display all the fields of the Address record in a reasonable viewing format. At line 60, we use the ignore function to pause the display so that the user can view the information before the screen is cleared and the menu is redisplayed. The ignore function will keep reading from the input stream until the user presses Enter. Any other characters are ignored. There is no particular limit to the number of characters we want to ignore, so we set the size limit to INT_MAX, a macro evaluating to (surprise) the largest value that can be stored in an int.

The INT_MAX macro (along with similar macros, such as INT_MIN, UINT_MAX, LONG_MAX, and so on) is defined in the <climits> header, which is included in line 9 of Listing 8.5. Because INT_MAX is a macro, it is not scoped in the std namespace. Note that there is also a <limits> header (no leading c) that contains similar information. However, this is in a more difficult-to-use template format that is more suitable for authoring complex templates that must determine the numeric limits of their template parameters.

The createEntry Function

If the user chooses C to create a new record, we want to start an edit session on an empty Address object. After the edit session is complete, we must check for duplicate names, giving the user the option of deliberately adding a duplicate name, editing the record so that it is no longer a duplicate, or canceling. The function returns when the record is successfully added to the address book or the user cancels the operation. Listing 8.7 shows the implementation of createEntry.

Listing 8.7   The createEntry Function

```
63:   void AddressBookMenu::createEntry()
64:   {
65:     // Edit an empty address
66:     AddressEditor   editor;
67:     Address addr;
68:
69:     // Continue editing until a record is saved or canceled.
70:     while (editor.edit())
71:     {
72:       addr = editor.addr();
73:       if (addr.lastname().empty())
74:       {
75:         std::cout << "Last name must not be empty." << std::endl;
76:         continue;     // Loop and re-edit
77:       }
78:
79:       // Search for existing entries with the same name
80:       int duplicates = addressBook_.countName(addr.lastname(),
81:                                     addr.firstname());
82:
83:       int recordId = 0;
84:       if (duplicates == 0)
85:       {
86:         // No duplicates, just insert record.
87:         recordId = addressBook_.insertAddress(addr);
88:
89:         // Scroll to display new record
90:         displayList_.scrollToTop(recordId);
91:         return;
92:       }
```

```
 93:        else
 94:        {
 95:          // Duplicate name. Check to see what user wants to do.
 96:          std::cout << "There are already " << duplicates
 97:                       << " records with this name.\n";
 98:          switch (getMenuSelection(
 99:                       "(S)ave as new record, (E)dit record or (C)ancel? ",
100:                       "SEC"))
101:          {
102:          case 'S':    // Save record (create a duplicate)
103:            recordId = addressBook_.insertAddress(addr);
104:            displayList_.scrollToTop(recordId);
105:            return;
106:
107:          case 'E':    // Edit record again
108:            continue;    // Loop back and re-edit
109:
110:          case 'C':    // Cancel or
111:          default:     // I/O error
112:            return;     // Return without changing AddressBook
113:          } // End switch
114:        } // end else
115:    } // end while
116: }
117:
```

The first thing we do, in line 70, is start an edit session on an empty Address record, addr, declared in line 67. We do this in a loop because we might have to edit the record again, if a duplicate is detected and the user chooses to continue editing. The loop is terminated in the middle if the record is stored successfully in the address book. The user can also terminate the loop by aborting the edit (with !x), causing editor.edit() to return false. In lines 73–77, we check to make sure that the Address record has a nonempty last name field. If not, we display an error and continue looping so that the user can edit the record again.

In lines 80 and 81, we get a count of the number of records in the address book that already have the name we entered for our new record. If no such records exist, this is a unique name, and we insert the record into the address book, scroll the new record to the top of the screen, and return—in lines 87, 90, and 91, respectively. If records already exist with the same name, we inform the user that there are duplicates in lines 96 and 97. Then we create another menu, in line 99, prompting the user for what he or she wants to do with the duplicate. The user may choose S to save the record anyway, E to reedit the record (to change the name so that it is no longer a duplicate), or C to cancel the whole create-record operation. As with the preceding menu, we switch on the results and handle each possible option. Note that the while loop exits only if a record is saved or the create operation is canceled.

8

The `deleteEntry` and `editEntry` Functions

Deleting or editing an entry can cause the display list cache to become invalid. Deleting an entry causes a record to disappear, thus leaving a false entry in the cache. Editing an entry can cause it to move in the sort order (for example, if the name changes), thus causing the cache to become out of sync with the address book. The simplest solution in both cases is to reset the cache, forcing it to reload the data from the address book, as seen in Listing 8.8.

Listing 8.8   The `deleteEntry` and `editEntry` Functions

```
118: void AddressBookMenu::deleteEntry()
119: {
120:   int recordId = displayList_.selectRecord();
121:   if (recordId == 0)
122:     return;
123:
124:   // Find first visible record on screen. If it is the record
125:   // we are erasing, then find second visible record on screen
126:   int firstVisible = displayList_.screenRecord(0);
127:   if (firstVisible == recordId)
128:     firstVisible = displayList_.screenRecord(1);
129:
130:   // Erase the address
131:   addressBook_.eraseAddress(recordId);
132:
133:   // Deleting the entry invalidates the display list cache.
134:   // Reset it, then scroll back to the previous position
135:   displayList_.reset();
136:   if (firstVisible != 0)
137:     displayList_.scrollToTop(firstVisible);
138: }
139:
140: void AddressBookMenu::editEntry()
141: {
142:   int recordId = displayList_.selectRecord();
143:   if (recordId == 0)
144:     return;
145:
146:   // Create an editor for the selected address
147:   Address addr = addressBook_.getAddress(recordId);
148:   AddressEditor editor(addr);
149
150:   // Edit the address
151:   if (editor.edit())
152:   {
153:     // Replace address with modified version.
154:     addressBook_.replaceAddress(editor.addr());
155:
156:     // Address's sort order might have changed. We need to reset
157:     // the display list.
```

```
158:        displayList_.reset();
159:
160:        // Scroll modified item to top of screen
161:        displayList_.scrollToTop(recordId);
162:    }
163: }
164:
```

In `deleteEntry`, we ask the user to select a record to delete in line 120, and then we actually delete the record in line 131. Because deleting the record will invalidate the display list cache, we reset the display list in line 135. However, to keep the display list from losing its place, we gather enough information to reestablish the scroll position before erasing the record. In line 126, we find out the current first line of the display. If the first line is the record we are deleting, we look at the second line instead, in lines 127 and 128. Then, after erasing the record and resetting the cache, we scroll the old first or second line back to the top of the screen in line 137. This keeps the display list from jumping back to the first record in the address book, which would be jarring for the user.

At line 142 in `editEntry`, we again ask the user to select a record from those displayed on the screen. We then retrieve the address in line 147 and create an editor object for it in line 148. If the editor terminates normally (that is, the user did not abort) in line 151, we replace the record in the address book in line 154. Because the record might have changed names and thus order in the list, we again must reset the display list in line 158. This time, we will scroll the record that we just edited to the top of the screen, in line 161. We could be more sophisticated in determining whether we really have to reset the display list, but this method performs quite adequately.

Lookups and Searches

Name lookups work by scrolling the display list to the record that most closely matches the name entered by the user. String searches work by filtering the records in the display list to include only those records that match the user's search string. The implementation of these functions is shown in Listing 8.9.

Listing 8.9   Implementation of Lookup and Search Functions

```
165: void AddressBookMenu::lookup()
166: {
167:    // Prompt for lastname and (optional) firstname
168:    std::string lkupname;
169:    std::cout << "lookup name (lastname [,firstname]): ";
170:    std::getline(std::cin, lkupname);
171:    if (lkupname.empty())
```

continues

Listing 8.9   continued

```
172:    return;
173:
174:    // Find end of last name and start of first name
175:    std::string::size_type lastNameEnd = lkupname.find(',');
176:    std::string::size_type firstNameStart = std::string::npos;
177:    if (lastNameEnd != std::string::npos)
178:      firstNameStart = lkupname.find_first_not_of(", \t\f\n\v",
179:                                                  lastNameEnd);
180:
181:    if (firstNameStart == std::string::npos)
182:      // Lookup using last name only
183:      displayList_.findNameStartsWith(lkupname.substr(0, lastNameEnd));
184:    else
185:      displayList_.findNameStartsWith(lkupname.substr(0, lastNameEnd),
186:                                      lkupname.substr(firstNameStart));
187: }
188:
189: void AddressBookMenu::search()
190: {
191:    std::string searchString;
192:    std::cout << "Search for string: ";
193:    std::getline(std::cin, searchString);
194:    if (searchString.empty())
195:      return;
196:
197:    displayList_.listContainsString(searchString);
198: }
199:
200: void AddressBookMenu::listAll()
201: {
202:    displayList_.listAll();
203: }
```

In lines 168 and 169, we ask the user for a name to look up, consisting of a last name and an optional first name. The user is likely to type just the first few letters of the last name because the lookup is a near match, not an exact match. However he or she might type in the entire last name and first name, to quickly retrieve a specific record. In line 170, we read from the standard input stream using getline, which, as you recall, reads up to the next newline character, which it discards.

In line 175, we look for the end of the last name part of the input stream by searching for a comma. In line 177, we check whether the comma was found. If so, we go to line 178, which skips the comma and any whitespace characters to give us the start of the first name portion of the input string. If the comma is not found, or if there is no nonwhitespace part of the first name, firstNameStart will be equal to npos. In lines 183 and 185, we extract the last name from the input string using the substr function, using a starting position of 0 and a length that take us up to the comma. In line 186, we extract the first name portion using substr again, passing firstNameStart as the starting position and letting the length default to the end of the string. In line 181, we detect whether the user entered a first name. If not, we call findNameStartsWith on line 183 with only the last name parameter (the first name defaults to the empty string). If we do have a last name, we call findNameStartsWith using two parameters on lines 185 and 186. The findNameStartsWith function of AddressDisplayList will scroll the desired name (or its closest match not smaller than the name) to the top of the screen.

The search function works similarly. Again, it reads a single line from the input stream in line 193. However, this function does not require breaking up the string into last name and first name, so the resulting input string is simply passed to AddressDisplayList's listContainsString function, which modifies the fetchMore operation to filter the displayed records. The user can undo the effect of search by selecting the List (A)ll menu item, which invokes the listAll function. The listAll function is simply a pass-through to AddressDisplayList's listAll function.

Putting the Pieces Together

In the previous chapter, we developed a display list but didn't test it. Now we have created a menu framework and implemented the address book menu, which makes extensive use of the display list. We are ready to put all the pieces together and give it a whirl.

The Main Program

Listing 8.10 shows a main program that invokes the address book menu. To create a working program, we will link this with the most recent version of all the classes we have developed so far. (See the note before Listing 8.1 to find this code on the Web.)

Listing 8.10 The Main Program

```
 1:  // TinyPIM (c) 1999 Pablo Halpern. File TinyPIM.cpp
 2:
 3:  #ifdef _MSC_VER
 4:  #pragma warning(disable : 4786)
 5:  #endif
 6:
 7:  #include <iostream>
 8:
 9:  #include "AddressBook.h"
10:  #include "AddressBookMenu.h"
11:
12:  // Main program just calls main menu, for now.
```

continues

Listing 8.10   continued

```
13:   int main()
14:   {
15:     AddressBook addrBook;
16:
17:     // Create address book menu and push on menu stack.
18:     AddressBookMenu addrBookMenu(addrBook);
19:     Menu::enterMenu(&addrBookMenu);
20:
21:     // Process menu choices until menu exits.
22:     while (Menu::isActive())
23:       Menu::activeMenu()->mainLoop();
24:
25:     std::cout << "\nThank you for using TinyPIM!\n" << std::endl;
26:
27:     return 0;
28:   }
```

In line 15, we create an AddressBook object, and on line 18, we create an
AddressBookMenu object. We push the menu onto the menu stack on line 19. Our
main loop is lines 22 and 23, where we look at the *active* menu (the menu on the top
of the menu stack) and call its main menu until no more menus appear on the menu
stack (Menu::isActive returns false). There will be no more menus on the menu
stack when the user selects (Q)uit and the address book menu pops itself off the
stack. When the loop terminates, we print out a final message in line 25 and then
exit. Listing 8.11 shows the result of running this program and interacting with the
menu and display list.

Listing 8.11   Output of a Simple Run

```
** Address Book ***

============= No records selected ===============

(P)revious, (N)ext, (V)iew, (C)reate, (D)elete, (E)dit,
list (A)ll, (L)ookup, (S)earch  (R)edisplay  (Q)uit ? C
Last name: Clinton
First name: William
Phone Number: 5551993
Address: 9 Monica Blvd
Address: Little Rock, AK
Address: .
```

```
                          Form Feed (new page)
```

```
*** Address Book ***

 1: Clinton, William......................555-1993
=============== End of list ===============
```

```
(P)revious, (N)ext, (V)iew, (C)reate, (D)elete, (E)dit,
list (A)ll, (L)ookup, (S)earch  (R)edisplay  (Q)uit ? C
Last name: Ford
First name: Gerald
Phone Number: 555-1974
Address: 8 Golf Dr.
Address: Washington, DC
Address: .
```

Form Feed (new page)

```
*** Address Book ***

  1: Ford, Gerald.........................555-1974
=============== End of list ===============

(P)revious, (N)ext, (V)iew, (C)reate, (D)elete, (E)dit,
list (A)ll, (L)ookup, (S)earch  (R)edisplay  (Q)uit ? a
```

Form Feed (new page)

```
*** Address Book ***

=============== Start of list ===============
  1: Clinton, William.....................555-1993
  2: Ford, Gerald.........................555-1974
=============== End of list ===============

(P)revious, (N)ext, (V)iew, (C)reate, (D)elete, (E)dit,
list (A)ll, (L)ookup, (S)earch  (R)edisplay  (Q)uit ? s
Search for string: Monica
```

Form Feed (new page)

```
*** Address Book ***

=============== Start of list ===============
  1: Clinton, William.....................555-1993
=============== End of list ===============

(P)revious, (N)ext, (V)iew, (C)reate, (D)elete, (E)dit,
list (A)ll, (L)ookup, (S)earch  (R)edisplay  (Q)uit ? v
Choose a record number between 1 and 1
Record number (0 to cancel)? 1

Name:  Clinton, William
Phone: 555-1993
Address:
9 Monica Blvd
Little Rock, AK

Press [RETURN] when ready.
```

continues

Listing 8.11   continued

Form Feed (new page)

```
*** Address Book ***

=============== Start of list ===============
 1: Clinton, Bill.........................555-1993
=============== End of list ===============

(P)revious, (N)ext, (V)iew, (C)reate, (D)elete, (E)dit,
list (A)ll, (L)ookup, (S)earch  (R)edisplay  (Q)uit ? q

Thank you for using TinyPIM!
```

We could have gone on, adding records until we had several screenfuls that we could scroll back and forth, doing lookups and searches; creating, deleting, and editing records; and confirming that the list scrolls as desired. However, this would become tedious. We must somehow add lots of records with a minimum of effort so that our testing can be more thorough.

A Data-Generating Function Using String Streams

Listing 8.12 shows a function, generateAddresses, that creates real-looking random addresses and inserts them into the address book.

Listing 8.12   A Function to Generate Random Addresses

```
 1:  // TinyPIM (c) 1999 Pablo Halpern. File TestData.cpp
 2:
 3:  #ifdef _MSC_VER
 4:  #pragma warning(disable : 4786)
 5:  #endif
 6:
 7:  #include <cstdlib>
 8:  #include <sstream>
 9:  #include <iomanip>
10:
11:  #ifdef _MSC_VER
12:  namespace std {
13:    inline int rand() { return ::rand(); }
14:    inline void srand(unsigned s) { ::srand(s); }
15:  }
16:  #endif
17:
18:  #include "AddressBook.h"
19:
20:  // Return a string at random from a constant array of strings
21:  template <class A>
22:  inline const char* randomString(A& stringArray)
23:  {
```

```
24:     int size = sizeof(A) / sizeof(stringArray[0]);
25:     int index = std::rand() % size;
26:     return stringArray[index];
27: }
28:
29: void generateAddresses(AddressBook& addrbook, int numAddresses)
30: {
31:     // Seed the random number generator with a constant so that the
32:     // same sequence of "random" numbers will be generated every time.
33:     std::srand(100);
34:
35:     static const char* const lastnames[] = {
36:       "Clinton", "Bush", "Reagan", "Carter", "Ford", "Nixon", "Johnson",
37:       "Kennedy"
38:     };
39:
40:     static const char* const firstnames[] = {
41:       "William", "George", "Ronald", "Jimmy", "Gerald", "Richard",
42:       "Lyndon", "Jack", "Hillary", "Barbara", "Nancy", "Rosalynn",
43:       "Betty", "Pat", "Ladybird", "Jackie"
44:     };
45:
46:     // The names of trees are used to generate street and town names.
47:     static const char* const trees[] = {
48:       "Maple", "Oak", "Willow", "Pine", "Hemlock", "Redwood", "Fir",
49:       "Holly", "Elm"
50:     };
51:
52:     static const char* const streetSuffixes[] = {
53:       "St.", "Rd.", "Ln.", "Terr.", "Ave."
54:     };
55:
56:     static const char* const townSuffixes[] = {
57:       "ton", "vale", "burg", "ham"
58:     };
59:
60:     // State abbreviations, U.S. and its territories.
61:     // Thanks to the USPS Web page:
62:     // http://www.usps.gov/cpim/ftp/pubs/201html/addrpack.htm#abbr
63:     static const char* const states[] = {
64:       "AL", "AK", "AS", "AZ", "AR", "CA", "CO", "CT", "DE",
65:       "DC", "FM", "FL", "GA", "GU", "HI", "ID", "IL", "IN",
66:       "IA", "KS", "KY", "LA", "ME", "MH", "MD", "MA", "MI",
67:       "MN", "MS", "MO", "MT", "NE", "NV", "NH", "NJ", "NM",
68:       "NY", "NC", "ND", "MP", "OH", "OK", "OR", "PA", "PR",
69:       "RI", "SC", "SD", "TN", "TX", "UT", "VT", "VA", "VI",
70:       "WA", "WV", "WI", "WY"
71:     };
72:
73:     for (int i = 0; i < numAddresses; ++i)
74:     {
```

8

continues

Listing 8.12   continued

```
75:        Address addr;
76:        addr.lastname(randomString(lastnames));
77:        addr.firstname(randomString(firstnames));
78:
79:        // Construct a phone number by streaming to a stringstream
80:        std::stringstream phonestream;
81:        phonestream << '(' << (std::rand() % 800 + 200) << ") "
82:                    << (std::rand() % 800 + 200) << '-'
83:                    << std::setfill('0') << std::setw(4)
84:                    << (std::rand() % 10000);
85:        addr.phone(phonestream.str());
86:
87:        std::stringstream addrstream;
88:        // Generate number and street.
89:        addrstream << (std::rand() % 100 + 1) << " "
90:                   << randomString(trees) << " "
91:                   << randomString(streetSuffixes) << '\n';
92:
93:        // Generate town name, state, and zip.
94:        addrstream << randomString(trees) << randomString(townSuffixes)
95:                   << ", " << randomString(states) << " "
96:                   << std::setfill('0') << std::setw(5)
97:                   << (std::rand() % 99999 + 1);
98:        addr.address(addrstream.str());
99:
100:   addrbook.insertAddress(addr);
101:   }
102: }
```

We will be using two functions in `<cstdlib>` (included in line 7): `rand` and `srand`. Because these functions are inherited from C, the Microsoft library will fail to put them into namespace `std`. In lines 12–15, we have an workaround to this problem. Rather than import these functions into the global namespace, we define them in the `std` namespace. Thus, there will be two versions of `rand`: The `std::rand` function is simply an inline call-through to the global `::rand` function—similarly for `srand`. Either workaround—importing into the global namespace or adding them to the `std` namespace—would work, but I like the clarity of using the `std::` prefix.

Lines 21–27 define an interesting template function, `randomString`. This function does not actually generate a random string of characters, but rather chooses a string at random from an array of strings. The array is passed in as the only argument. Because the size of the array is part of its type, each array will cause `randomString` to be instantiated with a different template parameter, `A`. In line 24, we calculate the number of elements in the array by dividing the total size of the array by the size of its first element. Thus, if `A` is `const char*[15]`, `size` will be computed as 15.

In line 25, we call the `rand` function, which returns a pseudorandom number in the range 0ñRAND_MAX (`RAND_MAX` is at least 32767 and is usually `INT_MAX`). We then apply the modulus operator to the result, giving `index` a value in the range 0ñsize. In other words, `index` is a randomly generated index into the `stringArray` variable. In line 26, we return the value at the randomly generated index. This function can work only for arrays of `const char*` because the return value is of type `const_char*`.

The `generateAddresses` function, starting at line 29, will use `randomString` to generate a plausible name and address in the U.S. Line 33 uses the `srand` function to set the *seed* of the random number generator. It is important to know that the return value of `rand` is only *pseudo*random, not truly random. It is computed using a mathematical formula that returns values in the same distribution pattern as truly random numbers. The sequence of numbers returned by `rand` is determined by a *seed* value set at the start. Each seed causes `rand` to generate a different sequence of numbers; each sequence seems random. We use the constant, 100, to seed the random number generator. It is common practice to get better randomness by setting the seed using the `time` function, which returns the current date and time as an integer. (We'll be using `time` more in the next chapter). In this case, however, we prefer the sequence of pseudorandom numbers to be the same every time, so it is easier to see the effect of changes in our program.

Lines 35–38 define an array of string literals containing possible last names. Lines 40–44 define another such array containing possible first names. The array in lines 47–50 contains tree names, which are commonly used names for streets or for towns. Lines 52–54 define an array of street-name suffixes, and lines 56–59 define an array of town-name suffixes. Lines 63–71 define an array of postal abbreviations for the states and territories of the U.S. (Thanks to the United States Postal Service for the list.) All these arrays will be used to generate strings for our synthetic `Address` records. An address record will consist of a randomly selected last name, a randomly selected first name, a randomly generated phone number, a randomly generated street number, a randomly selected street name and suffix, a randomly selected town name and suffix, a randomly selected state, and a randomly generated zip code (postal code).

The loop starting at line 73 will execute `numAddresses` times, creating an `Address` object each time around and inserting it into the address book. Lines 76 and 77 select random last name and first name fields for the `Address`. Generating a phone number is trickier than it seems. Neither the first nor fourth digit of a 10-digit U.S. phone number may be 0 or 1. Furthermore, the number should be displayed in the format *(ddd) ddd-dddd*, in which each *d* is a digit. The job would be easier if instead of creating a string, we were simply writing formatted data to an output stream. C programmers do this using the `sprintf` function. C++ programmers use *string streams*.

8

A string stream is an object of the class `stringstream`, which is derived from `iostream`. It is declared in the header `<sstream>`, included in line 8. Like the I/O streams we have already seen (for example, `cout` and `cin`), a string stream supports operators `<<` and `>>` to insert or extract formatted data to or from the stream. However, instead of sending text to the console or reading it from the keyboard, the formatted text is stored in a `string` object or read from a `string` object. In line 80, we define a string stream named `phonestream`, which we will use to format the randomly generated phone number. The formula, `(std::rand() % 800 + 200)`, in line 81 will generate a random number in the range 200–999, that is, a three-digit number not starting with 0 or 1. We will create a phone number using two such three-digit random numbers and a four-digit random number with the necessary punctuation in between. Lines 81–84 do this formatting and send the result to the `phonestream` string stream. Notice that all aspects of I/O streams are supported by string streams, including manipulators like `setfill` and `setw`. The `str` member function of `stringstream` returns the result of the formatted output, which we use to set the phone number in our `Address` object.

Beginning with line 87, we construct an address string using the same technique we used for the phone number. In lines 89–91, we insert a random number in the range 1–100 (the house number), a randomly selected tree name (the street name), a randomly selected street suffix, and a newline character. In lines 94–97, we add a randomly selected tree name with a town suffix, a comma, a randomly selected state, and a random five-digit postal zip code. Notice that we set the fill character to `0` and the width to `5` so that a number like 102 is formatted as `00102`. In line 98, we take the resulting string and use it to set the address field. Finally, we insert the new `Address` object into the address book in line 100. This process is repeated as many times as specified in the `numAddresses` argument to the `generateAddresses` function.

EXCURSION

`fstream`s *and* `strstream`s

The C++ Standard Library defines three types of I/O streams: `stringstream`, `fstream`, and `strstream`. Each of these has three variants for doing output, input, or both. The classes `ostringstream`, `ofstream`, and `ostrstream` are derived from `ostream` and are used for output; `ostringstream`, `ifstream`, and `istrstream` are derived from `istream` and are used for input; and `stringstream`, `fstream`, and `strstream` are derived from `iostream` and are used for both input and output. The formatting features of all these stream types are the same. They differ only in the source or destination for the data. We have already seen string streams, so let's now explore `fstream`s and `strstream`s.

The `fstream` classes are declared in `<fstream>` and are used for input and output from files. All the `fstream` classes have a member function, `open`, which takes a filename argument and an optional file mode argument. The file mode argument is constructed by or'ing together the bit flags `ios::in` for input mode, `ios::out` for output mode, and `ios::binary` for binary mode I/O, as well as others, as found in the quick reference. The `open` function opens the file and prepares it for input or output. The corresponding `close` function closes the file. The `ifstream` and `ofstream` constructors can also be passed a filename and flags argument, causing them to automatically call the `open` function. The destructor will always call `close` if a file is open.

If an `fstream` is opened in text mode (the default), newline characters are translated to and from the underlying file system representation when writing or reading. (For example, in DOS or Windows, a newline is translated on output to two characters: carriage return and linefeed.) If an `fstream` is opened in binary mode using the `ios::binary` file mode flag, this translation does not occur.

The `strstream` class works like `stringstream` except that the formatted text is sent to a memory buffer instead of a `string` object. Because of the availability of `stringstream`, the standard *deprecates* the `strtream` class, meaning that it is considered obsolete and might be removed in the next C++ standard (in 5 to 10 years). If you have used `strstream` before, be aware that the `eos` manipulator—which is used to tack a null terminator onto the end of a `strstream` buffer—should not be used with `fstreams` or `stringstreams` because it will insert a spurious null character into the stream.

Listing 8.13 shows the change to our main program to use the `generateAddresses` test function.

Listing 8.13   The Main Program Using the Random Address Generator

```
1:  // TinyPIM (c) 1999 Pablo Halpern. File TinyPIM.cpp
2:
3:  #ifdef _MSC_VER
4:  #pragma warning(disable : 4786)
5:  #endif
6:
7:  #include <iostream>
8:
9:  #include "AddressBook.h"
10: #include "AddressBookMenu.h"
11:
12: // Test function to generate addresses (in TestAddrData.cpp)
13: extern void generateAddresses(AddressBook& addrbook,
14:                                int numAddresses);
15:
16: // Main program just calls main menu, for now.
17: int main()
18: {
19:    AddressBook addrBook;
20:
21:    // Generate 50 random address-book entries
22:    generateAddresses(addrBook, 50);
23:
24:    // Create address book menu and push on menu stack
25:    AddressBookMenu addrBookMenu(addrBook);
```

continues

Listing 8.13   continued

```
26:     Menu::enterMenu(&addrBookMenu);
27:
28:     // Process menu choices until menu exits.
29:     while (Menu::isActive())
30:       Menu::activeMenu()->mainLoop();
31:
32:     std::cout << "\nThank you for using TinyPIM!\n" << std::endl;
33:
34:     return 0;
35:   }
```

Lines 13 and 14 declare the `generateAddress` function. We didn't bother creating a separate header file for this one function. In line 22, we use it to generate 50 random address values. When we fire up this program, we get the output shown in Listing 8.14. (You might see different values, depending on the sequence generated by your compiler's implementation of rand.)

Listing 8.14   Initial Output Screen When Using the Data Generation Function

```
*** Address Book ***

=============== Start of list ===============
  1: Bush, Barbara..........................(994) 342-1167
  2: Bush, Jack.............................(793) 651-9982
  3: Bush, Jack.............................(932) 794-5662
  4: Bush, Lyndon...........................(491) 421-9782
  5: Bush, Nancy............................(420) 672-5507
  6: Carter, Barbara........................(642) 628-2442
  7: Carter, George.........................(581) 409-9816
  8: Carter, George.........................(483) 515-8945
  9: Carter, Lyndon.........................(741) 590-6004
 10: Carter, Rosalynn.......................(568) 301-0648
 11: Carter, William........................(620) 256-2045
 12: Clinton, Jimmy.........................(547) 348-2090
 13: Clinton, Jimmy.........................(499) 318-5124
 14: Clinton, Ladybird......................(676) 341-0043
 15: Clinton, Lyndon........................(264) 471-2286


(P)revious, (N)ext, (V)iew, (C)reate, (D)elete, (E)dit,
list (A)ll, (L)ookup, (S)earch  (R)edisplay  (Q)uit ? v
Choose a record number between 1 and 15
Record number (0 to cancel)? 11

Name:  Carter, William
Phone: (620) 256-2045
Address:
27 Hemlock Ln.
Maplevale, VA 13217


Press [RETURN] when ready.
```

I'll leave it as an exercise for you to play with this program at length, scrolling forward and backward, inserting, editing and deleting records, performing lookups and searches, and so on. The complete code is available on the accompanying Web page.

Room for Improvement: Non–Case-Sensitive Searches

Let's run our program again and do a couple of lookups. We will first find the first entry beginning with the letter *R* and then try another lookup using a lowercase *r*. The result is in Listing 8.15.

Listing 8.15   Searching for *R* and Then *r*

```
 1:
 2:  *** Address Book ***
 3:
 4:  =============== Start of list ===============
 5:   1: Bush, Barbara...........................(994) 342-1167
 6:   2: Bush, Jack..............................(793) 651-9982
 7:   3: Bush, Jack..............................(932) 794-5662
 8:   4: Bush, Lyndon............................(491) 421-9782
 9:   5: Bush, Nancy.............................(420) 672-5507
10:   6: Carter, Barbara.........................(642) 628-2442
11:   7: Carter, George..........................(581) 409-9816
12:   8: Carter, George..........................(483) 515-8945
13:   9: Carter, Lyndon..........................(741) 590-6004
14:  10: Carter, Rosalynn........................(568) 301-0648
15:  11: Carter, William.........................(620) 256-2045
16:  12: Clinton, Jimmy..........................(547) 348-2090
17:  13: Clinton, Jimmy..........................(499) 318-5124
18:  14: Clinton, Ladybird.......................(676) 341-0043
19:  15: Clinton, Lyndon.........................(264) 471-2286
20:
21:
22:  (P)revious, (N)ext, (V)iew, (C)reate, (D)elete, (E)dit,
23:  list (A)ll, (L)ookup, (S)earch  (R)edisplay  (Q)uit ? L
24:  lookup name (lastname [,firstname]): R
25:
                          Form Feed
27:
28:  *** Address Book ***
29:
30:   1: Reagan, Barbara.........................(577) 755-4801
31:   2: Reagan, Jackie..........................(393) 699-0036
32:   3: Reagan, Jackie..........................(705) 203-7648
33:   4: Reagan, Ladybird........................(625) 867-5077
34:   5: Reagan, Nancy...........................(981) 896-2771
```

continues

8

Listing 8.15   continued

```
35:    6: Reagan, Ronald.........................(336) 634-1605
36:    7: Reagan, Ronald.........................(461) 478-6096
37:    8: Reagan, Rosalynn.......................(636) 506-9142
38:    =============== End of list ===============
39:
40:    (P)revious, (N)ext, (V)iew, (C)reate, (D)elete, (E)dit,
41:    list (A)ll, (L)ookup, (S)earch  (R)edisplay  (Q)uit ? L
42:    lookup name (lastname [,firstname]): r
43:

                              Form Feed

45:
46:    *** Address Book ***
47:
48:    =============== Start of list ===============
49:     1: Bush, Barbara..........................(994) 342-1167
50:     2: Bush, Jack.............................(793) 651-9982
51:     3: Bush, Jack.............................(932) 794-5662
52:     4: Bush, Lyndon...........................(491) 421-9782
53:     5: Bush, Nancy............................(420) 672-5507
54:     6: Carter, Barbara........................(642) 628-2442
55:     7: Carter, George.........................(581) 409-9816
56:     8: Carter, George.........................(483) 515-8945
57:     9: Carter, Lyndon.........................(741) 590-6004
58:    10: Carter, Rosalynn.......................(568) 301-0648
59:    11: Carter, William........................(620) 256-2045
60:    12: Clinton, Jimmy.........................(547) 348-2090
61:    13: Clinton, Jimmy.........................(499) 318-5124
62:    14: Clinton, Ladybird......................(676) 341-0043
63:    15: Clinton, Lyndon........................(264) 471-2286
64:
65:
66:    (P)revious, (N)ext, (V)iew, (C)reate, (D)elete, (E)dit,
67:    list (A)ll, (L)ookup, (S)earch  (R)edisplay  (Q)uit ?
```

In lines 23 and 24, we ask to look up names beginning with *R*; as expected, the display list scrolls to the first names beginning with *R*, as seen in lines 30–37. However, in lines 41 and 42, when we ask to look up names beginning with lowercase *r*, nothing is found and the display list scrolls to the beginning. This does not seem very friendly. Moreover, if we were to create a record with the name *clinton, Kenny*, it would not show up between *Clinton, Jimmy* and *Clinton, Ladybird* because it starts with a lowercase *c* and the sort order is case sensitive. What must we do to change our sort and search operations so that they are not case sensitive?

Creating a Non–Case-Sensitive Comparison Function Object

To get sorting and searching that is not case sensitive in our address book, we must change the way in which the `multiset` class does its sorting. We can do this by supplying another template parameter to the `multiset` instantiation. The `set` and `multiset` templates take three parameters: element type, comparison function object, and allocator. Similarly the `map` and `multimap` templates take four parameters: key type, content type, key comparison function object, and allocator. By default, the comparison function object is `less<T>`, where `T` is the element type. (The allocator also has a default that is almost never overridden. See "The Gory Details: Default Allocator Parameters" in Chapter 3, "Creating the `AddressBook` Using Container Classes.") The `less` function object class template uses the < operator. To cause our `multiset` to sort the way we want, we must instantiate it with a new function object that does a non–case-sensitive less-than operation on `Address` objects. Listing 8.16 shows the changes to the `AddressBook` class.

 Note   **Code Note**   Listings 8.16 and 8.17 correspond to files on the companion Web page in the `Chapter 8 Code\Case_insensitive` directory. The files in this directory can be compiled and linked together to create an executable program.

Listing 8.16   A Non–Case-Sensitive Address Comparison Added to `AddressBook`

```
 1:  // TinyPIM (c) 1999 Pablo Halpern
 2:
 3:  #ifndef AddressBook_dot_h
 4:  #define AddressBook_dot_h
 5:
 6:  #include <set>
 7:  #include <map>
 8:  #include <functional>
 9:  #include "Address.h"
10:
11:  // Case-insensitive Address less-than function object.
12:  struct AddressLess
13:    : public std::binary_function<Address, Address, bool>
14:  {
15:    bool operator()(const Address& a1,const Address& a2) const;
16:  };
17:
18:  class AddressBook
19:  {
20:    // Data structure abbreviations
21:    typedef std::multiset<Address, AddressLess>   addrByName_t;
22:    typedef std::map<int, addrByName_t::iterator> addrById_t;
23:
24:    // rest of AddressBook unchanged
```

In lines 12–16, we define a function object, `AddressLess`, that performs a less-than comparison of `Address` objects that is not case sensitive. Unlike simpler function objects we've seen before, the definition for `operator()` is not expanded inline. In line 21, we change the declaration of `addrByName_t` by adding our new function object type to the parameter list for `multiset`. All sorting and searching operations on this multiset will be performed using the new comparison function object class. Aren't you glad we defined `addrByName_t` using a typedef?

EXCURSION

Pointers as Associative Keys

It is possible to use a pointer type as the key type in an associative container. In fact, a `set` of pointers can be useful for keeping track of one-to-many relationships between objects. (One object keeps a set of pointers to all the objects to which it is related.) A potential problem is that the C and C++ standards do not define a less-than operator that is guaranteed to be useful when applied to pointers to objects that don't belong to the same array. The standard library solves this problem by providing a specialized version of the `less<T>` template that produces meaningful results if `T` is a pointer type, even if the built-in < operator does not produce meaningful results.

If you use containers of pointers, you must pay attention to the fact that deleting the container does not automatically delete the pointers contained within it. Doing the proper cleanup can be trickier than it seems. Your first attempt might look like this (warning, this doesn't work):

```
set<myclass*> myset;
for (set<myclass*>::iterator j = myset.begin(); j != myset.end(); ++j)
{
  myclass* p = *j;
  myset.erase(j);
  delete p;
}
```

This won't work because the call to `erase` invalidates your loop iterator. The simplest correct way to remove and delete all the pointers in a container is as follows:

```
set<myclass*> myset;
while (! myset.empty())
{
  myclass* p = *myset.rend();
  myset.erase(myset.rend());
  delete p;
}
```

This code simply removes and deletes the last element in the container until the container is empty. This idiom works for all standard container types.

Writing a New Algorithm

Writing the code for `AddressLess::operator()` is a multilayer process. The basic logic for comparing two sequences of things to find out which comes first in *lexicographical order* is a well-known algorithm. Therefore, it is not surprising that an algorithm for this already exists in the standard library. The `lexicographical_compare` algorithm takes as arguments two iterator ranges and an optional comparison function object (it uses < by default) and returns true if the first range compares less than the second range. Using this as a starting point, we implement our comparison as shown in Listing 8.17.

Lexicographical ordering is the concept of dictionary ordering extended to data types that are not necessarily characters. Given two sequences of items, the items are compared one by one until a mismatch is found. The sequence containing the smaller item in the first mismatch is the lower ranked item in the ordering. If there is no mismatch, the shorter sequence is the lower ranked one. Otherwise, if they are the same length, they have equivalent rank.

Listing 8.17 Implementation of a Non–Case-Sensitive Comparison

```
1:  // TinyPIM (c) 1999 Pablo Halpern. File AddressBook.cpp
2:
3:  #ifdef _MSC_VER
4:  #pragma warning(disable : 4786)
5:  #endif
6:
7:  #include <algorithm>
8:  #include <cctype>
9:
10: #include "AddressBook.h"
11:
12: #if ! (_MSC_VER || __GCC__)
13: using std::tolower;
14: using std::toupper;
15: #endif
16:
17: // Non-case-sensitive character less-than function object
18: struct ci_less_char : public std::binary_function<char, char, bool>
19: {
20:   bool operator()(char c1, char c2) const
21:   {
22:     return toupper(c1) < toupper(c2);
23:   }
24: };
25:
26: // Algorithm for non-case-sensitive lexicographical comparison
27: // of two character sequences
28: template <class FwdIter1, class FwdIter2>
29: bool ci_less(FwdIter1 b1, FwdIter1 e1, FwdIter2 b2, FwdIter2 e2)
30: {
31:   return std::lexicographical_compare(b1, e1, b2, e2,
32:                                       ci_less_char());
```

continues

Listing 8.17   continued

```
33:   }
34:
35:   // Non-case-sensitive string comparison function
36:   bool ciStringLess(const std::string& s1, const std::string& s2)
37:   {
38:     return ci_less(s1.begin(), s1.end(), s2.begin(), s2.end());
39:   }
40:
41:   bool AddressLess::operator ()(const Address& a1,
42:                                 const Address& a2) const
43:   {
44:     if (ciStringLess(a1.lastname(), a2.lastname()))
45:       return true;
46:     else if (ciStringLess(a2.lastname(), a1.lastname()))
47:       return false;
48:     else
49:       return ciStringLess(a1.firstname(), a2.firstname());
50:   }
```

In lines 18–24, we create a function object class that performs a non–case-sensitive comparison of two single characters, the heart of the logic for string comparison that is not case sensitive. Line 22 converts both characters to uppercase before comparing them. If the characters are not letters, toupper returns them unchanged.

In lines 28–33, we do something new: We define our own algorithm. We are taking advantage of the extensibility of the standard library, particularly the part known as the *STL*. Our algorithm is called ci_less (for *case-insensitive-less*). It takes two sequences in the form of iterator ranges and returns true if the first is less than the second using a non–case-sensitive lexicographical comparison. The ci_less function takes four parameters comprising two iterator ranges, as seen in line 29. The first and second arguments must be iterators of the same type, FwdIter1, and the third and fourth arguments must be iterators of the same type, FwdIter2, which may or may not be of the same type as FwdIter1. Line 28 declares FwdIter1 and FwdIter2 as template parameters, indicating that ci_less can be instantiated with any types that meet the requirements of a forward iterator (that is, bidirectional or random access iterators will also work).

The ci_less function is implemented in lines 31 and 32 as a single call to the standard library function lexicographical_compare, using the ci_less_char comparison object. (Remember, the empty parentheses after ci_less_char are to construct a ci_less_char *object* from the ci_less_char *class*.) Because the ci_less_char::operator() function expects two char arguments, you will get a compile-time error if you attempt to call ci_less with iterators that don't point to char elements or elements that can be converted to char.

What can we do with our `ci_less` algorithm? Well, if we have a `vector<char>` and a `list<char>`, we can compare them using `ci_less`. That doesn't seem very useful, though. Using pointers as iterators, we could also compare two arrays of `char`, which can be useful for comparing C-style strings. But what can we use as iterators to compare objects of type `std::string`? It turns out that `string` has iterators—as well as the requisite `begin` and `end` (and `rbegin` and `rend`) functions—and meets all the requirements of a standard sequence container. This lets strings play in the algorithm world, which is exactly what we need for this task. Lines 36–39 define a function, `ciStringLess`, that takes two strings and returns true if the first is less than the second using a comparison that is not case sensitive. It is implemented as a single call to the `ci_less` algorithm in line 38, passing it `begin()` and `end()` iterators to the two strings.

We now reach the top layer of our logic for comparing `Address` records using string comparisons that are not case sensitive. In lines 41–50, we define `operator()` for the `AddressLess` function object class. This is the function object that is used to keep our `multiset` properly ordered. In line 44, we compare the last names and return true if the first is less than the second. In line 47, we return false if the second is less than the first. If neither last name is less than the other, we get to line 49 and return the result of comparing the first names.

The Gory Details: Strict Weak Ordering

The sorted associative containers—as well as sorting-related algorithms such as `sort`, `lower_bound`, and `binary_search`—all require that elements be compared using an operation that defines a *strict weak ordering*. The simplest way to define a strict weak ordering is to go backward from a *total ordering*. The less-than operator defines a total ordering on integers; given any two nonequal integers, one is always less than the other. Furthermore, if a < b and b < c, then a < c. (This property is called *transitivity*.) A total ordering certainly meets the requirements for sorted associative containers and sorting-related algorithms. In most cases, though, the requirement is looser than a total ordering. A strict weak ordering is like a total ordering except that it permits two items such that neither compares less than the other, even if the items are not equal. Two such items are called *equivalent*. In our address book, we might have entries for two people named *George Carter*. Assuming that they really are two people, their entries in the address book are *equivalent* in the sort order even though the records are not *equal*. Our non–case-sensitive comparison function defines a strict weak ordering.

8

If we run the program again and insert *clinton, kenny*, the new list looks like Listing 8.18.

```
*** Address Book ***

=============== Start of list ===============
 1: Bush, Barbara...........................(994) 342-1167
 2: Bush, Jack..............................(793) 651-9982
 3: Bush, Jack..............................(932) 794-5662
 4: Bush, Lyndon............................(491) 421-9782
 5: Bush, Nancy.............................(420) 672-5507
 6: Carter, Barbara.........................(642) 628-2442
 7: Carter, George..........................(581) 409-9816
 8: Carter, George..........................(483) 515-8945
 9: Carter, Lyndon..........................(741) 590-6004
10: Carter, Rosalynn........................(568) 301-0648
11: Carter, William.........................(620) 256-2045
12: Clinton, Jimmy..........................(547) 348-2090
13: Clinton, Jimmy..........................(499) 318-5124
14: clinton, kenny..........................(123) 456-7890
15: Clinton, Ladybird.......................(676) 341-0043


(P)revious, (N)ext, (V)iew, (C)reate, (D)elete, (E)dit,
list (A)ll, (L)ookup, (S)earch  (R)edisplay  (Q)uit ?
```

I'll leave it to you to try the lookup function and prove to yourself that it is not case sensitive. The search function does not use the sort order, so it will not work in a non–case-sensitive way. However, the same approach can be used to solve this problem. The `std::search` algorithm can be used to find a subsequence within a larger sequence. You would supply it with iterators to the two strings and a comparison function that implements a non–case-sensitive equality test on individual characters. You are now familiar enough with the concepts that I will leave it as an exercise for you to implement a non–case-sensitive search feature.

Next Steps

We finally have something that is beginning to look like a PIM. We implemented a menu system that pulls the pieces together. Along the way, we learned about the `stack` adapter, the `<climits>` header, and string streams. We tested our program with a random data generator that used the `rand` and `srand` functions. When we wanted non–case-sensitive sorting and searching, we implemented our own `ci_less` algorithm, extending the STL by following the STL's rules.

We are now ready to embark on the date book part of TinyPIM. Our first task will be to represent dates and times. We will rely on the standard library's time facilities to implement our own date and time classes. We will also learn how to make the stream I/O system savvy enough to handle our date and time classes.

A Date and Time Class with User-Defined I/O

Implementing a Date and Time Class

With the address book portion of TinyPIM complete, we can now turn our attention to the date book. Each appointment in the date book has a start date and time and an end date and time. The start date and time are used to sort the entries. Obviously, the concept of date and time is key to implementing our date book, so we need a class to represent date and time before we go any further. You learn about the time features of the standard library as well as some advanced input/output concepts.

Using the time_t Type

At this point, you are probably eagerly waiting for me to introduce some sort of date and time class provided in the C++ Standard Library. Sadly, the C++ Standard Library doesn't provide much more time and date support than what was inherited from C. What additional support it does provide is imbedded in the arcane localization library, which is not yet implemented in many compilers' libraries. This sorry state of affairs, like many other shortcomings of the standard library, was caused by an absence of reasonable proposals for a new time library within the time allotted for adding new features. Most people agree that we are better off with an imperfect standard today than waiting for a perfect standard to be done in 10 years. We will make do with the time_t type inherited from the C Standard Library.

To make the C date and time facilities more usable, we will create a small DateTime class to use in the date book. We will not try to plug the hole in the standard by designing a comprehensive date and time library, but will create a minimal interface tailored to our needs. The header file for this class is shown in Listing 9.1.

Code Note   Listings 9.1–9.5 correspond to files on the companion Web page in the Chapter 9 Code\Basic DateTime directory. The files in this directory can be compiled and linked together to create an executable program. See the end of the Introduction for information on accessing this book's companion Web page.

Listing 9.1 The DateTime Class

```
 1:  // TinyPIM (c) 1999 Pablo Halpern. File DateTime.h
 2:
 3:  #ifndef DateTime_dot_h
 4:  #define DateTime_dot_h 1
 5:
 6:  #include <iostream>
 7:  #include <string>
 8:  #include <ctime>
 9:
10:  #ifdef _MSC_VER
11:  // Make sure these types and functions are in namespace std:
12:  namespace std {
13:    typedef ::time_t time_t;
14:    typedef ::tm tm;
15:    inline double difftime(time_t t1, time_t t0)
16:      { return ::difftime(t1, t0); }
17:  }
18:  #endif
19:
20:  class DateTime
21:  {
22:  public:
23:    DateTime() : theTime_(0) { }
24:    DateTime(int year, int month, int day, int hour, int min);
25:
26:    // Use compiler-generated copy constructor, assignment, destructor
27:
28:    // Read accessors
29:    void get(int& year, int& month, int& day,
30:             int& hour, int& min) const;
31:
32:    // Write accessors
33:    DateTime& set(int year, int month, int day, int hour, int min);
34:
35:    // Get the current date and time
36:    static DateTime now();
37:
38:    friend bool operator==(const DateTime& dt1, const DateTime& dt2)
```

```
39:         { return dt1.theTime_ == dt2.theTime_; }
40:
41:     friend bool operator<(const DateTime& dt1, const DateTime& dt2)
42:         { return std::difftime(dt1.theTime_, dt2.theTime_) < 0; }
43:
44:     friend std::ostream& operator<<(std::ostream& os,
45:                                     const DateTime& dt);
46:     friend std::istream& operator>>(std::istream& is, DateTime& dt);
47:
48:  private:
49:
50:     std::time_t theTime_;
51:  };
52:
53:
54:  #endif // DateTime_dot_h
```

In line 50, we declare a single member variable, of type std::time_t. The time_t type is an arithmetic type (integral or floating point) declared in <ctime> that can hold a date and time value. The encoding of the date and time into time_t is up to the implementation. Our DateTime class will use the time functions in the C Standard Library to manipulate time_t values.

Like other components inherited from C, the Microsoft 6.0 compiler fails to put the time types and functions into namespace std. Our workaround, in lines 10–18, is to create aliases for these components within namespace std. The time_t and tm types are aliased using simple typedefs. The difftime function is aliased by creating an inline pass-through function. I chose this workaround because these components have names that are so generic that it is easier to understand the code if we use the std:: prefix. Although putting these names in namespace std does not remove them from the global namespace, it does enable us to distinguish them from local types or functions with the same names by prefixing the standard library names with the std:: qualifier.

The interface to DateTime lets us compose a time value from the year, month, day, hour, and minute using the constructor in line 24 or using the set function in line 33. We can decompose a time value into the same components using the get function in line 29. For our purposes, we don't have to resolve time with precision better than one minute. Line 36 defines a now static function that retrieves the current date and time from the system clock. Because time values are used for sorting and searching in the date book, we provide relational operators in lines 38–42.

Notice that in line 42 we use the difftime function, which returns the difference, in seconds, between two time_t values. If the difference is negative, we know that the first time is less than the second. Because time_t is an arithmetic value, the compiler would not complain if we compared them directly, using the < operator. However, the encoding of the time values is not specified in the standard, so we have no guarantee that later times are numerically larger than smaller values in a particular implementation. The temptation to perform straight arithmetic using `time_t` is very seductive because Windows, DOS and UNIX compilers all use the same, simple integer encoding for `time_t`, which is the number of seconds since midnight, January 1, 1970. Other operating systems use similar integer encodings with different base years. If you are sure that you will be using one of these operating systems, you can make your code simpler and more efficient by adding, subtracting, and comparing `time_t` values. In this book, however, I will stick to the most portable uses of `time_t`.

In our application, two of the most common manipulations we will be performing with time values are input and output. The operators declared in lines 44 and 46 effectively extend the stream library to include our `DateTime` class. Here's how it works. If `myTime` is a `DateTime` object, when the compiler sees code like this,

```
std::cout << myTime;
```

it calls the operator declared in line 44, passing `std::cout` as the `os` parameter and passing `myTime` as the `dt` parameter. The `<<` operator is defined as a `friend` of class `DateTime`, which means that it is a global function (not a member of `DateTime`, even though it is declared within the class) but it has access to the private members of `DateTime`. The implementation of this function uses the steam I/O facilities that we've already seen to format the date and time and send them to the output stream, which in this case is `cout`. It then returns the `os` parameter to the caller. Because the result of `operator<<` is the same as its `os` parameter, calls can be chained together like this:

```
std::cout << "The time is " << myTime << std::endl;
```

Each insertion into `cout` returns a reference to `cout` that is then used by the next insertion. The C++ language's support for overloading lets the compiler choose the correct `operator<<` for each value, based on the type of the value. If the type is `DateTime`, our own `operator<<` is called. Input works the same way, except using `>>` instead of `<<` and `istream` instead of `ostream`. Notice that we did not have to modify the `ostream` or `istream` classes to extend the stream library in this way. Moreover, these functions must be implemented only once and will work with any kind of stream (`stringstream`, `fstream`, `strstream`, or others as defined by you or the implementation). This extensibility is not available with the old C I/O functions `printf` and `scanf`.

Composing and Decomposing a `time_t` Value

We will get to the implementation of the I/O functions in a moment. First, we must see how to implement the basic `DateTime` member functions for composing a

DateTime from year, month, day, hour, and minute components and decomposing them back again. Listing 9.2 shows our implementation up to that point.

Listing 9.2   Composition and Decomposition Functions in `DateTime`

```
 1:  // TinyPIM (c) 1999 Pablo Halpern. File DateTime.cpp
 2:
 3:  #include <iomanip>
 4:  #include "DateTime.h"
 5:
 6:  #ifndef _MSC_VER
 7:  using std::mktime;
 8:  using std::localtime;
 9:  using std::time_t;
10:  #endif
11:
12:  DateTime::DateTime(int year, int month, int day, int hour, int min)
13:  {
14:    set(year, month, day, hour, min);
15:  }
16:
17:  void DateTime::get(int& year, int& month, int& day,
18:                     int& hour, int& min) const
19:  {
20:    std::tm* mytm = localtime(&theTime_);
21:    year  = mytm->tm_year + 1900;
22:    month = mytm->tm_mon + 1;
23:    day   = mytm->tm_mday;
24:    hour  = mytm->tm_hour;
25:    min   = mytm->tm_min;
26:  }
27:
28:  DateTime& DateTime::set(int year, int month, int day,
29:                          int hour, int min)
30:  {
31:    // Years from 0-49 are assumed to mean 2000-2049.
32:    // Years 1900 or over are assumed to be 4-digit years.
33:    // Other years are assumed to mean 1950 - 1999.
34:    if (year < 50)
35:      year += 2000;
36:    else if (year < 1900)
37:      year += 1900;
38:
39:    std::tm mytm;
40:    mytm.tm_year = year - 1900;
41:    mytm.tm_mon  = month - 1; // zero based
42:    mytm.tm_mday = day;
43:    mytm.tm_hour = hour;
44:    mytm.tm_min  = min;
45:    mytm.tm_sec  = 0;
46:    mytm.tm_isdst = -1;
```

continues

9

Listing 9.2   continued

```
47:
48:    theTime_ = mktime(&mytm);
49:
50:    return *this;
51: }
52:
53: // Get the current date and time
54: DateTime DateTime::now()
55: {
56:   DateTime ret;
57:   ret.theTime_ = time(0);  // Call std::time
58:   return ret;
59: }
60:
```

In line 20, the get function uses the standard `localtime` function to convert a `time_t` value into a `std::tm` structure. The input argument to `localtime` is a pointer to a const `time_t`. The `tm` structure is defined as follows:

```
struct tm
{
  int tm_sec;      /* seconds after the minute - [0,60] */
  int tm_min;      /* minutes after the hour - [0,59] */
  int tm_hour;     /* hours since midnight - [0,23] */
  int tm_mday;     /* day of the month - [1,31] */
  int tm_mon;      /* months since January - [0,11] */
  int tm_year;     /* years since 1900 */
  int tm_wday;     /* days since Sunday - [0,6] */
  int tm_yday;     /* days since January 1 - [0,365] */
  int tm_isdst;    /* daylight savings time flag */
};
```

At first, it looks like a straightforward breakdown of the date and time, but it has some maddening quirks. The first day of a month would have the `tm_mday` member set to 1. However, the first month of the year would have the `tm_mon` member set to 0, not 1. Thus, in line 22 of Listing 9.2, we must add one to the `tm_mon` member to get the month number as it is normally counted. The `tm_year` member is the number of years since 1900, which means that the year 2000 is represented as 100. Although this data structure does not suffer from a Y2K problem, it is certainly counter-intuitive to use this formula rather than simply store the full (4-digit) year, which would fit easily in even a 16-bit integer. In line 21, we adjust for this representation by adding 1900 to the value in `tm_year`.

Note that the `localtime` function returns a pointer to a static data structure that is owned by the library. You must not try to `delete` or `free` this data structure. Because this data structure is overwritten by each subsequent call to `localtime`, you must either use the data right away or copy it into a `tm` structure over which you have control. This use of static data is *nonreentrant*, which means that `localtime` is not suitable for applications where multiple concurrent threads may call `localtime` and thus overwrite one another's data structures. The POSIX operating system standard defines thread-safe variants of `localtime` and similar routines, but these variants are not part of the C or C++ standards, per se.

In line 48 of Listing 9.2, the `set` function uses the `mktime` function, which is the inverse of `localtime`. It takes the address of a `tm` structure and converts it into the corresponding `time_t` value. If the `tm` structure cannot be represented as a `time_t`, `mktime` returns `time_t(-1)`. When creating the `tm` structure, we subtract 1900 from the year and subtract one from the month. The `tm_isdst` member of `tm` indicates whether `mktime` should use *daylight savings time* to compute the `time_t` value. (Daylight savings time is the U.S. term for the standardized practice of setting the clock ahead one hour during the summer months.) If `tm_isdst` is zero, standard time is used; if it is positive, daylight savings time is used. If it is negative, `mktime` figures out whether daylight savings time would be in effect for the specified date in the current locale. In line 46, we make sure that it is negative so that the time correctly reflects the local convention. The `tm_wday` and `tm_yday` members are ignored by `mktime`.

The `now` function calls the standard `time` function in line 57. The `time` function returns a `time_t` value corresponding to the current date and time according to the system clock. If a non-null pointer to a `time_t` is passed to `time`, the result is also stored in that location, as well as being returned. Thus, line 57 could also have been written `time(&ret.theTime);`.

Implementing I/O Functions for Time

The input and output operators (>> and <<, respectively) are global operator functions that are friends of the `DateTime` class. This gives them access to the private `theTime_` member of `DateTime`. Starting simple, we will now evolve a set of input and output operators.

Basic Input and Output

Listing 9.3 shows a basic implementation of the output operator, which formats the date and time in standard U.S. style (mm/dd/yyyy hh::mmAM).

Listing 9.3   The Output Operator for `DateTime`

```
61:  std::ostream& operator<<(std::ostream& os, const DateTime& dt)
62:  {
63:      std::tm theTm = *localtime(&dt.theTime_);
```

continues

Listing 9.3   continued

```
64:
65:     os << (theTm.tm_mon + 1) << '/'
66:        << theTm.tm_mday << '/'
67:        << (theTm.tm_year + 1900) << ' ';
68:
69:     int hour = theTm.tm_hour % 12;
70:     const char* ampm = (theTm.tm_hour < 12 ? "am" : "pm");
71:
72:     if (hour == 0)
73:       hour = 12;
74:
75:     os << std::setfill(' ') << std::right << std::setw(2) << hour
76:        << ':' << std::setfill('0') << std::right << std::setw(2)
77:        << theTm.tm_min << ampm;
78:
79:     return os;
80:  }
81:
```

In line 63, we use `localtime` to break down the date and time, storing a copy of the result in `theTm`. In lines 65–67, we output the month, day, and year, separated by slashes. Lines 69–73 convert the hour from 24-hour format to 12-hour format with an `am` or `pm` suffix. In lines 75–77, we send the hour, minute, and am/pm indicator to the stream. We use the I/O manipulators `setfill`, `setw`, and `right` to ensure that the output looks correct. In line 79, we return the stream so that another output operation can be chained onto this one.

The input side takes the standard format and converts it into a `DateTime` object. Listing 9.4 shows how this is done.

Listing 9.4   The Input Operator for `DateTime`

```
82:  std::istream& operator>>(std::istream& is, DateTime& dt)
83:  {
84:    char slash1, slash2, colon;
85:    int mon, day, year, hour, min;
86:    char ampm[3];
87:
88:    is >> mon >> slash1 >> day >> slash2 >> year
89:       >> hour >> colon >> min >> std::setw(3) >> ampm;
90:
91:    // Check for error
92:    if (is.fail())
93:      return is;
94:
95:    // Convert hour from 12-hour to 24-hour format (0-23)
96:    if (hour == 12)
97:      hour = 0;
```

```
98:     if (ampm[0] == 'p' || ampm[0] == 'P')
99:       hour += 12;
100:
101:    dt = DateTime(year, mon, day, hour, min);
102:
103:    return is;
104: }
```

Note, in line 82, that the dt argument is a writeable reference. This is required so that operator>> can set it to the value read from the stream. In lines 88 and 89, we read all the components at once: the month, day, year, hour, minute, and am/pm indicator, as well as the punctuation marks. The space between the year and the hour is automatically skipped by the extraction operator, so we don't try to read it. The am/pm indicator is read into a fixed-length buffer with a maximum length of three characters. We use the setw manipulator on line 89 to ensure that the string read from the stream does not overflow the buffer.

If any components fail to read in correctly (for example, a letter is found where a number is expected), is.fail() will be true on line 92, and all subsequent components will fail to read. We don't modify the dt result object in this case and simply return, with the stream still in a failed state. Otherwise, in lines 96–99, we convert the hour and am/pm indicator to 24-hour format. Finally, in line 101 we construct the result, and in line 103, we return the input stream for chaining purposes.

Because we now have enough code for a working DateTime class, we will test it with the test program shown in Listing 9.5.

Listing 9.5   Test Program for the DateTime Class

```
1:  // TinyPIM (c) 1999 Pablo Halpern. File timeTest.cpp
2:
3:  #include <iomanip>
4:  #include "DateTime.h"
5:
6:  int main()
7:  {
8:    // Test now() function
9:    std::cout << "Now = " << DateTime::now() << std::endl;
10:
11:   // Test contructor
12:   std::cout << "Party = " << DateTime(0, 1, 1, 0, 0) << std::endl;
13:
14:   DateTime dt;
15:
16:   while (std::cin)
17:   {
18:     std::cout << "\nEnter a date and time: ";
```

continues

Listing 9.5   continued

```
19:        if (std::cin.peek() == 'q' || std::cin.peek() == 'Q' )
20:          break;
21:
22:        std::cin >> dt;
23:        if (std::cin.fail())
24:        {
25:          std::cout << "Bad input" << std::endl;
26:          std::cin.clear();
27:        }
28:        else
29:        {
30:          std::cout << "DateTime = " << dt << std::endl;
31:
32:          std::cout << std::setfill('*') << std::left << std::setw(30)
33:                    << std::hex << dt
34:                    << ' ' << std::setw(10) << 0xff << std::endl;
35:        }
36:
37:        std::cin.ignore(INT_MAX, '\n');   // If fails, loop will exit
38:      }
39:
40:      return 0;
41:    }
```

Line 9 tests the now and output functions. Line 12 constructs a DateTime for Midnight, January 1, 2000, and outputs it. Line 16 begins a loop that reads DateTime objects from cin until the input stream goes bad. (Using a stream in a Boolean context is the same as calling the good function.) You can terminate the loop by entering q (for *quit*) instead of a date and time. Line 19 checks for this by peeking at the next character in the input stream.

In line 22, we call the >> operator that we just implemented in Listing 9.3. If successful, a date and time entered by the user will be stored in dt. Line 23 of Listing 9.5 checks for the failure condition. On failure, it informs the user and clears the failure state. Otherwise, we get to line 30, which tests the output operator for DateTime that we implemented in Listing 9.2.

Lines 32–34 also test the output operator, but in a more advanced way; here, we check to see what would happen if we called the output operator with the output stream fill character and width set to interesting values and the numeric base set to hexadecimal (base 16). We output the date and time with the field width set to 30 and the fill character set to asterisk. We then output the hexadecimal value 0xff with a field width of 10. If everything works correctly, we should see the date come out, followed by some number of asterisks up to column 30, then a space, and then ff followed by eight more asterisks. In other words, both the date and the hex number should print out left justified in a field of asterisks. Listing 9.6 shows an actual run (*italic* indicates user input).

Listing 9.6   Output of a Small Run of the Test Program

```
 1:  Now = 9/5/1999  3:39pm
 2:  Party = 1/1/2000 12:00am
 3:
 4:  Enter a date and time: 4/5/1996 3:11am
 5:  DateTime = 4/5/1996  3:11am
 6:  4****************************/5/7cc  3:0bam 00000000ff
 7:
 8:  Enter a date and time: 4/5#96 3:74am
 9:  DateTime = 4/5/7cc  4:0eam
10:  4****************************/5/7cc  4:0eam 00000000ff
11:
12:  Enter a date and time: q
```

Lines 1 and 2 correctly show the current time (at the time I ran the program, of course) and the big party time. Line 5 successfully echoed back the date and time that were entered in line 4. Things become strange, though, in line 6. Let's trace what is happening here. The test program set the fill character to asterisk and the alignment to left justified. Just before outputting the date and time, it set the field width to 30. Remember that the field width affects only the very next output operation. Although it looks as if the outputting dt is a single operation, we know in the implementation that every component of the date and time is output separately. Thus, we see the 4 left justified in a 30-character field filled with asterisks.

The next problem we run into is that the year is being output in hexadecimal. You might have a different opinion, but I don't consider dates to be numbers, and I don't believe that they should ever be expressed in hex. The same problem exists for the minutes. Unfortunately, our problems are not limited to the output of the date and time itself. The 0xff value was supposed to show up left justified in a 10-character–wide field of asterisks. Instead, it is right justified in a 10-character field of zeros. If we look at the output code for DateTime, we see that we change the fill character to zero and the alignment to right in order to output minutes correctly (two digits with a possible leading zero). Unlike setw, these stream settings persist and override the settings that were in effect before calling the output operator.

Listing 9.6 shows a problem with input as well. On line 8, we used the wrong punctuation between the month and the year, and our minutes value was invalid. These errors should have been detected but weren't. The quality of our I/O routines might be okay for casual use, but not for a quality product like TinyPIM.

9

Being a Good I/O Citizen

A good I/O citizen is a class that behaves like a built-in type when it is used with the `iostream` operators. It should honor format settings that apply and should not alter any format settings on output. On input, it should detect errors and leave the object unchanged if an error occurs.

Listing 9.7 shows a rewrite of the output and input operators for `DateTime` that attempt to make `DateTime` a good I/O citizen.

> **Code Note**   Listing 9.7 corresponds to a file on the companion Web page in the `Chapter 9 Code\Good IO citizen` directory. The files in this directory can be compiled and linked together to create an executable program.

Listing 9.7   Output and Input Operators to Make `DateTime` a Good I/O Citizen

```
61:  std::ostream& operator<<(std::ostream& os, const DateTime& dt)
62:  {
63:    char oldfill = os.fill('0');              // Save fill value
64:    std::ios::fmtflags oldflags = os.flags(); // Save old flags
65:
66:    std::tm theTm = *localtime(&dt.theTime_);
67:
68:    os << std::setw(0) << std::dec << (theTm.tm_mon + 1) << '/'
69:       << theTm.tm_mday << '/'
70:       << (theTm.tm_year + 1900) << ' ';
71:
72:    int hour = theTm.tm_hour % 12;
73:    const char* ampm = (theTm.tm_hour < 12 ? "am" : "pm");
74:
75:    if (hour == 0)
76:      hour = 12;
77:
78:    os << std::setfill(' ') << std::right << std::setw(2) << hour
79:       << ':' << std::setfill('0') << std::right << std::setw(2)
80:       << theTm.tm_min << ampm;
81:
82:    os.flags(oldflags);
83:    os.fill(oldfill);
84:    return os;
85:  }
86:
87:  std::istream& operator>>(std::istream& is, DateTime& dt)
88:  {
89:    char slash1, slash2, colon;
90:    int mon, day, year, hour, min;
91:    char ampm[3];
92:
```

```
93:     is >> mon >> slash1 >> day >> slash2 >> year
94:        >> hour >> colon >> min >> std::setw(3) >> ampm;
95:
96:     // Check for I/O error
97:     if (is.fail())
98:       return is;
99:
100:    // Do a range check
101:    if (slash1 != '/' || slash2 != '/' || colon != ':' ||
102:            mon < 1 || 12 < mon || day < 1 || 31 < day ||
103:            hour < 1 || 12 < hour || min < 0 || 59 < min ||
104:            (ampm[0] != 'a' && ampm[0] != 'p'))
105:    {
106:      // format error, set fail bit and return
107:      is.clear(std::ios::failbit);
108:      return is;
109:    }
110:
111:    // Convert hour from 12-hour to 24-hour format (0-23)
112:    if (hour == 12)
113:      hour = 0;
114:    if (ampm[0] == 'p' || ampm[0] == 'P')
115:      hour += 12;
116:
117:    dt = DateTime(year, mon, day, hour, min);
118:
119:    return is;
120: }
```

Line 63 sets the fill character to zero. The `fill` member function returns the old fill character, which we save for later. (The `fill` function can also be called without any parameters to get the fill character without changing it.) In line 64, we save a copy of the format flags. The value returned by `flags` is an integral value with bits set for things like alignment, decimal/hex/octal, and so on. In line 82, we restore the flags to the value they had when we entered. In line 83, we restore the fill character. Because we don't want the month to use up the entire field width, we set the width to zero in line 68. This will cause the month to take up only as much space as it needs. We also set the stream for decimal output in line 68 so that the date is not printed in hex or octal.

Lines 100–104 contain checks for bad input. If any punctuation marks are incorrect or any numeric values are out of the valid range, the `if` condition will evaluate to true. In that case, we get to line 107, which puts the stream into the failure state. The `clear` function is somewhat misnamed. In its usual form, with no arguments, it clears all the state bits, putting the stream back into the `good()` state. However, with an argument, it actually sets rather than clears the state bit in question. The `badbit` constant (as well as `badbit` and `eofbit`) is defined in `std::ios`, which is a base class of `std::istream` and `std::ostream`. After detecting the error, we return in line 108.

Notice that we return without having modified the dt argument. It is good practice to leave the argument unchanged if an error is detected.

If we run the test program again, we get better results, though still not perfect, as shown in Listing 9.8.

Listing 9.8 Test Program Output After Making DateTime a Good I/O Citizen

```
 1:  Now = 9/5/1999 11:44pm
 2:  Party = 1/1/2000 12:00am
 3:
 4:  Enter a date and time: 4/5/1996 3:11am
 5:  DateTime = 4/5/1996  3:11am
 6:  4/5/1996  3:11am ff********
 7:
 8:  Enter a date and time: 4/5#96 3:11am
 9:  Bad input
10:
11:  Enter a date and time: 4/5/96 3:74pm
12:  Bad input
13:
14:  Enter a date and time: 4/5/96 3:11
15:  am
16:  DateTime = 4/5/1996  3:11am
17:  4/5/1996  3:11am ff********
18:
19:  Enter a date and time: q
```

On line 6, we see that the date and time are no longer in hex. Also, a string of asterisks no longer appear after the month number. The 0xff is now correctly left adjusted in a 10-character field filled with asterisks. However, the date and time are not correctly formatted within a 30-character field filled with asterisks. We will address this problem in our next attempt.

On the input side, in lines 8 and 11, we input invalid date and time values. Both were correctly diagnosed, causing cin to go into a failure state and causing the test program to print the error message. However, in line 14, we input an incomplete time. Rather than accept it or detect an error, the input operator continued waiting for the rest of the input. We provided the am in line 15 and it was happy, but *we* were not happy. A time value should probably not have a newline in the middle. The solution to this problem is similar to the solution for the output problem.

Using Intermediate Strings for More Flexibility

How do we fix the output operator so that it correctly fills and adjusts the date and time according to the fill, width, and alignment settings? The hard way would be to calculate the number of characters necessary for the string, taking into account that single-digit months and days take less space than double-digit months and days, and so on. Then we would have to read the fill and width settings and test the alignment bits from the stream and pad the output before or after the field.

The easier way is to store the formatted output in a string and then simply output the string in one piece. Because the string class already has the intelligence to do alignment and padding, we don't have to do the work ourselves. The stringstream class is a convenient way to format the data to a string. Conversely for input, we can sometimes read a string from the input stream and then analyze it. With the entire string available at once, we can more easily detect missing pieces or accept multiple input formats. For example, in the case of reading a DateTime value, we can allow users to enter the time in 24-hour format, omitting the am/pm indicator if they want. Listing 9.9 shows the output and input operators modified to use strings and stringstreams in this way.

Note   **Code Note**   Listing 9.9 corresponds to a file on the companion Web page in the Chapter 9 Code\String based IO directory. The files in this directory can be compiled and linked together to create an executable program.

Listing 9.9   More Powerful and Less Error-Prone I/O Using Intermediate Strings

```
62:  std::ostream& operator<<(std::ostream& os, const DateTime& dt)
63:  {
64:    std::ostringstream tmpstrm;
65:
66:    std::tm theTm = *localtime(&dt.theTime_);
67:
68:    tmpstrm << (theTm.tm_mon + 1) << '/'
69:            << theTm.tm_mday << '/'
70:            << (theTm.tm_year + 1900) << ' ';
71:
72:    int hour = theTm.tm_hour % 12;
73:    const char* ampm = (theTm.tm_hour < 12 ? "am" : "pm");
74:
75:    if (hour == 0)
76:      hour = 12;
77:
78:    tmpstrm << std::setfill(' ') << std::right << std::setw(2) << hour
79:            << ':' << std::setfill('0') << std::right << std::setw(2)
80:            << theTm.tm_min << ampm;
81:
82:    return os << tmpstrm.str();
83:  }
84:
85:  std::istream& operator>>(std::istream& is, DateTime& dt)
```

continues

Listing 9.9   continued

```
86:  {
87:    // First, read the date part
88:    std::string date;
89:    is >> date;
90:    if (is.fail())
91:      return is;  // I/O error
92:
93:    char slash1, slash2, colon;
94:    int mon, day, year, hour, min;
95:    char ampm[3];
96:
97:    // Unpack the date part using a stringstream
98:    std::istringstream tmpstrm(date);
99:    tmpstrm >> mon >> slash1 >> day >> slash2 >> year;
100:
101:   // Check for error in date
102:   if (tmpstrm.fail() || slash1 != '/' || slash2 != '/' ||
103:       mon < 1 || 12 < mon || day < 1 || 31 < day)
104:   {
105:     // format error, set fail bit and return
106:     is.clear(std::ios::failbit);
107:     return is;
108:   }
109:
110:   // Now read the time part
111:   std::string time;
112:   is >> time;
113:   if (is.fail())
114:     return is;  // I/O error
115:
116:   // Unpack the time part using the stringstream
117:   // Do not read am/pm indicator yet
118:   tmpstrm.clear();
119:   tmpstrm.str(time);
120:   tmpstrm >> hour >> colon >> min;
121:
122:   // Check for error in time
123:   if (tmpstrm.fail() || hour < 0 || 23 < hour || min < 0 || 59 < min)
124:   {
125:     // format error, set fail bit and return
126:     is.clear(std::ios::failbit);
127:     return is;
128:   }
129:
130:   // Check for am/pm indicator
131:   tmpstrm >> std::setw(3) >> ampm;
132:   bool useAmPm = ! tmpstrm.fail();
133:
134:   // Convert hour from 12-hour to 24-hour format (0-23)
135:   if (useAmPm)
```

```
136:    {
137:      if (hour == 12)
138:        hour = 0;
139:      if (ampm[0] == 'p' || ampm[0] == 'P')
140:        hour += 12;
141:    }
142:
143:    dt = DateTime(year, mon, day, hour, min);
144:
145:    return is;
146: }
```

In line 64, we declare a `stringstream` into which we will format the date and time. Lines 68–80 output the formatted date to the `stringstream`. We no longer have to set decimal mode or fill characters or field widths, because the `stringstream` will automatically be created with reasonable defaults. In line 82, we extract the formatted string from the `stringstream` and send it to the os stream. The return value of this operation is the os stream itself, which we return as usual. Notice that we did not have to save and restore format information. We tampered only with the format of `tmpstrm`, never of os, so there was no need to do the save and restore. The only operation involving os is the output of a single string, which will be aligned and padded as set in the os stream's format state.

In the input operator, we read the date and time as two consecutive words, separated by whitespace. In lines 89–91, we read the first word, representing the date, and detect input errors. In line 98, we create a `stringstream` from which we will read the formatted date in line 99. Remember that `tmpstrm` contains only the date string without the time portion, so we read only the month, day, and year fields.

In lines 112–114, we read the second word, representing the time, and detect input errors. In line 118, we reuse the `tmpstrm stringstream`. Because `tmpstrm` is likely to be in an `eof()` state (because we read to the end of the date string), we clear its state in line 118. Then we assign a new string to it in line 119. In line 120, we read the hour and minute. After checking for errors in lines 123–128, we are ready to try to read the am/pm indicator. If the indicator is present, we decode the time in 12-hour format; otherwise, we use 24-hour format. In line 131, we attempt to read the am/pm indicator. If it is not there, we will reach the end of the string and fail. In line 132, we set `useAmPm` to false if the attempt to read the am/pm indicator fails. Because we are reading from a string rather than from the standard input device, there is no danger that the program will hang at this point, waiting for more input. In addition, the failure to read the am/pm indicator does not mean that the input operation as a whole failed.

With these changes, the `DateTime` appears much more like a single object for input and output purposes. We see the result in Listing 9.10.

Listing 9.10   Test Program Output for the Intermediate Strings Version of the `DateTime` I/O

```
 1:  Now = 9/6/1999 12:37am
 2:  Party = 1/1/2000 12:00am
 3:
 4:  Enter a date and time: 4/5/1996 3:11am
 5:  DateTime = 4/5/1996  3:11am
 6:  4/5/1996  3:11am************** ff********
 7:
 8:  Enter a date and time: 4/5/96 3:
 9:  Bad input
10:
11:  Enter a date and time: 4/5/96 3:11
12:  DateTime = 4/5/1996  3:11am
13:  4/5/1996  3:11am************** ff********
14:
15:  Enter a date and time: 4/5/96 15:11
16:  DateTime = 4/5/1996  3:11pm
17:  4/5/1996  3:11pm************** ff********
18:
19:  Enter a date and time: q
```

In line 6, we finally see the date and time left aligned as a unit in a 30-character field filled with asterisks, just as the format specifications in the test program indicated. In lines 8 and 9, we see that a partial time is still invalid. However, in lines 11–13, we see that it is now valid to omit the am/pm indicator. Lines 15–17 show the same thing using a time after 12 noon. We could have gone further and allowed dates without the year (meaning *the current year*) or times without the minutes (meaning *on the hour*). In general, it is a good idea to make your input functions as forgiving as possible and accept as many variants of the input format as possible. I recommend that you try these enhancements as an exercise.

Some Extensions to `DateTime` for Use in the Date Book

Before we consider the `DateTime` class complete, let's see if it will meet our needs in the date book. The date book will certainly have to represent dates and times, compare them, read them from the input stream, and write them to the output stream. However, dates together with times do not always work. When displaying a day's appointments, for example, we will want to print the date once at the top and then display only the time, without the date, for each appointment. We will also want to display the names of the days of the week and the months of the year.

The date book requires knowledge of day, week, and month boundaries (for example, What is the beginning and end of this month?). It must also be capable of advancing

through the calendar one day at a time. We will thus extend the definition of
DateTime as shown in Listing 9.11.

Note

Code Note   Unless otherwise noted, Listings 9.11–9.13 correspond to files on
the companion Web page in the Chapter 9 Code\Final Version directory. The
files in this directory can be compiled and linked together to create an executable
program.

Listing 9.11   Extended DateTime Class

```
 1:  // TinyPIM (c) 1999 Pablo Halpern. File DateTime.h
 2:
 3:  #ifndef DateTime_dot_h
 4:  #define DateTime_dot_h 1
 5:
 6:  #include <iostream>
 7:  #include <string>
 8:  #include <ctime>
 9:
10:  #ifdef _MSC_VER
11:  // Make sure these types and functions are in namespace std:
12:  namespace std {
13:    typedef ::time_t time_t;
14:    typedef ::tm tm;
15:    inline double difftime(time_t t1, time_t t0)
16:      { return ::difftime(t1, t0); }
17:  }
18:  #endif
19:
20:  class DateTime
21:  {
22:  public:
23:    DateTime() : theTime_(0) { }
24:    DateTime(int year, int month, int day, int hour, int min);
25:
26:    // Use compiler-generated copy constructor, assignment, destructor
27:
28:    // Read accessors
29:    void get(int& year, int& month, int& day,
30:             int& hour, int& min) const;
31:    void getDate(int& year, int& month, int& day) const;
32:    void getTime(int& hour, int& min) const;
33:
34:    // Return the day of the week (range 0 = Sunday to 6 = Saturday)
35:    int dayOfWeek() const;
36:
37:    // Write accessors
```

continues

Listing 9.11   continued

```
38:     DateTime& set(int year, int month, int day, int hour, int min);
39:     DateTime& setDate(int year, int month, int day);
40:     DateTime& setTime(int hour, int min);
41:
42:     // Return this day at midnight
43:     DateTime startOfDay() const;
44:
45:     // Return most recent Sunday at midnight
46:     DateTime startOfWeek() const;
47:
48:     // Return first day of this month
49:     DateTime startOfMonth() const;
50:
51:     // Add a certain number of days to the date
52:     DateTime addDay(int days = 1) const;
53:
54:     // Return string quantities
55:     std::string dateStr() const;      // Date in string form
56:     std::string timeStr() const;      // Time in string form
57:     std::string wdayName() const;     // Name of day of the week
58:     std::string monthName() const;    // Name of month of the year
59:
60:     // Following functions parse the string and set the date or time.
61:     // They return false on error
62:     bool dateStr(const std::string&);
63:     bool timeStr(const std::string&);
64:
65:     // Get the current date and time
66:     static DateTime now();
67:
68:     friend bool operator==(const DateTime& dt1, const DateTime& dt2)
69:       { return dt1.theTime_ == dt2.theTime_; }
70:
71:     friend bool operator<(const DateTime& dt1, const DateTime& dt2)
72:       { return std::difftime(dt1.theTime_, dt2.theTime_) < 0; }
73:
74:     friend std::ostream& operator<<(std::ostream& os,
75:                                     const DateTime& dt);
76:     friend std::istream& operator>>(std::istream& is, DateTime& dt);
77:
78: private:
79:
80:     std::time_t theTime_;
81: };
82:
83:
84: #endif // DateTime_dot_h
```

To support separate operations on the time and date portions of a DateTime, we define getDate and getTime operations in lines 31 and 32 and setDate and setTime operations in lines 39 and 40. Lines 43, 46, and 49 declare functions that, for a given DateTime, return DateTime objects representing the start of the day, week, or month, respectively. The addDay function declared in line 52 allows simple DateTime arithmetic (the number of days to add may be negative).

Lines 55–58 declare a set of functions that return string representations of the date, the time, the name of the day of the week, or the name of the month. In lines 61 and 62, we declare functions that convert from string representations of the date or time. These functions work much like the input operator, so we will be able to borrow code from the input operator. If the string is malformed, these functions return false to indicate an error condition.

Listing 9.12 shows the final version of DateTime.cpp, with all the new extensions implemented.

Listing 9.12   Final Version of DateTime.cpp

```
 1:  // TinyPIM (c) 1999 Pablo Halpern. File DateTime.cpp
 2:
 3:  #include <iomanip>
 4:  #include <sstream>
 5:  #include "DateTime.h"
 6:
 7:  #ifndef _MSC_VER
 8:  using std::mktime;
 9:  using std::localtime;
10:  using std::time_t;
11:  using std::strftime;
12:  #endif
13:
14:  DateTime::DateTime(int year, int month, int day, int hour, int min)
15:  {
16:     set(year, month, day, hour, min);
17:  }
18:
19:  void DateTime::get(int& year, int& month, int& day,
20:                     int& hour, int& min) const
21:  {
22:     std::tm* mytm = localtime(&theTime_);
23:     year  = mytm->tm_year + 1900;
24:     month = mytm->tm_mon + 1;
25:     day   = mytm->tm_mday;
26:     hour  = mytm->tm_hour;
27:     min   = mytm->tm_min;
28:  }
29:
30:  void DateTime::getDate(int& year, int& month, int& day) const
31:  {
```

continues

Listing 9.12   continued

```
32:    int hour, min;
33:    get(year, month, day, hour, min);
34: }
35:
36: void DateTime::getTime(int& hour, int& min) const
37: {
38:    int year, month, day;
39:    get(year, month, day, hour, min);
40: }
41:
42: // Return the day of the week (range 0 = Sunday to 6 = Saturday)
43: int DateTime::dayOfWeek() const
44: {
45:    return localtime(&theTime_)->tm_wday;
46: }
47:
48: DateTime& DateTime::set(int year, int month, int day,
49:                         int hour, int min)
50: {
51:    // Years from 0-49 are assumed to mean 2000-2049.
52:    // Years 1900 or over are assumed to be 4-digit years.
53:    // Other years are assumed to mean 1950-1999.
54:    if (year < 50)
55:      year += 2000;
56:    else if (year < 1900)
57:      year += 1900;
58:
59:    std::tm mytm;
60:    mytm.tm_year = year - 1900;
61:    mytm.tm_mon  = month - 1; // zero based
62:    mytm.tm_mday = day;
63:    mytm.tm_hour = hour;
64:    mytm.tm_min  = min;
65:    mytm.tm_sec  = 0;
66:    mytm.tm_isdst = -1;
67:
68:    theTime_ = mktime(&mytm);
69:
70:    return *this;
71: }
72:
73: DateTime& DateTime::setDate(int year, int month, int day)
74: {
75:    int hour, min;
76:    getTime(hour, min);
77:    set(year, month, day, hour, min);
78:
79:    return *this;
80: }
81:
```

```
 82:   DateTime& DateTime::setTime(int hour, int min)
 83:   {
 84:     int year, month, day;
 85:     getDate(year, month, day);
 86:     set(year, month, day, hour, min);
 87:
 88:     return *this;
 89:   }
 90:
 91:   std::string DateTime::dateStr() const
 92:   {
 93:     char buf[20];
 94:     strftime(buf, 20, "%x", localtime(&theTime_));
 95:     return buf;
 96:   }
 97:
 98:   std::string DateTime::timeStr() const
 99:   {
100:     char buf[20];
101:     strftime(buf, 20, "%I:%M%p", localtime(&theTime_));
102:     return buf;
103:   }
104:
105:   // Name of day of the week
106:   std::string DateTime::wdayName() const
107:   {
108:     char buf[30];
109:     strftime(buf, 30, "%A", localtime(&theTime_));
110:     return buf;
111:   }
112:
113:   // Name of month of the year
114:   std::string DateTime::monthName() const
115:   {
116:     char buf[30];
117:     strftime(buf, 30, "%B", localtime(&theTime_));
118:     return buf;
119:   }
120:
121:   bool DateTime::dateStr(const std::string& s)
122:   {
123:     char slash1, slash2;
124:     int mon, day, year;
125:
126:     // Unpack the date part using a stringstream
127:     std::istringstream tmpstrm(s);
128:     tmpstrm >> mon >> slash1 >> day >> slash2 >> year;
129:
130:     // Check for error in date
131:     if (tmpstrm.fail() || slash1 != '/' || slash2 != '/' ||
```

continues

Listing 9.12   continued

```
132:       mon < 1 || 12 < mon || day < 1 || 31 < day)
133:     return false;
134:
135:   setDate(year, mon, day);
136:   return true;
137: }
138:
139: bool DateTime::timeStr(const std::string& s)
140: {
141:   char colon;
142:   int hour, min;
143:   char ampm[3];
144:
145:   std::istringstream tmpstrm(s);
146:   tmpstrm >> hour >> colon >> min;
147:
148:   // Check for error in time
149:   if (tmpstrm.fail() || hour < 0 || 23 < hour || min < 0 || 59 < min)
150:     return false;
151:
152:   // Check for am/pm indicator
153:   tmpstrm >> std::setw(3) >> ampm;
154:   bool useAmPm = ! tmpstrm.fail();
155:
156:   // Convert hour from 12-hour to 24-hour format (0-23)
157:   if (useAmPm)
158:   {
159:     if (hour == 12)
160:       hour = 0;
161:     if (ampm[0] == 'p' || ampm[0] == 'P')
162:       hour += 12;
163:   }
164:
165:   setTime(hour, min);
166:   return true;
167: }
168:
169: // Return this day at midnight
170: DateTime DateTime::startOfDay() const
171: {
172:   std::tm theTm = *localtime(&theTime_);
173:   theTm.tm_hour = 0;
174:   theTm.tm_min = 0;
175:   theTm.tm_sec = 0;
176:   theTm.tm_isdst = -1;
177:
178:   DateTime result;
179:   result.theTime_ = mktime(&theTm);
180:   return result;
181: }
```

```
182:
183: // Return most recent Sunday at midnight
184: DateTime DateTime::startOfWeek() const
185: {
186:   std::tm theTm = *localtime(&theTime_);
187:   theTm.tm_mday -= theTm.tm_wday;     // Subtract current day-of week
188:   theTm.tm_hour = 0;
189:   theTm.tm_min = 0;
190:   theTm.tm_sec = 0;
191:   theTm.tm_isdst = -1;
192:
193:   DateTime result;
194:   result.theTime_ = mktime(&theTm);
195:   return result;
196: }
197:
198: // Return first day of this month
199: DateTime DateTime::startOfMonth() const
200: {
201:   std::tm theTm = *localtime(&theTime_);
202:   theTm.tm_mday = 1;
203:   theTm.tm_hour = 0;
204:   theTm.tm_min = 0;
205:   theTm.tm_sec = 0;
206:   theTm.tm_isdst = -1;
207:
208:   DateTime result;
209:   result.theTime_ = mktime(&theTm);
210:   return result;
211: }
212:
213: // Add a certain number of days to the date
214: DateTime DateTime::addDay(int days) const
215: {
216:   std::tm theTm = *localtime(&theTime_);
217:   theTm.tm_mday += days;
218:   theTm.tm_isdst = -1;
219:
220:   DateTime result;
221:   result.theTime_ = mktime(&theTm);
222:   return result;
223: }
224:
225: // Get the current date and time
226: DateTime DateTime::now()
227: {
228:   DateTime ret;
229:   ret.theTime_ = time(0);  // Call std::time
230:   return ret;
231: }
```

9

continues

Listing 9.12   continued

```
232:
233: std::ostream& operator<<(std::ostream& os, const DateTime& dt)
234: {
235:   return os << (dt.dateStr() + " " + dt.timeStr());
236: }
237:
238: std::istream& operator>>(std::istream& is, DateTime& dt)
239: {
240:   DateTime result;
241:
242:   // First, read the date part
243:   std::string date;
244:   is >> date;
245:   if (is.fail())
246:     return is;  // I/O error
247:
248:   if (! result.dateStr(date))
249:   {
250:     is.clear(std::ios::failbit);
251:     return is;  // Format error
252:   }
253:
254:   std::string time;
255:   is >> time;
256:   if (is.fail())
257:     return is;  // I/O error
258:
259:   if (! result.timeStr(time))
260:   {
261:     is.clear(std::ios::failbit);
262:     return is;  // Format error
263:   }
264:
265:   dt = result;
266:   return is;
267: }
```

Let's briefly look at these new functions. The getDate and getTime functions, defined in lines 30–40, simply call get and then discard some of the elements. In line 45, the dayOfWeek function calls localtime and then returns the tm_wday member of the resulting tm structure. The setDate function, in lines 73–80, first extracts the time components and then combines them with the date arguments, creating a new DateTime. The setTime function in lines 82–89 works in a similar way.

In line 94, we see another function call, std::strftime, which takes four parameters: a character array, a length for the character array, a format string, and a tm structure pointer. This strftime function copies the format string to the character array, replacing certain substitution codes with date and time elements. A substitution code consists of a percent symbol (%) within the format string, followed by a single letter. The letter indicates which component(s) of the date and time should be inserted at that point in the resulting character array. For example, "%y" is replaced by the last two digits of the year ("00" to "99"). Thus, if the year in the tm structure represents the year 2001, and the format string is "The year is '%y", the resulting (null-terminated) character string will be "The year is '01". In line 94, we use the format string "%x", which is replaced by the current date in *locale-specific* format.

Locale specific is something that varies from region to region in the world. Common locale-specific attributes are the format of dates, times, currency, and so on.

In line 101, we use strftime again, this time to format the time. Here we use three substitution strings: %I, which substitutes the hour from 1 to 12, %M, which substitutes the minutes from 1 to 60 and %p, which substitutes the am/pm indicator in locale-specific format. Our format string inserts a colon between the hours and minutes. We could instead have used the %X substitution code, which is replaced by the time in locale specific format, but on my compiler, this format includes the seconds, which is not desirable here. Some other codes we use are %A, for the name of the day of the week (in line 109), and %B, for the name of the month (in line 117). For a complete list of substitution codes, see your compiler's documentation. By concatenating the results of the dateStr and timeStr functions, we can replace the logic of the output function with a single statement, at line 235.

The dateStr function uses a stringstream to parse the date, in lines 127 and 128. The code for this function was borrowed almost unchanged from the input operator. We do the same for the time string in lines 145 and 146 in the timeStr function. Again, the code was taken from the input operator. Rather than repeat the same logic, we modified the input operator to call dateStr and timeStr in lines 248 and 259, respectively.

We begin our implementation of startOfDay at line 172 by decomposing the time into a tm structure. In lines 173–175, we set the hour, minute, and seconds to zero (midnight). It is possible that in doing this, the time crossed a daylight-savings–time/standard-time boundary. Therefore, in line 176, we set the tm_isdst flag to -1, which will cause mktime to recompute whether daylight saving time is in effect at the new time. The call to mktime in line 179 computes a new time_t that represents midnight on the same day as the original. Note that the original DateTime object has not been changed. The new DateTime object is separate and is returned to the caller in line 180.

The startOfWeek function works mostly like startOfDay. In addition to zeroing the hour, minute, and seconds in lines 188–190, we subtract some number of days in line 187. The tm_wday value is the day of the week expressed as a number in the range 0

9

(Sunday) to 6 (Saturday). Thus, if `tm_wday` is 3 (Wednesday), we subtract three days from `tm_mday`, to get the date of the preceding Sunday. What happens if the subtraction yields a number less than 1? It so happens that the `mktime` function allows the members of the `tm` structure to be out of the normal range so that, for example, a `tm_mon` of 13 is treated as February of the following year and `tm_mday` of 0 is treated as the last day of the preceding month. Not only will the resulting `time_t` be valid, but the `tm` structure itself is *normalized* to valid values. This is an extremely useful feature for doing calendar arithmetic.

To *normalize* is to convert values to a more useful, or *normal*, form. For example, the fraction 3/2 can be normalized to 1 1/2.

The `startOfMonth` function again converts a `DateTime` to a `tm` structure and back. This time, we set the day of the month to 1, in line 202. The `addDay` function works mostly the same way. In line 217, it adds the specified number of days to `tm_mday`, relying on `mktime` to normalize the structure in case we go past the beginning or end of the month. Unlike `startOfWeek`, `addDay` does not zero out the hours and minutes.

To test these new features, we modify our test program as shown in Listing 9.13.

Listing 9.13   Test Program for Extended `DateTime` Features

```
 1:  // TinyPIM (c) 1999 Pablo Halpern. File timeTest.cpp
 2:
 3:  #include <iomanip>
 4:  #include "DateTime.h"
 5:
 6:  int main()
 7:  {
 8:    // Test now() function
 9:    std::cout << "Now = " << DateTime::now() << std::endl;
10:
11:    // Test constructor
12:    std::cout << "Party = " << DateTime(0, 1, 1, 0, 0) << std::endl;
13:
14:    DateTime dt;
15:
16:    while (std::cin)
17:    {
18:      std::cout << "\nEnter a date and time: ";
19:      if (std::cin.peek() == 'q' || std::cin.peek() == 'Q' )
20:        break;
21:
22:      std::cin >> dt;
23:      if (std::cin.fail())
24:      {
25:        std::cout << "Bad input" << std::endl;
26:        std::cin.clear();
27:      }
```

```
28:     else
29:     {
30:       std::cout << "DateTime = " << dt << std::endl;
31:       std::cout << "Next day = " << dt.addDay() << std::endl;
32:       std::cout << "Midnight = " << dt.startOfDay() << std::endl;
33:       std::cout << "Week     = " << dt.startOfWeek() << std::endl;
34:       std::cout << "Month    = " << dt.startOfMonth() << std::endl;
35:       std::cout << "Month name = " << dt.monthName() << std::endl;
36:       std::cout << "Day name = " << dt.wdayName() << std::endl;
37:       std::cout << "Day number = " << dt.dayOfWeek() << std::endl;
38:
39:       std::cout << std::setfill('*') << std::left << std::setw(30)
40:                 << std::hex << dt
41:                 << ' ' << std::setw(10) << 0xff << std::endl;
42:     }
43:
44:     std::cin.ignore(INT_MAX, '\n');   // If fails, loop will exit
45:   }
46:
47:   return 0;
48: }
```

The major change, as you can see, is in lines 30–37, where we print the various attributes of the DateTime object. There is no need to directly test the dateStr and timeStr functions because they are already indirectly tested through the input and output operators. A quick run of this program yields the output shown in Listing 9.14.

Listing 9.14　Output of Test Program for Final Version of DateTime

```
 1:  Now = 09/06/99 02:06PM
 2:  Party = 01/01/00 12:00AM
 3:
 4:  Enter a date and time: 4/5/1996 3:11
 5:  DateTime = 04/05/96 03:11AM
 6:  Next day = 04/06/96 03:11AM
 7:  Midnight = 04/05/96 12:00AM
 8:  Week     = 03/31/96 12:00AM
 9:  Month    = 04/01/96 12:00AM
10:  Month name = April
11:  Day name = Friday
12:  Day number = 5
13:  04/05/96 03:11AM************** ff********
14:
15:  Enter a date and time: 4/5/96 3:75
16:  Bad input
17:
18:  Enter a date and time: q
```

On line 8, you can see that the startOfWeek function successfully found the beginning of the week, even though it was in the preceding month. Alignment and error checking seem to work as before, as seen on lines 13 and 16. Two things that have changed, though, are that the year is now being represented with only two digits and the am/pm indicator is uppercase. The former is simply the date format chosen by the %x code for strftime. The latter is the am/pm format chosen by the %p code. Although strftime has many codes to format dates and times in almost any format imaginable, it is remarkably difficult to get it to do what you want. Only a few of the substitution codes do things in a locale-specific way, and there is no way to modify the behavior of those codes to, for example, include or exclude the seconds, use four-digit years, or use lowercase am/pm indicators. If you don't mind committing to a single locale, you can use strftime to format the date and time any way you want. Alternatively, you can choose a dozen or so formats suitable for a variety of locales and give users a choice as to which they want.

Next Steps

We now have a DateTime class that is suitable for use in our date book. Along the way, we learned to use the time_t and tm types and the mktime, localtime, and strftime functions. The majority of our work, however, was in writing input and output operators that seamlessly extend the standard stream I/O system to include DateTime. Our DateTime class is general enough to warrant ironing out all the quirks of the I/O mechanism. Less general classes might be used in more restrictive contexts where format is less of an issue.

Our next step is to build a date book around our DateTime class. We will be sorting on DateTime objects, as well as building menus and display lists. The auto_ptr template will help us manage memory. We will bring together everything we have learned as we work to complete the TinyPIM program.

Putting It All Together

At this point, we are ready to put everything together and complete the project. We still need to write the classes related to the date book as well as the main menu class. In writing these classes, we will use most of the skills and knowledge we have learned up until now.

The approach I will take in introducing the rest of the project will be a top-down walk through the code execution. Up until now, we have built new components on top of other components; for example, the `AddressBook` class was built using the `Address` class. This bottom-up approach worked well for introducing concepts, but the top-down approach used in this chapter is better suited for tying the concepts together. We will, however, see an occasional new concept as we go along.

Referring to the design in Chapter 1, "Introducing TinyPIM," the classes we have yet to write are the following:

- `PIMData`
- `MainMenu`
- `Appointment`
- `DateBook`
- `DateBookMenu`
- `AppointmentDisplayList`
- `AppointmentEditor`

As we need each class to proceed, I will show you listings of the class definition and implementation and will highlight the interesting points. Because we are walking through the execution of the program, I will often introduce a new class before finishing with the previous one, eventually returning to the description of the unfinished class. Where needed, I will repeat parts of the listings, but expect to do a certain amount of page flipping anyway. Let's begin.

Writing the Main Program

The main program is responsible for setting up our data structures and launching the main menu. It is shown in Listing 10.1.

Code Note   Unless otherwise noted, the listings in this chapter correspond to files on the companion Web page in the `Chapter 10 Code\TinyPIM` directory. The files in this directory can be compiled and linked together to create an executable program. See the end of the Introduction for information on accessing this book's companion Web page.

Listing 10.1   The `TinyPIM` Main Program

```
 1:  // TinyPIM (c) 1999 Pablo Halpern. File TinyPIM.cpp
 2:
 3:  #ifdef _MSC_VER
 4:  #pragma warning(disable : 4786)
 5:  #endif
 6:
 7:  #include <iostream>
 8:  #include <cstdlib>
 9:
10:  #ifndef _MSC_VER
11:  using std::exit;
12:  #endif
13:
14:  #include "PIMData.h"
15:  #include "AddressBookMenu.h"
16:  #include "DateBookMenu.h"
17:  #include "MainMenu.h"
18:
19:  // Test function to generate addresses (in TestAddrData.cpp)
20:  extern void generateAddresses(AddressBook& addrbook,
21:                                   int numAddresses);
22:
23:  // Test function to generate appointments (in TestAddrData.cpp)
24:  extern void generateAppointments(DateBook& dateBook, int numDays);
25:
26:  // Global data object
27:  PIMData myPIMData;
28:
29:  int main()
```

```
30:    {
31:      try
32:      {
33:        // Create address book and date book
34:        std::auto_ptr<AddressBook> addrBookPtr(new AddressBook);
35:        std::auto_ptr<DateBook>    dateBookPtr(new DateBook);
36:
37:        // Will only get here if no exception was thrown
38:        myPIMData.addressBook(addrBookPtr);
39:        myPIMData.dateBook(dateBookPtr);
40:      }
41:      catch (...)
42:      {
43:        std::cerr << "Could not create address and date books.\n";
44:        exit(EXIT_FAILURE);
45:      }
46:
47:    #ifndef NOGENERATE
48:      // Generate 50 random address-book entries
49:      generateAddresses(myPIMData.addressBook(), 50);
50:
51:      // Generate a year's worth of appointments
52:      generateAppointments(myPIMData.dateBook(), 366);
53:    #endif
54:
55:      // Create address book menu and date book menus
56:      AddressBookMenu addrBookMenu(myPIMData.addressBook());
57:      DateBookMenuCatalog dateBookMenus(myPIMData.dateBook());
58:
59:      // Create the main menu and push it on the menu stack
60:      MainMenu mainMenu(&addrBookMenu, dateBookMenus.monthlyMenu());
61:      Menu::enterMenu(&mainMenu);
62:
63:      // Process menu choices until menu exits.
64:      while (Menu::isActive())
65:        Menu::activeMenu()->mainLoop();
66:
67:      std::cout << "\nThank you for using TinyPIM!\n" << std::endl;
68:
69:      return 0;
70:    }
```

10

Lines 7 and 8 bring in two standard headers. The <iostream> header includes definitions for stream I/O. The <cstdlib> header is needed for the definition of the exit function. The c at the beginning of <cstdlib> tells us that this header has basically the same contents as the C standard header, <stdlib.h>. However, <cstdlib> puts all nonmacro identifiers into namespace std. Because exit is inherited from C, we run across the Microsoft 6.0 compiler library bug that fails to put it into namespace std, and we must use the workaround in lines 10–12. After line 12, the standard function `exit` is in the global namespace for all compilers and can be used without the `std::` prefix. (See the discussion of Listing 2.5 in Chapter 2, "Implementing the Address Class with Text Strings," for a description of this Microsoft workaround.)

Lines 20 and 24 declare functions that generate random data for testing purposes. We've seen `generateAddresses` already. The `generateAppointments` function does basically the same thing for the date book as `generateAddresses` does for the address book. We'll look at `generateAppointments` later in this chapter.

Implementing the `PIMData` Class Using `auto_ptr`

Line 27 in Listing 10.1 creates an object of type `PIMData`. `PIMData` is a core class that acts as a vessel to hold an `AddressBook` and a `DateBook` object. The definition of `PIMData` is shown in Listing 10.2.

Listing 10.2   The `PIMData` Class

```
 1:  // TinyPIM (c) 1999 Pablo Halpern. File PIMData.h
 2:
 3:  #ifndef PIMData_dot_h
 4:  #define PIMData_dot_h 1
 5:
 6:  #ifdef _MSC_VER
 7:  #pragma warning(disable : 4786)
 8:  #endif
 9:
10:  #include <memory>
11:  #include "AddressBook.h"
12:  #include "DateBook.h"
13:
14:  // Class to encapsulate all of the data for a given PIM file.
15:  class PIMData
16:  {
17:  public:
18:    PIMData() { }
19:    AddressBook& addressBook() { return *addressBook_; }
20:    DateBook& dateBook() { return *dateBook_; }
21:
22:    void addressBook(std::auto_ptr<AddressBook> ab)
23:      { addressBook_ = ab; }
24:    void dateBook(std::auto_ptr<DateBook> db) { dateBook_ = db; }
25:
26:  private:
27:    std::auto_ptr<AddressBook>     addressBook_;
28:    std::auto_ptr<DateBook>        dateBook_;
29:
30:    // Because this class contains auto_ptrs, it does not have proper
31:    // copy semantics. We disable copying to avoid problems.
```

```
32:    PIMData(const PIMData&);
33:    PIMData& operator=(const PIMData&);
34:  };
35:
36:  #endif // PIMData_dot_h
```

The functions in `PIMData` are entirely inline, so there is no need for a separate `PIMData.cpp` file. Lines 27 and 28 declare a pointer to an `AddressBook` and a pointer to a `DateBook` object. However, instead of normal pointers, we use a template class called `auto_ptr`, which is defined in the `<memory>` header included in line 10. An auto pointer is a type of smart pointer that implements the semantics of *strict ownership*. Strict ownership means that only one `auto_ptr` can point to a given object at a time. That `auto_ptr` is said to *own* the object. When the owner of an object is destroyed, it also deletes the object that it points to. Like many other standard library facilities, `auto_ptr` is very handy for preventing errors that can cause memory leaks. Notice, for example, that `PIMData` does not define a destructor. That is because the compiler-generated destructor will automatically call the `auto_ptr` destructor, which will delete the owned `AddressBook` and `DateBook` objects.

The most surprising aspect of strict ownership is what happens when one `auto_ptr` is assigned to another. If a and b are of type `std::auto_ptr<sometype>`, the statement

```
a = b;
```

will cause the following sequence of events:

1. The object owned by a is deleted.
2. Ownership of the object owned by b is transferred to a so that a now points to and owns that object.
3. The value of b becomes `NULL`.

An important consequence of these semantics is that both objects are modified, not just the one on the left. The same is true for the `auto_ptr` copy constructor. Strict ownership prevents ambiguities about who owns an object and, therefore, who is responsible for deleting it.

10

After one `auto_ptr` is constructed from or is assigned the value of another `auto_ptr`, the two `auto_ptr`s are not equal. This violates the rule that a copy constructor and assignment operator should make a copy. Because all containers rely on this rule, `auto_ptr` is not suitable as an element type in any container. Beware, also, that this strange noncopy behavior is automatically transferred to any class that contains an `auto_ptr`.

The `auto_ptr` template is a quirky thing. You can make an object owned by an `auto_ptr` in one of the following ways:

```
auto_ptr<sometype> ptr1(new sometype);
auto_ptr<sometype> ptr2 = auto_ptr<sometype>(new sometype);
```

You cannot give ownership to an `auto_ptr` in this way:

```
auto_ptr<sometype> ptr3 = new sometype;
```

The reason for this has to do with `auto_ptr`'s constructor, which is declared `explicit`, meaning that there is no invisible conversion from a normal pointer to an `auto_ptr`. Some compilers do not yet support the `explicit` keyword and will erroneously allow the third definition.

An `auto_ptr` should only be constructed with a pointer to an object that was created using the non-array form of `new`. The reason for this is that the `auto_ptr` destructor uses the non-array form of `delete`, and it could cause resource leaks or worse if the pointer were to point to an array. Never make an `auto_ptr` point to a non-heap object or construct two `auto_ptrs` pointing to the same object.

In addition to the constructor and destructor, `auto_ptr` provides dereference operators * and ->, so that it works like a pointer. It also provides the function `get`, which returns a normal pointer to the object owned by the `auto_ptr`, and the function `release`, which works like `get` but also causes the `auto_ptr` to give up ownership of the object (and become null). The `reset` function takes a pointer argument and causes the `auto_ptr` to delete its owned object and assume ownership of its argument.

Compiler Note   The `auto_ptr` class was modified late in the standardization process. Many compiler libraries, including the Microsoft 6.0 library, still have the version of `auto_ptr` specified in the December, 1996 draft standard. The biggest practical difference between the old and new versions is that the older `auto_ptr` releases ownership without becoming null. Also, there is no `reset` function in the older version. Your code will work with both the old and new definitions of `auto_ptr` if it never uses an `auto_ptr` after it has given up ownership and if it does not use the `reset` function.

In lines 19 and 20 of Listing 10.2, we dereference the `auto_ptrs` to return references to the actual `AddressBook` and `DateBook` objects. The `addressBook` function in lines 22 and 23 takes an `auto_ptr<AddressBook>` and assigns it to the `addressBook_` member. To see what happens when this version of the `addressBook` function is called, let's look at the beginning of the `main` program, repeated here from Listing 10.1:

```
31:     try
32:     {
33:        // Create address book and date book
34:        std::auto_ptr<AddressBook> addrBookPtr(new AddressBook);
35:        std::auto_ptr<DateBook>    dateBookPtr(new DateBook);
36:
37:        // Will only get here if no exception was thrown
38:        myPIMData.addressBook(addrBookPtr);
39:        myPIMData.dateBook(dateBookPtr);
40:     }
41:     catch (...)
42:     {
43:        std::cerr << "Could not create address and date books.\n";
44:        exit(EXIT_FAILURE);
45:     }
```

Lines 34 and 35 (of Listing 10.1) create `auto_ptr`s to `AddressBook` and `DateBook` objects, respectively. When `addressBook` is called in line 38, two transfers of ownership take place. The `main` function transfers ownership of the `AddressBook` object from `addrBookPtr` to the `ab` argument of `PIMData::addressBook`. Then, ownership is transferred from the `ab` argument to the `addressBook_` member variable within `myPIMData`. The net result is that `myPIMData` winds up owning the `AddressBook` object, and `addrBookPtr` becomes null. The `dateBook` function called in line 39 works the same way. To transfer ownership from the caller, it is important that the `auto_ptr` argument be passed by value, not reference. An `auto_ptr` should be passed by `const` reference if no transfer of ownership is desired or by non-`const` reference if it is intended to be the *recipient* rather than the source of a transfer of ownership.

An important aspect of this code fragment is the exception safety created by using `auto_ptr`. What would happen if an exception were thrown in the creation of the `DateBook` object? The `try` block would immediately end, and control would jump to the start of the `catch` clause at line 43. If `addrBookPtr` were a normal pointer, a memory leak would result from the pointer going out of scope without being deleted. However, because `addrBookPtr` is an `auto_ptr`, the `addrBookPtr` object effectively deletes itself when it goes out of scope, calling the destructor for the owned `AddressBook`. We could have inserted the `AddressBook` object directly into the `PIMData` object without the intermediate pointer. However, this causes a different problem. If an exception is thrown, `myPIMData` would effectively be half initialized. In this (somewhat contrived) situation, the consequences would be unimportant, but in other situations there is a real benefit to temporarily holding a bunch of objects until the last object is constructed successfully. The exception safety provided by `auto_ptr` is one of the main reasons it is included in the C++ Standard Library.

10

Before we leave this code fragment, look at line 44, which is reached if our attempt to create the `AddressBook` or `DateBook` objects fails with an exception. The `std::exit` function does what its name implies: It terminates the program and calls the destructors for all global and static variables. However, it does not call destructors for local variables. Thus, it is often a bad idea to call `exit` anywhere but in `main` and even then only if there are no local variables that have destructors. The program can be terminated gracefully by instead throwing an exception and catching it in `main`. To make sure that local variables in `main` are properly destroyed, you can simply return `EXIT_FAILURE` instead of calling `exit(EXIT_FAILURE)`. Thus, the `exit` function is much less useful in C++ than it was in C. (In fact, I can't recall ever having used `exit` in C++, except for this example.)

The Appointment and DateBook Classes

The first thing the `main` program does is create an `AddressBook` object and a `DateBook` object (as we have just seen in lines 34 and 35 of Listing 10.1). We've already visited the `AddressBook` class in previous chapters. Let's take a quick look at the `DateBook` class, shown in Listing 10.3.

Listing 10.3   The DateBook Class Definition

```
 1:  // TinyPIM (c) 1999 Pablo Halpern. File DateBook.h
 2:
 3:  #ifndef DateBook_dot_h
 4:  #define DateBook_dot_h 1
 5:
 6:  #include <set>
 7:  #include <map>
 8:
 9:  #include "Appointment.h"
10:
11:  class DateBook
12:  {
13:    // Data structure abbreviations
14:    typedef std::multiset<Appointment>              apptByTime_t;
15:    typedef std::map<int, apptByTime_t::iterator> apptById_t;
16:
17:  public:
18:    DateBook();
19:    ~DateBook();
20:
21:    // Exception classes
22:    class appointmentNotFound { };
23:    class DuplicateId { };
24:
25:    int insertAppointment(const Appointment& appt, int recordId = 0)
26:      throw (DuplicateId);
```

```
27:        void eraseAppointment(int recordId) throw (appointmentNotFound);
28:        void replaceAppointment(const Appointment& appt, int recordId = 0)
29:          throw (appointmentNotFound);
30:        const Appointment& getAppointment(int recordId) const
31:          throw (appointmentNotFound);
32:
33:        // Iterator to traverse Appointment records
34:        typedef apptByTime_t::const_iterator const_iterator;
35:
36:        // Functions to traverse all Appointment records
37:        const_iterator begin() const { return appointments_.begin(); }
38:        const_iterator end()   const { return appointments_.end();   }
39:
40:        // Find first Appointment with start time greater-than-or-equal to
41:        // specified time.
42:        const_iterator findAppointmentAtTime(const DateTime& dt) const;
43:
44:        // Find next Appointment in which any field contains the specified
45:        // string. Indicate starting point for search with start parameter.
46:        const_iterator findNextContains(const std::string& searchStr,
47:                                        const_iterator start) const;
48:
49:        // Return iterator to specified records ID.
50:        const_iterator findRecordId(int recordId) const
51:          throw (appointmentNotFound);
52:
53:    private:
54:        // Disable copying
55:        DateBook(const DateBook&);
56:        DateBook& operator=(const DateBook&);
57:
58:        static int nextId_;
59:
60:        apptByTime_t appointments_;
61:        apptById_t   apptById_;
62:
63:        // Get the index of the record with the specified ID.
64:        apptByTime_t::iterator getById(int recordId)
65:          throw (appointmentNotFound);
66:        apptByTime_t::const_iterator getById(int recordId) const
67:          throw (appointmentNotFound);
68:    };
69:
70:
71:    #endif // DateBook_dot_h
```

The DateBook class has the same basic architecture as the AddressBook class, so much of this header file should look familiar. Lines 14 and 15 contain abbreviations for the main data structures defined in lines 60 and 61. The Appointment objects are kept in a multiset container, sorted in their natural order (by start time). The multiset enables us to insert, delete, and find Appointment records quickly by start time.

Because we also want to be able to find records quickly by record ID, we have a second index, `apptById`, which associates record IDs to `Appointment` records using a `map` container. The key to the map is the integer record ID. The contents of each map entry is an iterator pointing to an `Appointment` within the `appointments_` multiset. (See Chapter 6, "An Enhanced `AddressBook` Using Algorithms and Sorted Containers," for a full description of these data structures.)

The `DateBook` class provides iterators and `begin` and `end` functions (lines 34–38) that make it possible to traverse the `Appointment` records. (A description of iterators is in Chapter 4, "An Alternative Implementation Using a List Container.") The `findAppointmentAtTime` function, declared on line 42, returns an iterator to the first appointment starting no earlier than the specified time. The iterator can then be used to get the next few appointments, for example, to examine the rest of the appointments on the same day. The `findNextContains` function on lines 46 and 47 returns an iterator to the next `Appointment` containing the specified string. It works the same way that the corresponding function works in the `AddressBook`. The other functions, declared in lines 25–31, are straightforward insert, erase, and retrieve functions just as we have for `AddressBook`. We will delve into the implementation of `DateBook` a bit later in this chapter.

The `DateBook` depends, of course, on the `Appointment` class, which is defined in Listing 10.4.

Listing 10.4   The `Appointment` Class

```
 1:  // TinyPIM (c) 1999 Pablo Halpern. File Appointment.h
 2:
 3:  #ifndef Appointment_dot_h
 4:  #define Appointment_dot_h 1
 5:
 6:  #include <string>
 7:  #include "DateTime.h"
 8:
 9:  class Appointment
10:  {
11:  public:
12:    Appointment() : recordId_(0) { }
13:
14:    // Field accessors
15:    int recordId() const { return recordId_; }
16:    void recordId(int i) { recordId_ = i; }
17:
18:    DateTime startTime() const { return startTime_; }
19:    void startTime(const DateTime& dt);
20:
21:    DateTime endTime() const { return endTime_; }
22:    void endTime(const DateTime& dt);
```

```
23:
24:    std::string description() const { return description_; }
25:    void description(const std::string& s);
26:
27: private:
28:    int          recordId_;
29:    DateTime     startTime_;
30:    DateTime     endTime_;
31:    std::string description_;
32: };
33:
34: inline bool operator< (const Appointment& a1, const Appointment& a2)
35:    { return a1.startTime() < a2.startTime(); }
36:
37: #endif //  Appointment_dot_h
```

The `Appointment` class, like the `Address` class, is a very basic data structure consisting of a bunch of scalar fields. There are accessors to set and retrieve these fields and very little else. The `startTime_` and `endTime_` fields in lines 29 and 30 are `DateTime` objects, as defined in the previous chapter. The less-than operator for `Appointment`, in lines 34 and 35, works by comparing the start times of the arguments. This is the operation that defines the sort order of appointments in the date book. Specifically, the `multimap` used in the `DateBook` class uses the less-than operator by default and thus will sort `Appointment` objects by start time.

The rest of the implementation of `Appointment` is trivial and is shown in Listing 10.5.

Listing 10.5   Implementation of Non-Inline `Appointment` Functions

```
1: // TinyPIM (c) 1999 Pablo Halpern. File Appointment.cpp
2:
3: #include "Appointment.h"
4:
5: void Appointment::startTime(const DateTime& dt)
6: {
7:   startTime_ = dt;
8: }
9:
10: void Appointment::endTime(const DateTime& dt)
11: {
12:   endTime_ = dt;
13: }
14:
15: void Appointment::description(const std::string& s)
16: {
17:   description_ = s;
18: }
```

10

The `generateAppointments` Function

After `AddressBook` and `DateBook` objects are created, the main program (Listing 10.1) usually calls functions that generate artificial data for testing the address book and date book. (These calls can be turned off by defining the `NOGENERATE` preprocessor symbol.) These functions are implemented in a separate file, shown in Listing 10.6.

Listing 10.6   The Test Data Generation Functions

```
 1:  // TinyPIM (c) 1999 Pablo Halpern. File TestData.cpp
 2:
 3:  #ifdef _MSC_VER
 4:  #pragma warning(disable : 4786)
 5:  #endif
 6:
 7:  #include <cstdlib>
 8:  #include <sstream>
 9:  #include <iomanip>
10:
11:  #ifdef _MSC_VER
12:  namespace std {
13:    inline int rand() { return ::rand(); }
14:    inline void srand(unsigned s) { ::srand(s); }
15:  }
16:  #endif
17:
18:  #include "AddressBook.h"
19:  #include "DateBook.h"
20:
21:  // Return a string at random from a constant array of strings
22:  template <class A>
23:  inline const char* randomString(A& stringArray)
24:  {
25:    int size = sizeof(A) / sizeof(stringArray[0]);
26:    int index = std::rand() % size;
27:    return stringArray[index];
28:  }
29:
30:  void generateAddresses(AddressBook& addrbook, int numAddresses)
31:  {
32:    // Seed the random number generator with a constant so that the
33:    // same sequence of "random" numbers will be generated every time.
34:    std::srand(100);
35:
36:    static const char* const lastnames[] = {
37:      "Clinton", "Bush", "Reagan", "Carter", "Ford", "Nixon", "Johnson",
38:      "Kennedy"
39:    };
40:
41:    static const char* const firstnames[] = {
42:      "William", "George", "Ronald", "Jimmy", "Gerald", "Richard",
43:      "Lyndon", "Jack", "Hillary", "Barbara", "Nancy", "Rosalynn",
```

```
44:        "Betty", "Pat", "Ladybird", "Jackie"
45:     };
46:
47:     // The names of trees are used to generate street and town names.
48:     static const char* const trees[] = {
49:        "Maple", "Oak", "Willow", "Pine", "Hemlock", "Redwood", "Fir",
50:        "Holly", "Elm"
51:     };
52:
53:     static const char* const streetSuffixes[] = {
54:        "St.", "Rd.", "Ln.", "Terr.", "Ave."
55:     };
56:
57:     static const char* const townSuffixes[] = {
58:        "ton", "vale", "burg", "ham"
59:     };
60:
61:     // State abbreviations, U.S. and its territories.
62:     // Thanks to the USPS web page:
63:     // http://www.usps.gov/cpim/ftp/pubs/201html/addrpack.htm#abbr
64:     static const char* const states[] = {
65:        "AL", "AK", "AS", "AZ", "AR", "CA", "CO", "CT", "DE",
66:        "DC", "FM", "FL", "GA", "GU", "HI", "ID", "IL", "IN",
67:        "IA", "KS", "KY", "LA", "ME", "MH", "MD", "MA", "MI",
68:        "MN", "MS", "MO", "MT", "NE", "NV", "NH", "NJ", "NM",
69:        "NY", "NC", "ND", "MP", "OH", "OK", "OR", "PA", "PR",
70:        "RI", "SC", "SD", "TN", "TX", "UT", "VT", "VA", "VI",
71:        "WA", "WV", "WI", "WY"
72:     };
73:
74:     for (int i = 0; i < numAddresses; ++i)
75:     {
76:        Address addr;
77:        addr.lastname(randomString(lastnames));
78:        addr.firstname(randomString(firstnames));
79:
80:        // Construct a phone number by streaming to a stringstream
81:        std::stringstream phonestream;
82:        phonestream << '(' << (std::rand() % 800 + 200) << ") "
83:                    << (std::rand() % 800 + 200) << '-'
84:                    << std::setfill('0') << std::setw(4)
85:                    << (std::rand() % 10000);
86:        addr.phone(phonestream.str());
87:
88:        std::stringstream addrstream;
89:        // Generate number and street.
90:        addrstream << (std::rand() % 100 + 1) << " "
91:                    << randomString(trees) << " "
92:                    << randomString(streetSuffixes) << '\n';
93:
94:        // Generate town name, state, and zip.
```

continues

Listing 10.6   continued

```
95:       addrstream << randomString(trees) << randomString(townSuffixes)
96:                 << ", " << randomString(states) << " "
97:                 << std::setfill('0') << std::setw(5)
98:                 << (std::rand() % 99999 + 1);
99:       addr.address(addrstream.str());
100:
101:      addrbook.insertAddress(addr);
102:    }
103: }
104:
105: // Helper function to generate a random appointment
106: Appointment randomAppointment(DateTime date, int minHour,
107:                               int maxHour, int maxDuration,
108:                               const std::string desc)
109: {
110:    // Generate hour in the range minHour to maxHour
111:    int hour = std::rand() % (maxHour - minHour + 1) + minHour;
112:
113:    // Generate minute = 0, 15, 30 or 45
114:    int min = (std::rand() % 4) * 15;
115:
116:    // Generate duration (hours) in range 1 - maxDuration
117:    int duration = std::rand() % maxDuration + 1;
118:
119:    Appointment result;
120:    date.setTime(hour, min);
121:    result.startTime(date);
122:    date.setTime(hour + duration, min);
123:    result.endTime(date);
124:    result.description(desc);
125:
126:    return result;
127: }
128:
129: // Generate appointments between startDate and endDate
130: void generateAppointments(DateBook& dateBook, int numDays)
131: {
132:    // Seed the random number generator with a constant so that the
133:    // same sequence of "random" numbers will be generated every time.
134:    std::srand(50);
135:
136:    static const char* const meetingTypes[] = {
137:      "Meeting", "Review meeting", "Urgent meeting", "Status meeting"
138:    };
139:
140:    static const char* const activities[] = {
141:      "Golf", "Raquetball", "Dancing", "Piano Lesson"
142:    };
143:
144:    static const char* const firstnames[] = {
```

```
145:        "William", "George", "Ronald", "Jimmy", "Gerald", "Richard",
146:        "Lyndon", "Jack", "Hillary", "Barbara", "Nancy", "Rosalynn",
147:        "Betty", "Pat", "Ladybird", "Jackie"
148:    };
149:
150:    // Create appointments an equal number of days before and
151:    // after today.
152:    DateTime startDate=DateTime::now().startOfDay().addDay(-numDays/2);
153:    DateTime endDate = startDate.addDay(numDays);
154:    std::string desc;
155:    for (DateTime currDate = startDate; currDate < endDate;
156:        currDate = currDate.addDay(1))
157:    {
158:      // There is a 1 in 4 chance that there is a morning meeting
159:      // between 8:00 and 10:45am.
160:      desc = std::string(randomString(meetingTypes)) + " with " +
161:        randomString(firstnames);
162:      if (std::rand() % 4 < 1)
163:        dateBook.insertAppointment(randomAppointment(currDate, 8, 10,
164:                                                     3, desc));
165:
166:      // There is a 2 in 11 chance that there there is a lunch date
167:      desc = std::string("Lunch with ") + randomString(firstnames);
168:      if (std::rand() % 11 < 2)
169:        dateBook.insertAppointment(randomAppointment(currDate, 12, 12,
170:                                                     2, desc));
171:
172:      // There is a 1 in 6 chance that there is an evening activity
173:      desc = std::string(randomString(activities)) + " with " +
174:        randomString(firstnames);
175:      if (std::rand() % 6 < 1)
176:        dateBook.insertAppointment(randomAppointment(currDate, 18, 21,
177:                                                     4, desc));
178:    }
179: }
```

The operation of generateAppointments is in many ways similar to generateAddresses, which we saw in Chapter 8, "A Simple Menu System." The first thing we do, in line 134, is set a seed for the random number generator. By selecting a fixed constant for the seed, we ensure that the sequence of pseudorandom numbers will be the same for every run. In lines 152 and 153, we do some time arithmetic to calculate an equal number of days before and after the current date (DateTime::now()). The total number of days was passed in as an argument. Starting at line 155, we loop through all the dates in the range that we just calculated. Then, for each date, we "roll the dice" to decide whether there will be a morning meeting, lunch appointment, and/or evening activity scheduled for that day.

In line 160, we generate the description for our morning meeting by selecting a random meeting type from our array of meeting type strings and a random person from our array of first names. In line 162, we use the rand function to make a probabilistic choice as to whether to record the morning meeting in the date book. The expression std::rand() % 4 produces a random integer in the range 0–3. The condition in line 162 will insert the appointment into the date book if this random integer is zero, which will happen one out of four times, on average. The random appointment is created in the randomAppointment function, which starts at line 111. The generateAppointments function passes in an hour range of 8–10 (a.m.) and a duration of up to 3 hours. The expression in line 111 will generate a random integer in the range 8–10. The expression in line 114 will generate a random number equaling 0, 15, 30, or 45. The expression in line 117 will choose a random duration of at least 1 hour and up to maxDuration (3) hours. With all these numbers generated, we can create our Appointment object, in lines 119–124. The generateAppointments function repeats this logic for lunch time in lines 167–170 and for evening times in lines 173, 177 and then loops and does the same thing for the next day.

The Main Menu

After the AddressBook and DateBook objects have been created and random records added to each of them, we come to the following lines from Listing 10.1 (the main program):

```
55:    // Create address book menu and date book menus
56:    AddressBookMenu addrBookMenu(myPIMData.addressBook());
57:    DateBookMenuCatalog dateBookMenus(myPIMData.dateBook());
58:
59:    // Create the main menu and push it on the menu stack
60:    MainMenu mainMenu(&addrBookMenu, dateBookMenus.monthlyMenu());
61:    Menu::enterMenu(&mainMenu);
62:
63:    // Process menu choices until menu exits.
64:    while (Menu::isActive())
65:      Menu::activeMenu()->mainLoop();
```

Line 56 defines an AddressBookMenu object. We'll come back to the meaning of the DateBookMenuCatalog defined in line 57 later in this chapter. For now, it is only important to know that the dateBookMenus object contains pointers to menus used to access the date book. In line 60, we create the main menu object, passing it pointers to address book and date book menus, which will be used as submenus. The main menu mainloop function presents the user with the choice of using the address book, using the date book, or quitting.

Before we delve into the MainMenu class, let's finish tracing through main. In line 61, we make mainMenu, the active menu using the enterMenu static function of the Menu class.

The Menu class maintains a last-in, first-out (LIFO) menu stack using the stack standard container adapter. The enterMenu function pushes a new menu pointer on to the top of the menu stack, making it the currently active menu. The main menu will cease to be the active menu when it pushes one of its submenus on to the stack. Each submenu will eventually terminate by using the exitMenu function to remove itself from the top of the stack, thus causing the main menu to become active again. (See Chapter 8 for a detailed description of the use of the stack template in the menu subsystem.) In line 64 (of Listing 10.1), the main program loops until the stack is empty, which will happen when the main menu exits. Within the loop, main calls the currently active menu's mainLoop function in line 65.

The main menu class is defined in Listing 10.7.

Listing 10.7   The MainMenu Class

```
 1:  // TinyPIM (c) 1999 Pablo Halpern. File MainMenu.h
 2:
 3:  #ifndef MainMenu_dot_h
 4:  #define MainMenu_dot_h 1
 5:
 6:  #include "Menu.h"
 7:
 8:  class MainMenu : public Menu
 9:  {
10:  public:
11:    MainMenu(Menu* addrBookMenu,
12:             Menu* dateBookMenu)
13:      : addrBookMenu_(addrBookMenu), dateBookMenu_(dateBookMenu) { }
14:
15:    void mainLoop();
16:
17:  private:
18:    void addressBook();
19:    void dateBook();
20:    void quit();
21:
22:    Menu*  addrBookMenu_;
23:    Menu*  dateBookMenu_;
24:  };
25:
26:  #endif // MainMenu_dot_h
```

MainMenu is, of course, derived from Menu, in line 8. It provides the required mainloop function in line 15 and three private functions, one for each menu operation, in lines 18–20. The pointers defined in lines 22 and 23 are used to start the submenu corresponding to the user's selection. The implementation of MainMenu is shown in Listing 10.8.

Listing 10.8   Implementation of `MainMenu` Functions

```
 1:  // TinyPIM (c) 1999 Pablo Halpern. File MainMenu.cpp
 2:
 3:  #ifdef _MSC_VER
 4:  #pragma warning(disable : 4786)
 5:  #endif
 6:
 7:  #include <iostream>
 8:  #include "PIMData.h"
 9:  #include "MainMenu.h"
10:  #include "AddressBookMenu.h"
11:  #include "DateBookMenu.h"
12:
13:  void MainMenu::mainLoop()
14:  {
15:    clearScreen();
16:    std::cout << "Welcome to TinyPIM!\n\n"
17:              << "*** Main Menu ***\n\n";
18:
19:    static const char menu[] =
20:      "Please select from the following:\n\n"
21:      "  (A)ddress Book\n  (D)ate Book\n  (Q)uit\n\n"
22:      "Enter selection> ";
23:
24:    switch (getMenuSelection(menu, "ADQ"))
25:    {
26:    case 'A': addressBook();      break;
27:    case 'D': dateBook();         break;
28:    case 'Q':
29:    default: quit();              break;
30:    } // end switch
31:  }
32:
33:  void MainMenu::addressBook()
34:  {
35:    enterMenu(addrBookMenu_);
36:  }
37:
38:  void MainMenu::dateBook()
39:  {
40:    enterMenu(dateBookMenu_);
41:  }
42:
43:  void MainMenu::quit()
44:  {
45:    exitMenu();
46:  }
```

In line 24, `mainloop` calls the base class `getMenuSelection` function, passing the menu prompt and a string of valid selection letters. If the user enters D, the `dateBook` function in lines 38–41 is called, which pushes the date book menu onto the menu stack but does not call its main loop. `MainMenu::dateBook` then returns to `MainMenu::main-loop`, which then returns to `main`. The `main` program will loop and call `mainloop` on the active menu, which is now the date book menu.

Designing the Date Book Menus

Our original design from Chapter 1 had a single `DateBookMenu` class derived from `Menu`. However, the date book has several modes—monthly view, weekly view, daily view, and search view—each of which has a different interaction with the user. In monthly view mode, the user is presented with a month at a glance in the following format:

```
            1*  2*  3   4
 5   6*  7*  8*  9  10  11*
12  13  14  15* 16  17* 18*
19* 20* 21  22  23* 24  25*
26* 27  28* 29  30*
```

An asterisk next to a day number indicates that there is at least one appointment scheduled for that day. There is not much the user can do in the monthly view except look at other months or switch to a different mode.

The weekly view shows all the appointments for a week as follows:

```
1: Sunday 09/26/99
2:      12:45PM - 01:45PM  Lunch with Barbara
3: Tuesday 09/28/99
4:      12:00PM - 02:00PM  Lunch with Hillary
5: Thursday 09/30/99
6:      09:00AM - 10:00AM  Meeting with Pat
7:      12:45PM - 01:45PM  Lunch with Pat
8: Saturday 10/02/99
9:      12:15PM - 01:15PM  Lunch with Hillary
```

The daily view shows all the appointments for a day:

```
1: 09:00AM - 10:00AM  Meeting with Pat
2: 12:45PM - 01:45PM  Lunch with Pat
```

The search view shows all the appointments containing a specified search string (for example, `Pat`):

```
1: 03/30/99 06:15PM - 09:15PM  Dancing with Pat
2: 05/29/99 12:15PM - 02:15PM  Lunch with Pat
3: 09/07/99 10:45AM - 01:45PM  Status meeting with Pat
4: 09/30/99 09:00AM - 10:00AM  Meeting with Pat
5: 09/30/99 12:45PM - 01:45PM  Lunch with Pat
```

The weekly, daily, and search views permit similar operations—creating, viewing, deleting, and editing date book entries—but there are also differences in presentation.

10

To handle these different modes, we can modify our design to add more detail. Figure 10.1 shows a detailed class diagram of the `DateBookMenu` class hierarchy.

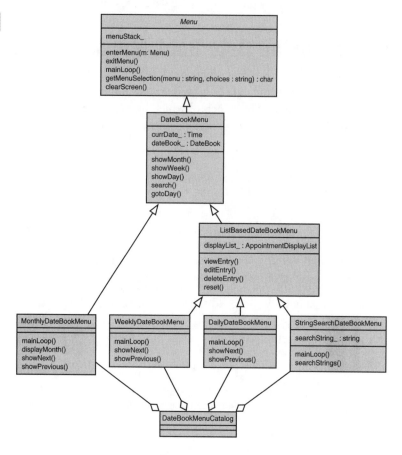

Figure 10.1

UML class diagram for the date book menus.

The `DateBookMenu` base class generalizes the functions to change modes and to set the date to be displayed, which are common to all the date book menus. The `MonthlyDateBookMenu` adds functions for displaying the month and moving to the previous or following month. The `ListBasedDateBookMenu` class is a base class for all the views that involve a scrolling display list. It encapsulates most of the functionality of those classes. The `WeeklyDateBookMenu` and `DailyDateBookMenu` each have functions for moving to the following or previous week or day. The `StringSearchDateBookMenu` class adds a search string member. All the *leaf* classes have their own `mainloop`, which produces a different menu interaction.

In any kind of hierarchy, a *leaf* is an element that has no subordinate elements. A diagram of a hierarchical structure usually looks like an upside down tree, with the leaves at the bottom.

The `DateBookMenuCatalog` Class

The `DateBookMenuCatalog` is a class that owns one instance of each of the leaf menu classes. When switching between view modes, the `DateBookMenu` consults the `DateBookMenuCatalog` to find the appropriate menu to make active. The `DateBookMenuCatalog` class is also responsible for creating and destroying the four menu objects.

All these classes are defined in the `DateBookMenu.h` header file, shown in Listing 10.9.

Listing 10.9   The `DateBookMenu` Classes

```
 1:  // TinyPIM (c) 1999 Pablo Halpern. File DateBookMenu.h
 2:
 3:  #ifndef DateBookMenu_dot_h
 4:  #define DateBookMenu_dot_h 1
 5:
 6:  #include <memory>
 7:  #include "Menu.h"
 8:  #include "AppointmentDisplayList.h"
 9:
10:  // Forward reference
11:  class DateBookMenuCatalog;
12:
13:  class DateBookMenu : public Menu
14:  {
15:  public:
16:    DateBookMenu(DateBook& dateBook, DateBookMenuCatalog* catalog)
17:      : dateBook_(dateBook), catalog_(catalog),
18:        currDate_(DateTime::now()) { }
19:
20:    void setDate(DateTime dt);
21:
22:  protected:
23:    void createEntry();
24:    void showDay();
25:    void showWeek();
26:    void showMonth();
27:    void search();
28:    void gotoDate();
29:
30:    virtual void reset();
31:
32:    DateBook&              dateBook_;
33:    DateTime               currDate_;
34:    DateBookMenuCatalog*   catalog_;
35:  };
36:
```

continues

Listing 10.9   continued

```
37:   // Derived class for Monthly view
38:   class MonthlyDateBookMenu : public DateBookMenu
39:   {
40:   public:
41:     MonthlyDateBookMenu(DateBook& dateBook,
42:                         DateBookMenuCatalog* catalog)
43:       : DateBookMenu(dateBook, catalog), cacheGood_(false) { }
44:
45:     void mainLoop();
46:
47:   private:
48:     void displayMonth();
49:     void showNext();
50:     void showPrevious();
51:
52:     virtual void reset();
53:
54:     bool scoreBoard_[32]; // Index zero unused
55:     bool cacheGood_;        // true if scoreBoard _ has valid data
56:   };
57:
58:   // Based class for all list-based date book views
59:   class ListBasedDateBookMenu : public DateBookMenu
60:   {
61:   public:
62:     ListBasedDateBookMenu(DateBook& dateBook,
63:                         DateBookMenuCatalog* catalog)
64:       : DateBookMenu(dateBook, catalog), displayList_(dateBook) { }
65:
66:   protected:
67:     void viewEntry();
68:     void editEntry();
69:     void deleteEntry();
70:
71:     virtual void reset();
72:
73:     AppointmentDisplayList  displayList_;
74:   };
75:
76:   // Derived class for Weekly view
77:   class WeeklyDateBookMenu : public ListBasedDateBookMenu
78:   {
79:   public:
80:     WeeklyDateBookMenu(DateBook& dateBook,
81:                         DateBookMenuCatalog* catalog);
82:
83:     void mainLoop();
84:
85:   private:
86:     void showNext();
```

```
 87:    void showPrevious();
 88: };
 89:
 90: // Derived class for Daily view
 91: class DailyDateBookMenu : public ListBasedDateBookMenu
 92: {
 93: public:
 94:    DailyDateBookMenu(DateBook& dateBook,DateBookMenuCatalog* catalog);
 95:
 96:    void mainLoop();
 97:
 98: private:
 99:    void showNext();
100:   void showPrevious();
101: };
102:
103: // Derived class for string search view
104: class StringSearchDateBookMenu : public ListBasedDateBookMenu
105: {
106: public:
107:    StringSearchDateBookMenu(DateBook& dateBook,
108:                             DateBookMenuCatalog* catalog);
109:
110:    std::string searchString() const { return searchString_; }
111:    void searchString(const std::string& s);
112:
113:    void mainLoop();
114:
115: private:
116:    std::string searchString_;
117: };
118:
119: // Class to collect all of the date book menus
120: class DateBookMenuCatalog
121: {
122: public:
123:    DateBookMenuCatalog(DateBook& dateBook);
124:
125:    // Use compiler-generated destructor
126:    // ~DateBookMenuCatalog();
127:
128:    DailyDateBookMenu* dailyMenu();
129:    WeeklyDateBookMenu* weeklyMenu();
130:    MonthlyDateBookMenu* monthlyMenu();
131:    StringSearchDateBookMenu* stringSearchMenu();
132:
133: private:
134:    // Copying would be very destructive, so disable it.
135:    DateBookMenuCatalog(const DateBookMenuCatalog&);
136:    DateBookMenuCatalog& operator=(const DateBookMenuCatalog&);
```

10

continues

Listing 10.9   continued

```
137:
138:     // This object "owns" a copy of each menu type
139:     std::auto_ptr<DailyDateBookMenu> dailyMenu_;
140:     std::auto_ptr<WeeklyDateBookMenu> weeklyMenu_;
141:     std::auto_ptr<MonthlyDateBookMenu> monthlyMenu_;
142:     std::auto_ptr<StringSearchDateBookMenu> stringSearchMenu_;
143: };
144:
145: #endif // DateBookMenu_dot_h
```

Very little in the header file isn't already described by the class diagram. In line 16, we see that the `DateBookMenu` constructor takes two parameters: a `DateBook` reference and a pointer to a `DateBookCatalog`. All the derived class constructors take the same two parameters and pass them up to the base class constructor. The base class also keeps track of the day currently being viewed. In line 18, this value is initialized to the current date (and time).

Because the `MonthlyDateBookMenu` doesn't have a display list, line 54 defines a special cache called the `scoreBoard_`, which keeps track of which days of the month have appointments scheduled. The `cacheGood_` flag defined in line 55 keeps track of whether the `scoreBoard_` is valid. The `ListBasedDateBookMenu` defines a display list object in line 73. The `AppointmentDisplayList` class is derived from `DisplayList`, and we will examine it shortly.

The `DateBookMenuCatalog` has an `auto_ptr` to one of each of the four `DateBookMenu` leaf classes. The copy constructor and assignment operator are disabled (made private and not implemented) in lines 135 and 136 because copying a `DateBookMenuCatalog` would not copy the menu objects but would instead transfer ownership to the so-called copy. The main program creates a `DateBookMenuCatalog` and passes a `DateBook` object to its constructor. The constructor and other functions of `DateBookMenuCatalog` are shown in Listing 10.10, which lists a part of the `DateBookMenu.cpp` file.

Listing 10.10   Implementation of `DateBookMenuCatalog`

```
455: DateBookMenuCatalog::DateBookMenuCatalog(DateBook& dateBook)
456:     : dailyMenu_(new DailyDateBookMenu(dateBook, this)),
457:       weeklyMenu_(new WeeklyDateBookMenu(dateBook, this)),
458:       monthlyMenu_(new MonthlyDateBookMenu(dateBook, this)),
459:       stringSearchMenu_(new StringSearchDateBookMenu(dateBook, this))
460: {
461: }
462:
```

```
463: DailyDateBookMenu* DateBookMenuCatalog::dailyMenu()
464: {
465:   return dailyMenu_.get();
466: }
467:
468: WeeklyDateBookMenu* DateBookMenuCatalog::weeklyMenu()
469: {
470:   return weeklyMenu_.get();
471: }
472:
473: MonthlyDateBookMenu* DateBookMenuCatalog::monthlyMenu()
474: {
475:   return monthlyMenu_.get();
476: }
477:
478: StringSearchDateBookMenu* DateBookMenuCatalog::stringSearchMenu()
479: {
480:   return stringSearchMenu_.get();
481: }
```

In lines 456–459, the constructor initializes each `auto_ptr` by creating the appropriate menu object on the heap. This causes the `DateBookMenuCatalog` to own all the menu objects, almost as if they were directly contained within it. After constructing the `DateBookMenuCatalog` object, the main function constructs a `MainMenu` object as follows:

```
MainMenu mainMenu(&addrBookMenu, dateBookMenus.monthlyMenu());
```

The second parameter to the `MainMenu` constructor is the result of calling `monthlyMenu` on the `DateBookMenuCatalog` object. This gets us to line 475 of Listing 10.10. The get member function of `auto_ptr` returns a pointer to the owned object but does not relinquish ownership. It is this pointer to the `MonthlyDateBookMenu` object that is pushed on to the menu stack by the main menu when the user chooses to enter the date book.

The `MonthlyDateBookMenu` Class

After the main menu pushes the `MonthlyDateBookMenu` pointer on to the menu stack, the `main` program calls `mainloop` for this object. Listing 10.11 shows the implementation of `MonthlyDateBookMenu`, which is also part of the `DateBookMenu.cpp` source file. Because `DateBookMenu.cpp` is such a large source file, I will continue to present it in pieces, in an order that makes sense for my exposition. You can find the complete source file on the companion Web page in `Chapter 10 Code\TinyPIM`.

```
187: void MonthlyDateBookMenu::mainLoop()
188: {
189:   clearScreen();
190:   int year, month, day;
191:   currDate_.getDate(year, month, day);
192:   std::cout << "*** Appointment Book ***\n"
193:             << "Month of " << currDate_.monthName() << ' ' << year
194:             << "\n\n";
195:
196:   displayMonth();
197:   std::cout << '\n';
198:
199:   const char menu[] =
200:     "(P)revious month, (N)ext month, (C)reate, (S)earch,\n"
201:     "(R)edisplay, d(A)ily view, (W)eekly view, (G)oto date, "
202:     "(Q)uit ? ";
203:   const char choices[] = "PNCSRAWGQ";
204:
205:   switch (getMenuSelection(menu, choices))
206:   {
207:   case 'P': showPrevious();                 break;
208:   case 'N': showNext();                     break;
209:   case 'C': createEntry();                  break;
210:   case 'S': search();                       break;
211:   case 'R': /* do nothing, just loop */     break;
212:   case 'A': showDay();                      break;
213:   case 'W': showWeek();                     break;
214:   case 'G': gotoDate();                     break;
215:   case 'Q': exitMenu();                     break;
216:   default:  exitMenu();                     break;
217:   }
218: }
219:
220: void MonthlyDateBookMenu::reset()
221: {
222:   cacheGood_ = false;
223: }
224:
225: void MonthlyDateBookMenu::displayMonth()
226: {
227:   using namespace std::rel_ops;
228:
229:   // Calculate start of current month and next month
230:   DateTime startOfMonth = currDate_.startOfMonth();
231:   DateTime nextMonth = startOfMonth.addDay(31).startOfMonth();
232:   int year, month, day;
233:
234:   if (! cacheGood_)
235:   {
236:     // Clear the scoreboard
```

```
237:     for (int i = 0; i < 32; ++i)
238:       scoreBoard_[i] = false;
239:
240:     // Iterate through every entry within the month
241:     DateBook::const_iterator iter =
242:       dateBook_.findAppointmentAtTime(startOfMonth);
243:     DateBook::const_iterator endIter =
244:       dateBook_.findAppointmentAtTime(nextMonth);
245:
246:     // For each entry, set the scoreboard value for that day to true.
247:     for ( ; iter != endIter; ++iter)
248:     {
249:       iter->startTime().getDate(year, month, day);
250:       scoreBoard_[day] = true;
251:     }
252:   }
253:
254:   // Calculate the day of the week for the first day of the month.
255:   int startWday = startOfMonth.dayOfWeek();
256:
257:   // Calculate last day of the month (== day zero of next month)
258:   nextMonth.addDay(-1).getDate(year, month, day);
259:   int monthLen = day;
260:
261:   std::cout << " ";
262:   int wday = 0;
263:
264:   // Print blank spaces for first few days of first week of month.
265:   for ( ; wday < startWday; ++wday)
266:     std::cout << "    ";
267:
268:   // Print each day of month
269:   std::cout.fill(' ');
270:   std::cout.setf(std::ios::dec, std::ios::basefield);
271:   std::cout.setf(std::ios::right, std::ios::adjustfield);
272:   for (int mday = 1; mday <= monthLen; ++mday)
273:   {
274:     if (wday == 0 && mday != 1)
275:       std::cout << "\n ";
276:     std::cout << std::setw(3) << mday
277:               << (scoreBoard_[mday] ? '*' : ' ');
278:     wday = (wday + 1) % 7;
279:   }
280:   std::cout << std::endl;
281: }
282:
283: void MonthlyDateBookMenu::showPrevious()
284: {
285:   // Subtract one month
286:   int year, month, day, hour, min;
```

continues

Listing 10.11   continued

```
287:    currDate_.get(year, month, day, hour, min);
288:    setDate(DateTime(year, month - 1, day, hour, min));
289: }
290:
291: void MonthlyDateBookMenu::showNext()
292: {
293:    // Add one month
294:    int year, month, day, hour, min;
295:    currDate_.get(year, month, day, hour, min);
296:    setDate(DateTime(year, month + 1, day, hour, min));
297: }
298:
```

The `mainLoop` function starting on line 187 is similar to the `mainLoop` functions from the other menu classes we have seen. In lines 192–194, it displays a header that announces the name of the month and year being displayed. The first time it is called, `currDate_` will contain the current date; thus the current month will be displayed. In line 196, we use `displayMonth` to show the month at a glance before giving the menu prompt.

The `displayMonth` function starts on line 225. In line 227, we import the namespace `std::rel_ops` into the current scope. This will automatically define operators `!=`, `>`, `<=`, and `>=` for the `DateTime` and `Appointment` classes, which define the operators `==` and `<`, but not the others. In lines 230–231, we compute the first and last days of the current month using functions from `DateTime`. In line 234, we test the state of the scoreboard cache. The cache will be good if we have displayed this month before and have not modified the date book in the interim. If the cache is not good, we first clear it in lines 237–238 and then begin the processes of iterating through all the appointments scheduled to start during the month, setting the appropriate scoreboard flag for each appointment. In lines 241–244, we obtain an iterator to the first appointment and an iterator to one record past the last appointment in this month.

The `DateBook` Implementation

At this point, we have `main` calling `mainloop` for the active menu, which belongs to the `MonthlyDateBookMenu`. The `MonthlyDateBookMenu::mainloop` function calls `MonthlyDateBook::displayMonth`, which then calls `DateBook::findAppointmentAtTime` to obtain start and end iterators for its loop. Now we will take another detour and look at the implementation of the `DateBook::findAppointmentAtTime` function, as well as the other functions in `DateBook`. The entire `DateBook.cpp` file is shown in Listing 10.12.

Listing 10.12   Implementation File for the DateBook Class

```cpp
 1: // TinyPIM (c) 1999 Pablo Halpern. File DateBook.cpp
 2:
 3: #ifdef _MSC_VER
 4: #pragma warning(disable : 4786)
 5: #endif
 6:
 7: #include <algorithm>
 8: #include "DateBook.h"
 9:
10: int DateBook::nextId_ = 1;
11:
12: DateBook::DateBook()
13: {
14: }
15:
16: DateBook::~DateBook()
17: {
18: }
19:
20: int DateBook::insertAppointment(const Appointment& appt,
21:                                 int recordId) throw (DuplicateId)
22: {
23:   if (recordId == 0)
24:     // If recordId is not specified, create a new record id.
25:     recordId = nextId_++;
26:   else if (recordId >= nextId_)
27:     // Make sure nextId is always higher than any known record id.
28:     nextId_ = recordId + 1;
29:   else if (apptById_.count(recordId))
30:     // recordId is already in map
31:     throw DuplicateId();
32:
33:   // Assign recordId to copy of Appointment
34:   Appointment apptCopy(appt);
35:   apptCopy.recordId(recordId);
36:
37:   // Insert record into set
38:   apptByTime_t::iterator i = appointments_.insert(apptCopy);
39:
40:   // Insert Appointment iterator into id-based map
41:   // apptById_.insert(std::make_pair(recordId, i));
42:   apptById_[recordId] = i;
43:
44:   return recordId;
45: }
46:
47: DateBook::apptByTime_t::iterator
48: DateBook::getById(int recordId) throw (appointmentNotFound)
```

continues

Listing 10.12   continued

```
49:  {
50:    // Find record by Id.
51:    apptById_t::iterator idIter = apptById_.find(recordId);
52:    if (idIter == apptById_.end())
53:      throw appointmentNotFound();
54:
55:    return idIter->second;
56:  }
57:
58:  DateBook::apptByTime_t::const_iterator
59:  DateBook::getById(int recordId) const throw (appointmentNotFound)
60:  {
61:    // Find record by Id.
62:    apptById_t::const_iterator idIter = apptById_.find(recordId);
63:    if (idIter == apptById_.end())
64:      throw appointmentNotFound();
65:
66:    return idIter->second;
67:  }
68:
69:  void DateBook::eraseAppointment(int recordId)
70:    throw (appointmentNotFound)
71:  {
72:    apptByTime_t::iterator i = getById(recordId);
73:
74:    // Remove entry from both containers
75:    appointments_.erase(i);
76:    apptById_.erase(recordId);
77:  }
78:
79:  void DateBook::replaceAppointment(const Appointment& appt,
80:                                    int recordId)
81:    throw (appointmentNotFound)
82:  {
83:    if (recordId == 0)
84:      recordId = appt.recordId();
85:
86:    eraseAppointment(recordId);
87:    insertAppointment(appt, recordId);
88:  }
89:
90:  const Appointment& DateBook::getAppointment(int recordId) const
91:    throw (appointmentNotFound)
92:  {
93:    return *getById(recordId);
94:  }
95:
96:  // Find first Appointment with start time greater-than-or-equal to
97:  // specified time.
98:  DateBook::const_iterator
```

```
 99:  DateBook::findAppointmentAtTime(const DateTime& dt) const
100: {
101:   Appointment searchAppt;
102:   searchAppt.startTime(dt);
103:
104:   return appointments_.lower_bound(searchAppt);
105: }
106:
107: // Function object class to search for a string within an Appointment
108: class AppointmentContainsStr
109:   : public std::unary_function<Appointment, bool>
110: {
111: public:
112:   AppointmentContainsStr(const std::string& str) : str_(str) { }
113:
114:   bool operator()(const Appointment& a)
115:   {
116:     // Return true if any Appointment field contains str_
117:     return (a.description().find(str_) != std::string::npos);
118:   }
119:
120: private:
121:   std::string str_;
122: };
123:
124: // Find next Appointment in which any field contains the specified
125: // string. Indicate starting point for search with start parameter.
126: DateBook::const_iterator
127: DateBook::findNextContains(const std::string& searchStr,
128:                            const_iterator start) const
129: {
130:   return std::find_if(start, appointments_.end(),
131:                       AppointmentContainsStr(searchStr));
132: }
133:
134: // Return iterator to specified records ID.
135: DateBook::const_iterator
136: DateBook::findRecordId(int recordId) const
137:   throw (appointmentNotFound)
138: {
139:   return getById(recordId);
140: }
```

10

The DateBook class works the same way that the AddressBook class works. To refresh your memory, look at the insertAppointment function. After we generate a record ID in lines 23–35, we insert the Appointment into the appointments_ variable, which is of type multiset<Appointment>. The insert function stores a copy of the Appointment and returns an iterator to the new element of the multiset. The elements in the multiset have a sorted order that is determined by the < operator for Appointment. Because the < operator simply compares the start dates of its two arguments, the multiset is sorted in ascending order by start time and allows quick lookups by start time. In line 42, we cross-reference the new element in the `apptById_` variable, which is of type `map<int, apptByTime_t::iterator>`. The map associates the record ID with the iterator returned from the previous step. With the `apptById_` map, we can look up an iterator by record ID and then dereference the associated iterator to get the `Appointment`. This allows quick lookup by either date or by record ID and is the same double-indexing scheme used in `AddressBook`. (The `AddressBook` class allowed quick lookup by name or by record ID.)

The `findAppointmentAtTime` function has no need for double-indexing. It simply creates a dummy `Appointment` object in line 101 and sets its start time to the desired time in line 102. The actual search is done by the `lower_bound` function, which executes in logarithmic time. The iterator returned by `lower_bound` points to the first element of `appointments_` with a start time not less than `dt`. If there is no such element, it returns `appointments_.end()`. We will return to `DateBook` in a little while. For now, let's follow the flow of execution back to `MonthlyDateBookMenu::displayMonth` in Listing 10.11.

Displaying the Month

The calls to `findAppointmentAtTime` in lines 242 and 244 of Listing 10.11 resulted in an iterator, `iter`, pointing to the first appointment starting no earlier than the first of the month and another iterator, `endIter`, pointing to the first appointment starting no earlier than the first of the next month. Thus, the iterator range, `[iter, endIter)`, comprises all the appointments in the current month. We begin looping through these appointments in line 247, using the typical termination test that stops before the end iterator is processed. For each entry, we extract the year, month, and day from the start time in line 249. Then, we use the day to index the `scoreboard_` value and set it to true. If there is more than one appointment on the same day, the same `scoreboard_` element will harmlessly be set twice.

That takes care of setting the score board. Now, we need to print out the days of the month, with an asterisk next to each day that has a true value in the `scoreboard_` array. On line 225, we find out on what day of the week the month starts. On line 258, we calculate the last day of the month by subtracting one from the first day of the next month. Lines 265–266 print out blanks for the days of the week from Sunday until the first of the month. Before we start printing days, we need to set some format parameters. Lines 269–271 set the output fill character to space, the numeric base to 10, and the field alignment to right. These three statements are equivalent to the following statement, which does the same thing using I/O manipulators:

```
std::cout << std::setfill(' ') << std::dec << std::right;
```

At line 272, we start looping through the days of the month. Lines 274–275 insert a newline and indent before the first day of each week; line 276 prints out the day number, right justified in a field of three blanks; line 277 prints an asterisk if the scoreboard_ array indicates that there is an appointment on that day or a space if the scoreboard_ does not indicate an appointment. In line 278, we update the wday variable, which keeps track of the day of the week to be printed next.

From displayMonth, we return to MonthlyDateBookMenu::mainloop, where, at line 205 (still in Listing 10.11), we present the user with the menu prompt and read the user's selection using the base class Menu::getMenuSelection function. The rest of mainloop is a straightforward switch on the user's selection. At the time getMenuSelection is called, the display looks as follows:

```
*** Appointment Book ***
Month of September 1999

             1*  2*  3*  4
  5   6   7*  8*  9* 10  11
 12* 13  14  15  16* 17  18*
 19* 20* 21* 22  23  24* 25
 26* 27* 28  29* 30

(P)revious month, (N)ext month, (C)reate, (S)earch,
(R)edisplay, d(A)ily view, (W)eekly view, (G)oto date, (Q)uit ?
```

Assume that the user enters N to see the next month. At line 208, we call the showNext function. At line 295 in showNext, we extract the components of the date and time. In line 296, we recombine these components, but we add one to the month. The DateTime constructor will normalize the date, in case the month gets set to 13. The result of this date arithmetic is passed to setDate, which is the DateBookMenu base class function for setting the date to be displayed. When showNext finishes, it returns to mainloop, which returns to main. Main then calls mainloop again, and the new month is displayed.

Switching Modes

If the user enters W in response to the menu prompt, control passes to the showWeek function, which belongs to DateBookMenu base class. The DateBookMenu implementation is the first part of DateBookMenu.cpp, as shown in Listing 10.13.

Listing 10.13   Implementation of DateBookMenu Base Class

```
1:  // TinyPIM (c) 1999 Pablo Halpern. File DateBookMenu.cpp
2:
3:  #ifdef _MSC_VER
4:  #pragma warning(disable : 4786)
```

continues

Listing 10.13   continued

```
 5:  #pragma warning(disable : 4355)
 6:  #endif
 7:
 8:  #include <iostream>
 9:  #include <iomanip>
10:  #include <sstream>
11:  #include <climits>
12:  #include "DateBookMenu.h"
13:  #include "Appointment.h"
14:  #include "DateBook.h"
15:  #include "AppointmentEditor.h"
16:
17:  void DateBookMenu::setDate(DateTime dt)
18:  {
19:    currDate_ = dt;
20:    reset();
21:  }
22:
23:  void DateBookMenu::reset()
24:  {
25:  }
26:
27:  void DateBookMenu::createEntry()
28:  {
29:    // Edit an empty appointment
30:    Appointment appt;
31:    appt.startTime(currDate_);
32:    appt.endTime(currDate_);
33:    AppointmentEditor    editor(appt);
34:
35:    // Continue editing until a record is saved or canceled.
36:    while (editor.edit())
37:    {
38:      appt = editor.appt();
39:      if (appt.description().empty())
40:      {
41:        std::cout << "Description must not be empty." << std::endl;
42:        continue;       // Loop and re-edit
43:      }
44:
45:      // insert record.
46:      dateBook_.insertAppointment(appt);
47:      setDate(appt.startTime());
48:      reset();
49:      break;
50:    } // end while
51:  }
52:
53:  void DateBookMenu::showDay()
54:  {
```

```
55:    // Go to daily mode for the current date
56:    exitMenu();
57:    catalog_->dailyMenu()->setDate(currDate_);
58:    enterMenu(catalog_->dailyMenu());
59: }
60:
61: void DateBookMenu::showWeek()
62: {
63:    // Go to weekly mode for the current date
64:    exitMenu();
65:    catalog_->weeklyMenu()->setDate(currDate_);
66:    enterMenu(catalog_->weeklyMenu());
67: }
68:
69: void DateBookMenu::showMonth()
70: {
71:    // Go to monthly mode for the current date
72:    exitMenu();
73:    catalog_->monthlyMenu()->setDate(currDate_);
74:    enterMenu(catalog_->monthlyMenu());
75: }
76:
77: void DateBookMenu::search()
78: {
79:    std::string searchString;
80:    std::cout << "Search for string: ";
81:    std::getline(std::cin, searchString);
82:
83:    // If no search string entered, abort.
84:    if (std::cin.fail() || searchString.empty())
85:      return;
86:
87:    // Set both search string and date
88:    exitMenu();
89:    catalog_->stringSearchMenu()->searchString(searchString);
90:    catalog_->stringSearchMenu()->setDate(currDate_);
91:    enterMenu(catalog_->stringSearchMenu());
92: }
93:
94: void DateBookMenu::gotoDate()
95: {
96:    std::string dateString;
97:    while (std::cin.good())
98:    {
99:      std::cout << "Goto date [" << currDate_.dateStr() << "]: ";
100:   std::getline(std::cin, dateString);
101:   if (dateString.empty())
102:     break;
103:   else if (dateString[0] == 't' || dateString[0] == 'T')
104:   {
```

continues

Listing 10.13   continued

```
105:        // User entered "today"
106:        setDate(DateTime::now());
107:        break;
108:     }
109:
110:     // Set date value
111:     DateTime newdate;
112:     if (! newdate.dateStr(dateString))
113:       std::cout << "Invalid date, please try again\n";
114:     else
115:     {
116:       setDate(newdate);
117:       break;
118:     } // end if
119:   } // end while
120: }
121:
122:
123:
```

Line 64 in showWeek exits the current menu, which up to now has been the monthly view menu. Because the current (monthly view) menu and the new (weekly view) menu have separate instances of the currDate_ member variable, it is necessary to set the current date for the weekly menu, which we do in line 57. Finally, we set the weekly view as the active menu by calling enterMenu in line 58.

Because showWeek is implemented in the base class, it is implemented once for all the DateBookMenu-derived classes. Thus, selecting W in any of the menus calls the same showWeek function. The showDay function in lines 53–59 and the showMonth function in lines 69–75 work the same way and are called when the user selects A or M, respectively. The search function, starting at line 77, also works the same way, except that we first prompt the user for a search string in line 80 and read the user's response in line 81, using the getline function from <string>. Remember that the getline function will read the rest of the line, including white space. If the input fails or if the user enters an empty line, we return from search without doing anything, in lines 84–85. Otherwise, we exit the current menu in line 88, set the search string and date for the search view menu in lines 89–90, and the set the search view as the active menu in line 91.

The Date Book Display List

DailyDateBookMenu, WeeklyDateBookMenu, and StringSearchDateBookMenu are all derived from ListBasedDateBookMenu (see Figure 10.1, earlier in this chapter). The ListBasedDateBookMenu class contains a AppointmentDisplayList object, which is the center of activity for all these menu classes. `AppointmentDisplayList` is derived from `DisplayList`, which was discussed in Chapter 7, "Scrolling Display Lists Using deques and I/O streams." The key aspect of `DisplayList` that interests us here is that derived classes must provide a function for retrieving records and a function for displaying a summary of a record. The class definition for `AppointmentDisplayList` is shown in Listing 10.14.

Listing 10.14   **Definition of the `AppointmentDisplayList` Class**

```
 1:  // TinyPIM (c) 1999 Pablo Halpern. File AppointmentDisplayList.h
 2:
 3:  #ifndef AppointmentDisplayList_dot_h
 4:  #define AppointmentDisplayList_dot_h 1
 5:
 6:  #include "DisplayList.h"
 7:  #include "DateTime.h"
 8:
 9:  class DateBook;
10:
11:  // Specialized DisplayList for Appointment records.
12:  class AppointmentDisplayList : public DisplayList
13:  {
14:  public:
15:      // Construct with a reference to the address book
16:      AppointmentDisplayList(DateBook& dateBook);
17:
18:      DateTime currDate() const { return currDate_; }
19:      void currDate(DateTime dt);
20:
21:      // List appointments for the day containing the specified DateTime
22:      void listDay(DateTime dt);
23:
24:      // List appointments for the week containing the specified DateTime
25:      void listWeek(DateTime dt);
26:
27:      // List all records that contain the specified string
28:      void listContainsString(const std::string&);
29:
30:  protected:
31:      // Display the specified appointment record in one-line format.
32:      // Implements pure virtual base-class function.
33:      virtual void displayRecord(int recordId);
34:
35:      // Override base-class function to retrieve more records.
36:      virtual bool fetchMore(int startId, int numRecords,
37:                             std::vector<int>& result);
38:
39:  private:
40:      DateBook&    dateBook_;
```

continues

10

Listing 10.14   continued

```
41:
42:     // Enumerate different listing modes
43:     enum listMode { dayMode, weekMode, stringMode };
44:     listMode      mode_;
45:
46:     // DateTime used for dayMode and weekMode
47:     DateTime      currDate_;
48:
49:     // String to use for stringMode.
50:     std::string   containsString_;
51: };
52:
53: #endif // AppointmentDisplayList_dot_h
```

The `listDay`, `listWeek`, and `listContainsString` functions are used to put the display list into one of three modes, defined in the `listMode` enumeration on line 43. The `displayRecord` overrides the base class `displayRecord` virtual function and is called by the `DisplayList` base class to format `Appointment` record summaries. The `fetchMore` function on lines 36–37 also overrides a base class function and is called to retrieve `Appointment` records from the date book. The implementation of the `AppointmentDisplayList` functions is shown in Listing 10.15.

Listing 10.15   Implementation of `AppointmentDisplayList`

```
 1: // TinyPIM (c) 1999 Pablo Halpern. File AppointmentDisplayList.cpp
 2:
 3: #ifdef _MSC_VER
 4: #pragma warning(disable : 4786)
 5: #endif
 6:
 7: #include <iostream>
 8: #include <iomanip>
 9: #include <algorithm>
10: #include "AppointmentDisplayList.h"
11: #include "Appointment.h"
12: #include "DateBook.h"
13:
14: #ifdef _MSC_VER
15: #define min _cpp_min
16: #define max _cpp_max
17: #endif
18:
19: // Construct with a reference to the appointment book
20: AppointmentDisplayList::AppointmentDisplayList(DateBook& apptBook)
21:   : dateBook_(apptBook), mode_(dayMode), currDate_(DateTime::now())
22: {
23: }
24:
```

```
25:   // Display the specified appointment record in one-line format
26:   void AppointmentDisplayList::displayRecord(int recordId)
27:   {
28:     if (recordId < 0)
29:     {
30:       // A negative recordId means a special date marker in the
31:       // range -1 (Sunday) to -7 (Saturday).
32:       // Print the date marker.
33:       DateTime startOfWeek = currDate_.addDay(-currDate_.dayOfWeek());
34:       DateTime marker = startOfWeek.addDay(-recordId - 1);
35:       std::cout << marker.wdayName() << ' ' << marker.dateStr();
36:       return;
37:     }
38:
39:     Appointment record = dateBook_.getAppointment(recordId);
40:
41:     // Print prefix for entry.
42:     switch (mode_)
43:     {
44:     case dayMode:
45:       break;
46:     case weekMode:
47:       // For week mode, indent each entry
48:       std::cout << "      ";
49:       break;
50:     case stringMode:
51:       // For string search view, put date on every line.
52:       std::cout << record.startTime().dateStr() << " ";
53:       break;
54:     }
55:
56:     // format start and end time
57:     std::cout << record.startTime().timeStr()
58:             << " - " << record.endTime().timeStr();
59:
60:     // Output 45 characters of the description or up to the first
61:     // newline, whichever is shorter.
62:     int outlen = std::min(45, (int) record.description().find('\n'));
63:     std::cout << "  " << record.description().substr(0, outlen);
64:   }
65:
66:   // Fetch more records from DateBook
67:   bool AppointmentDisplayList::fetchMore(int startId, int numRecords,
68:                                          std::vector<int>& result)
69:   {
70:     // Remove old contents of result
71:     result.clear();
72:
73:     if (numRecords == 0)
74:       return false;
```

continues

Listing 10.15   continued

```
 75:
 76:     bool forwards = true;
 77:     if (numRecords < 0)
 78:     {
 79:       forwards = false;
 80:       numRecords = -numRecords;
 81:     }
 82:
 83:     // Check for empty list
 84:     if (dateBook_.begin() == dateBook_.end())
 85:       return true;
 86:
 87:     // Declare an iterator
 88:     DateBook::const_iterator iter;
 89:
 90:     // Get iterator to record specified by startId.
 91:     // When fetching forward, increment iterator past matching record
 92:     // to avoid a duplicate insertion into the display list.
 93:     if (startId == 0)
 94:       iter = (forwards ? dateBook_.begin() : dateBook_.end());
 95:     else
 96:     {
 97:       iter = dateBook_.findRecordId(startId);
 98:       if (forwards)
 99:         ++iter;
100:     }
101:
102:     if (mode_ != stringMode)
103:     {
104:       // "List week" or "List day" mode
105:       DateTime firstDate, lastDate;
106:       if (mode_ == dayMode)
107:       {
108:         // Set time range from midnight at start of day to
109:         // midnight at end of day
110:         firstDate = currDate_.startOfDay();
111:         lastDate  = firstDate.addDay();
112:       }
113:       else
114:       {
115:         // Set time range from midnight on prior Sunday to
116:         // midnight on following Sunday.
117:         firstDate = currDate_.startOfDay();
118:         firstDate = firstDate.addDay(-firstDate.dayOfWeek());
119:         lastDate  = firstDate.addDay(7);
120:       }
121:
122:       // We will always fill the cache completely in one call,
123:       // so we force an empty cache to start with. We should never
124:       // actually reach this point unless the cache is already empty,
```

```
125:      // but just in case ...
126:      if (startId != 0)
127:        reset();
128:
129:      DateBook::const_iterator startIter =
130:        dateBook_.findAppointmentAtTime(firstDate);
131:      DateBook::const_iterator endIter =
132:        dateBook_.findAppointmentAtTime(lastDate);
133:
134:      // retrieve records starting at iter (doesn't matter whether
135:      // we are searching forwards or backwards because we are always
136:      // getting a complete set.
137:      DateTime prevDate;
138:      for (iter = startIter; iter != endIter; ++iter)
139:      {
140:        using namespace std::rel_ops; // To get != operator
141:        if (mode_ == weekMode &&
142:            iter->startTime().startOfDay() != prevDate)
143:        {
144:          // Start of a new day. Push a negative number for the
145:          // day of the week in the range -1 (Sunday) to -7 (Sat)
146:          result.push_back(-iter->startTime().dayOfWeek() - 1);
147:          prevDate = iter->startTime().startOfDay();
148:        }
149:        result.push_back(iter->recordId());
150:      }
151:
152:      // Return true because we reached end of the list
153:      return true;
154:    }
155:    else
156:    {
157:      // "Contains string" mode
158:
159:      if (forwards)
160:      {
161:        // Retrieve records AFTER startId
162:
163:        // Find matching record starting at iter
164:        iter = dateBook_.findNextContains(containsString_, iter);
165:        while (iter != dateBook_.end() && numRecords-- > 0)
166:        {
167:          result.push_back(iter->recordId());
168:
169:          // Find next matching record
170:          iter = dateBook_.findNextContains(containsString_,++iter);
171:        }
172:
173:        // Return true if we reached the end
174:        return iter == dateBook_.end();
```

continues

Listing 10.15   continued

```
175:    }
176:    else
177:    {
178:      // retrieve records BEFORE startId
179:
180:      // DateBook does not a function to search backwards.
181:      // Instead, we retrieve ALL records before iter
182:      DateBook::const_iterator endIter = iter;
183:      iter = dateBook_.findNextContains(containsString_,
184:                                        dateBook_.begin());
185:      while (iter != endIter)
186:      {
187:        result.push_back(iter->recordId());
188:        iter = dateBook_.findNextContains(containsString_,++iter);
189:      }
190:
191:      return true;   // Yes, we reached the start of the list.
192:    }
193:  }
194: }
195:
196: // Set the current date
197: void AppointmentDisplayList::currDate(DateTime dt)
198: {
199:   if (dt == currDate_)
200:     return;
201:
202:   currDate_ = dt;
203:   reset();
204:
205:   // Next call to display() will refill cache
206: }
207:
208: // List appointments for the day containing the specified DateTime
209: void AppointmentDisplayList::listDay(DateTime dt)
210: {
211:   if (mode_ == dayMode && currDate_ == dt)
212:     return;
213:
214:   mode_ = dayMode;
215:   currDate(dt);
216: }
217:
218: // List appointments for the week containing the specified DateTime
219: void AppointmentDisplayList::listWeek(DateTime dt)
220: {
221:   if (mode_ == weekMode && currDate_ == dt)
222:     return;
223:
224:   mode_ = weekMode;
```

```
225:   currDate(dt);
226: }
227:
228: // List all records that contain the specified string
229: void AppointmentDisplayList::listContainsString(const std::string& s)
230: {
231:   if (mode_ == stringMode && containsString_ == s)
232:     return;
233:
234:   containsString_ = s;
235:   mode_ = stringMode;
236:   reset();
237:
238:   // Next call to display() will refill cache
239: }
```

When one of the menus derived from `ListBasedDateBookMenu` enters its main loop, the first thing it does is call `displayList_.display()`, where `displayList_` is a member variable of type `AppointmentDisplayList`. The `display` function is implemented in the `DisplayList` base class and eventually calls `fetchMore` to retrieve records from the date book. Lines 71–100 in `fetchMore` are essentially the same as the `AddressDisplayList` that we saw in Chapter 7. These lines perform basic setup functions.

In line 102, we take one of two different major paths, depending on the mode. In the case of `dayMode` or `weekMode`, we end up at line 105, which declares variables for the beginning and end of the time range we will display. If `mode_` is `dayMode`, we set `firstDate` to the start of the current day and `lastDate` to the start of the next day, in lines 110–111. If `mode_` is `weekMode`, we compute the start of the week in line 118 by subtracting the current day of the week. Thus, if `currDate_` is a Tuesday, we subtract two to get the date of the previous Sunday. Then, we add seven days in line 119 to get the start of the following week.

The `fetchMore` function is intended to be able to fetch only enough records to fill a screen. However, it is unlikely that the number of appointments in one week will be very large (more than 50 would be unusual). It is reasonable to simply get all the records for the desired period. The iterators created in lines 129–132 define an iterator range [`startIter`, `endIter`) that comprises all the `Appointment` records starting in the current day or week. We use the usual idiomatic `for` loop to traverse this range, appending record IDs to the result vector using `push_back` in line 149. If `mode_` is `weekMode`, we want to keep track of the divisions between days. Before the first `Appointment` of each day, we will insert a special marker in the form of a fake record ID. The fake ID will encode the day of the week as a negative number from –1 (Sunday) to –7 (Saturday). In line 141–142, we detect that the next record is from a different day than the previous record. In line 146, we insert the fake record ID, and in line 147 we update the prevDate variable that we use to discover day boundaries. At the end of the loop, the result vector has a mixture of record IDs and special markers.

If mode_ is stringMode, we want to collect records that contain the containsString_ value. The logic for this code is the same as the logic for the string search code in AddressDisplayList. Depending on whether we are fetching records forward or backward, either the loop in lines 165–171 or the loop in lines 185–189 will be executed. Both loops call the findNextContains in DateBook, passing the previously returned iterator as the starting point for the search. The findNextContains function as well as the AppointmentContainsStr class from Listing 10.12 is repeated here:

```
107: // Function object class to search for a string within an Appointment
108: class AppointmentContainsStr
109:    : public std::unary_function<Appointment, bool>
110: {
111: public:
112:    AppointmentContainsStr(const std::string& str) : str_(str) { }
113:
114:    bool operator()(const Appointment& a)
115:    {
116:      // Return true if any Appointment field contains str_
117:      return (a.description().find(str_) != std::string::npos);
118:    }
119:
120: private:
121:    std::string str_;
122: };
123:
124: // Find next Appointment in which any field contains the specified
125: // string. Indicate starting point for search with start parameter.
126: DateBook::const_iterator
127: DateBook::findNextContains(const std::string& searchStr,
128:                            const_iterator start) const
129: {
130:    return std::find_if(start, appointments_.end(),
131:                        AppointmentContainsStr(searchStr));
132: }
```

Class AppointmentContainsStr is a function object class. Its constructor specifies the search string. Its function-call operator (operator()), in lines 114–118, uses the string class's find function to look for the search string, str_, within the argument string, a. If the search string is found, find returns a value other than npos and the function call operator returns true. (The find function and other functions belonging to the string class are discussed in Chapter 5, "Editing Addresses with Strings and I/O.")

In lines 130 and 131, the findNextContains function uses the standard find_if algorithm to look for a search string in the records in the date book. It constructs an AppointmentContainsStr object, passing the search string to its constructor, and then uses it as the predicate object that will be used to test every object in the iterator range [start, appointments_.end()). The findNextContains function returns an iterator to the first Appointment object in the range that satisfies the predicate, that is, the first Appointment that contains the search string. (For more information on the find_if algorithm and predicate objects, see Chapter 6.)

Let's restate where we are. The main program calls mainloop on whichever menu is active. If the active menu is one of the menus derived from ListBasedDateBookMenu, mainloop will call the display function on the AppointmentDisplayList object. The display function will fill its cache of record IDs by calling the fillCacheFwd function, which calls the fetchMore function. Depending on the mode, fetchMore will get record IDs using either the findAppointmentAtTime or the findNextContains function on the DateBook. When fetchMore is done, it returns a vector of record IDs to the fillCacheFwd function. The fillCacheFwd function uses the copy algorithm and back_inserter to copy the vector into its cache, as shown in the following code excerpted from Listing 7.2:

```
64:     std::copy(moreRecords.begin(), moreRecords.end(),
65:             std::back_inserter(cache_));
```

When fillCacheFwd returns to the display function, the display function loops through the cache and calls displayRecord for each record ID. That brings us back to Listing 10.15.

In line 28, we detect the special markers that we put in to mark the boundaries between days. We then do some date arithmetic in lines 33–34 to determine the day-of-the-week name and date corresponding to the marker. In line 35, we print the day-of-the-week name and date, which will serve as a header for each day in the weekly listing.

If the record ID is not a special marker, we come to line 39, where we look up the record in the DateBook object by record ID using the getAppointment function. In lines 42–54, we output a prefix that might include the date, and then in lines 57 and 58, we output the start and end times of the Appointment. Next, we want to output the first line of the description. In line 62, we use string functions to compute the smaller of the length of the first line of the description (that is, the number of characters before the first newline), or the number 45. On line 63, we use substr to extract that many characters of the description.

10

The `ListBasedDateBookMenu` Classes

At this point, we have entered D at the main menu to view the date book using the monthly view and then A, W, or S to switch to the daily, weekly, or search view. This gives us a display that looks something like this (assuming a weekly view):

```
*** Appointment Book ***
Week of 10/10/99 to 10/16/99


=============== Start of list ===============
 1: Monday 10/11/99
 2:      09:45AM - 12:45PM  Status meeting with Betty
 3:      09:45PM - 01:45AM  Raquetball with Barbara
 4: Wednesday 10/13/99
 5:      07:15PM - 11:15PM  Golf with George
 6: Friday 10/15/99
 7:      06:15PM - 08:15PM  Piano Lesson with Betty
=============== End of list ===============


(P)revious week, (N)ext week,
scroll (B)ackward, scroll (F)orward, (V)iew,
(C)reate, (D)elete, (E)dit, (S)earch, (R)edisplay,
d(A)ily view, (M)onthly view, (G)oto date, (Q)uit ?
```

In the execution sequence, we are now back at the `mainloop` function for either the `WeeklyDateBookMenu` object, the `MonthlyDateBookMenu` object, or the `StringSearchDateBookMenu` object. Listing 10.16 shows the `mainloop` and related functions of all these menu classes.

Listing 10.16 `mainloop` and Related Functions for List-Based Date Book Menu Classes

```
299: WeeklyDateBookMenu::WeeklyDateBookMenu(DateBook& datebook,
300:                                        DateBookMenuCatalog* catalog)
301:   : ListBasedDateBookMenu(datebook, catalog)
302: {
303:   displayList_.listWeek(DateTime::now());
304: }
305:
306: void WeeklyDateBookMenu::mainLoop()
307: {
308:   clearScreen();
309:   std::cout << "*** Appointment Book ***\n"
310:             << "Week of "
311:             << currDate_.startOfWeek().dateStr() << " to "
312:             << currDate_.startOfWeek().addDay(6).dateStr()
313:             << "\n\n";
314:
315:   displayList_.display();
316:   std::cout << '\n';
317:
318:   const char menu[] = "(P)revious week, (N)ext week,\n"
```

```
319:          "scroll (B)ackward, scroll (F)orward, (V)iew, \n"
320:          "(C)reate, (D)elete, (E)dit, (S)earch, (R)edisplay,\n"
321:          "d(A)ily view, (M)onthly view, (G)oto date, (Q)uit ? ";
322:    const char choices[] = "PNBFVCDESRAMGQ";
323:
324:    switch (getMenuSelection(menu, choices))
325:    {
326:    case 'P': showPrevious();              break;
327:    case 'N': showNext();                  break;
328:    case 'B': displayList_.pageUp();       break;
329:    case 'F': displayList_.pageDown();     break;
330:    case 'V': viewEntry();                 break;
331:    case 'C': createEntry();               break;
332:    case 'D': deleteEntry();               break;
333:    case 'E': editEntry();                 break;
334:    case 'S': search();                    break;
335:    case 'R': /* do nothing, just loop */  break;
336:    case 'A': showDay();                   break;
337:    case 'M': showMonth();                 break;
338:    case 'G': gotoDate();                  break;
339:    case 'Q': exitMenu();                  break;
340:    default:  exitMenu();                  break;
341:    }
342: }
343:
344: void WeeklyDateBookMenu::showPrevious()
345: {
346:    setDate(currDate_.addDay(-7));
347: }
348:
349: void WeeklyDateBookMenu::showNext()
350: {
351:    setDate(currDate_.addDay(7));
352: }
353:
354: DailyDateBookMenu::DailyDateBookMenu(DateBook& datebook,
355:                                     DateBookMenuCatalog* catalog)
356:    : ListBasedDateBookMenu(datebook, catalog)
357: {
358:    displayList_.listDay(DateTime::now());
359: }
360:
361: void DailyDateBookMenu::mainLoop()
362: {
363:    clearScreen();
364:    std::cout << "*** Appointment Book ***\n"
365:              << currDate_.wdayName() << ' ' << currDate_.dateStr()
366:              << "\n\n";
367:
368:    displayList_.display();
```

continues

Listing 10.16   continued

```
369:      std::cout << '\n';
370:
371:      const char menu[] = "(P)revious day, (N)ext day,\n"
372:          "scroll (B)ackward, scroll (F)orward, (V)iew, \n"
373:          "(C)reate, (D)elete, (E)dit, (S)earch, (R)edisplay,\n"
374:          "(W)eekly view, (M)onthly view, (G)oto date, (Q)uit ? ";
375:      const char choices[] = "PNBFVCDESRWMGQ";
376:
377:      switch (getMenuSelection(menu, choices))
378:      {
379:      case 'P': showPrevious();                     break;
380:      case 'N': showNext();                         break;
381:      case 'B': displayList_.pageUp();              break;
382:      case 'F': displayList_.pageDown();            break;
383:      case 'V': viewEntry();                        break;
384:      case 'C': createEntry();                      break;
385:      case 'D': deleteEntry();                      break;
386:      case 'E': editEntry();                        break;
387:      case 'S': search();                           break;
388:      case 'R': /* do nothing, just loop */         break;
389:      case 'W': showWeek();                         break;
390:      case 'M': showMonth();                        break;
391:      case 'G': gotoDate();                         break;
392:      case 'Q': exitMenu();                         break;
393:      default:  exitMenu();                         break;
394:      }
395: }
396:
397: void DailyDateBookMenu::showPrevious()
398: {
399:      setDate(currDate_.addDay(-1));
400: }
401:
402: void DailyDateBookMenu::showNext()
403: {
404:      setDate(currDate_.addDay(1));
405: }
406:
407: StringSearchDateBookMenu::StringSearchDateBookMenu(DateBook& db,
408:                                        DateBookMenuCatalog *catalog)
409:      : ListBasedDateBookMenu(db, catalog)
410: {
411:      displayList_.listContainsString("");
412: }
413:
414: void StringSearchDateBookMenu::mainLoop()
415: {
416:      clearScreen();
417:      std::cout << "*** Appointment Book ***\n"
418:              << "Records matching \"" << searchString_  << "\"\n\n";
```

```
419:
420:     displayList_.display();
421:     std::cout << '\n';
422:
423:     const char menu[] =
424:         "scroll (B)ackward, scroll (F)orward, (V)iew, \n"
425:         "(C)reate, (D)elete, (E)dit, (S)earch, (R)edisplay,\n"
426:         "d(A)ily view, (W)eekly view, (M)onthly view, (G)oto date, "
427:         "(Q)uit ? ";
428:     const char choices[] = "BFVCDESRAWMGQ";
429:
430:     switch (getMenuSelection(menu, choices))
431:     {
432:     case 'B': displayList_.pageUp();       break;
433:     case 'F': displayList_.pageDown();     break;
434:     case 'V': viewEntry();                 break;
435:     case 'C': createEntry();               break;
436:     case 'D': deleteEntry();               break;
437:     case 'E': editEntry();                 break;
438:     case 'S': search();                    break;
439:     case 'R': /* do nothing, just loop */  break;
440:     case 'A': showDay();                   break;
441:     case 'W': showWeek();                  break;
442:     case 'M': showMonth();                 break;
443:     case 'G': gotoDate(); showDay();       break;
444:     case 'Q': exitMenu();                  break;
445:     default:  exitMenu();                  break;
446:     }
447: }
448:
449: void StringSearchDateBookMenu::searchString(const std::string& s)
450: {
451:     searchString_ = s;
452:     displayList_.listContainsString(s);
453: }
454:
```

The three menu class implementations are largely the same as one another. The specific menu items vary a bit from menu to menu, but they all provide menu selections to view, create, delete, or edit an appointment entry. These operations are implemented by the `createEntry` function of the `DateBookMenu` base class and the `viewEntry`, `deleteEntry`, and `editEntry` functions of the `ListBasedDateBookMenu` base class, as shown in Listing 10.17.

Listing 10.17   Implementation of `ListBaseDateBookMenu` Functions

```
27:    void DateBookMenu::createEntry()
28:    {
29:        // Edit an empty appointment
```

continues

10

Listing 10.17   continued

```
30:     Appointment appt;
31:     appt.startTime(currDate_);
32:     appt.endTime(currDate_);
33:     AppointmentEditor    editor(appt);
34:
35:     // Continue editing until a record is saved or canceled.
36:     while (editor.edit())
37:     {
38:       appt = editor.appt();
39:       if (appt.description().empty())
40:       {
41:         std::cout << "Description must not be empty." << std::endl;
42:         continue;        // Loop and re-edit
43:       }
44:
45:       // insert record.
46:       dateBook_.insertAppointment(appt);
47:       setDate(appt.startTime());
48:       reset();
49:       break;
50:     } // end while
51:   }
52:
...    // Other functions already seen in Listing 10.13
124: void ListBasedDateBookMenu::reset()
125: {
126:   displayList_.reset();
127:   displayList_.currDate(currDate_);
128: }
129:
130: void ListBasedDateBookMenu::viewEntry()
131: {
132:   int recordId = displayList_.selectRecord();
133:   if (recordId <= 0)
134:     return;
135:
136:   setDate(dateBook_.getAppointment(recordId).startTime());
137:
138:   Appointment appt = dateBook_.getAppointment(recordId);
139:   std::cout << "Date: " << appt.startTime().dateStr() << '\n';
140:   std::cout << "From " << appt.startTime().timeStr()
141:             << " to " << appt.endTime().timeStr() << '\n';
142:   std::cout << appt.description();
143:
144:   std::cout << "\n\nPress [RETURN] when ready.";
145:   std::cin.ignore(INT_MAX, '\n');
146: }
147:
148: void ListBasedDateBookMenu::deleteEntry()
149: {
```

```
150:    int recordId = displayList_.selectRecord();
151:    if (recordId <= 0)
152:      return;
153:
154:    setDate(dateBook_.getAppointment(recordId).startTime());
155:
156:    // Erase the appointment
157:    dateBook_.eraseAppointment(recordId);
158:
159:    // Deleting the entry invalidates the display list cache.
160:    // Reset it, then scroll back to the previous position
161:    displayList_.reset();
162: }
163:
164: void ListBasedDateBookMenu::editEntry()
165: {
166:    int recordId = displayList_.selectRecord();
167:    if (recordId <= 0)
168:      return;
169:
170:    // Create an editor for the selected appointment
171:    Appointment appt = dateBook_.getAppointment(recordId);
172:    AppointmentEditor editor(appt);
173:
174:    // Edit the appointment
175:    if (editor.edit())
176:    {
177:      // Replace appointment with modified version.
178:      dateBook_.replaceAppointment(editor.appt());
179:
180:      // Appointment's sort order might have changed. We need to reset
181:      // the display list.
182:      displayList_.reset();
183:      setDate(editor.appt().startTime());
184:    }
185: }
186:
```

Creating an Appointment

If the user selects C in any date book menu, the mainloop for that menu calls
createEntry. In lines 30–32, createEntry creates an Appointment object with an
empty description field and a start and end time set to the day and time currently
being viewed (currDate_). In line 33, we create an editor object for this new appointment. The AppointmentEditor class works much like the AddressEditor class that we
saw in Chapter 5. We will return to the AppointmentEditor class in a moment. The
loop in lines 33–50 runs until the user enters a valid Appointment or until the user
cancels the editing session with !x. At line 46, we insert the new appointment into
the date book, and in lines 47–48, we make sure that the new appointment will be
visible the next time the screen is refreshed.

10

Editing an Appointment

If the user selects E in any date book menu (except in monthly view), the mainloop for that menu calls editEntry. In line 166, editEntry gets an item selection from the user. In line 167, we check for record IDs of less than zero, which indicate that the user either aborted the command or selected a day marker in weekly mode by accident. After retrieving the Appointment object in line 171, we create an editor object in line 172. The AppointmentEditor class is shown in Listing 10.18.

Listing 10.18   The `AppointmentEditor` Class

```
 1:  // TinyPIM (c) 1999 Pablo Halpern. File AppointmentEditor.h
 2:
 3:  #ifndef AppointmentEditor_dot_h
 4:  #define AppointmentEditor_dot_h 1
 5:
 6:  #include "Editor.h"
 7:  #include "Appointment.h"
 8:
 9:  // Class for editing an Appointment object.
10:  class AppointmentEditor : public Editor
11:  {
12:  public:
13:    // Start with an empty Appointment object
14:    AppointmentEditor();
15:
16:    // Edit an existing Appointment object
17:    AppointmentEditor(const Appointment& a);
18:
19:    // Use compiler-generated destructor
20:    // ~AppointmentEditor();
21:
22:    // Main loop returns true if appointment was successfully edited,
23:    // false if edit was aborted.
24:    bool edit();
25:
26:    // This accessor is used to retrieve the modified appointment.
27:    Appointment appt() const { return appt_; }
28:
29:    // This accessor is used to set the Appointment object to edit:
30:    void appt(const Appointment& a) { appt_ = a; }
31:
32:  private:
33:    // Disable copying
34:    AppointmentEditor(const AppointmentEditor&);
35:    const AppointmentEditor& operator=(const AppointmentEditor&);
36:
37:    // Member variables
38:    Appointment    appt_;
39:
40:  protected:
```

```
41:     // Protected functions
42:     bool editDate(const std::string& prompt, DateTime& dt);
43:     bool editTime(const std::string& prompt, DateTime& dt);
44: };
45:
46: #endif // AppointmentEditor_dot_h
```

The `AppointmentEditor` class is derived from `Editor`, which provides important common functionality. The `AppointmentEditor` derived class contains the logic specific to editing `Appointment` objects, implemented in the `edit`, `editDate`, and `editTime` functions, declared in lines 24, 42, and 43, respectively. After constructing an `AppointmentEditor` object, `editEntry` calls its `edit` function. We'll continue following the code by looking at the implementation of the `AppointmentEditor` in Listing 10.19.

Listing 10.19 **Implementation of `AppointmentEditor` Class**

```
 1: // TinyPIM (c) 1999 Pablo Halpern. File AppointmentEditor.cpp
 2:
 3: #include <iostream>
 4: #include <sstream>
 5:
 6: #include "AppointmentEditor.h"
 7:
 8: // Start with an empty Appointment object.
 9: AppointmentEditor::AppointmentEditor()
10: {
11: }
12:
13:
14: // Edit an existing Appointment object
15: AppointmentEditor::AppointmentEditor(const Appointment& a)
16:     : appt_(a)
17: {
18: }
19:
20: // Main loop returns true if appointment was successfully edited,
21: // false if edit was aborted.
22: bool AppointmentEditor::edit()
23: {
24:     // Unpack the appointment
25:     DateTime startTime(appt_.startTime());
26:     DateTime endTime(appt_.endTime());
27:     std::string description(appt_.description());
28:
29:     editDate("Date", startTime) &&
30:     editTime("Start Time", startTime) &&
31:     editTime("End Time", endTime) &&
```

continues

10

Listing 10.19   continued

```
32:     editMultiLine("Description", description);
33:
34:     if (status() == canceled)
35:       return false;
36:
37:     // Make sure that end time is after start time and that
38:     // they are less than 24-hours apart.
39:     int year, month, day;
40:     startTime.getDate(year, month, day);
41:     endTime.setDate(year, month, day);
42:
43:     // If endTime is after start time, advance end time to next day.
44:     if (endTime < startTime)
45:       endTime = endTime.addDay();
46:
47:     // Commit changes
48:     appt_.startTime(startTime);
49:     appt_.endTime(endTime);
50:     appt_.description(description);
51:
52:     return status() != canceled;
53:   }
54:
55:   bool AppointmentEditor::editDate(const std::string& prompt,
56:                                     DateTime& dt)
57:   {
58:     std::string dateStr = dt.dateStr();
59:
60:     for (;;)
61:     {
62:       if (! editSingleLine(prompt, dateStr))
63:         return false;
64:
65:       // Check for special string "today":
66:       if (! dateStr.empty() &&
67:           (dateStr[0] == 'T' ¦¦ dateStr[0] == 't'))
68:       {
69:         dt = DateTime::now();
70:         return true;
71:       }
72:
73:       // Convert back from string rep to DateTime
74:       if (! dt.dateStr(dateStr))
75:         std::cout << "Invalid date. Try again" << std::endl;
76:       else
77:         return true;
78:     }
79:   }
80:
81:   bool AppointmentEditor::editTime(const std::string& prompt,
```

```
82:                              DateTime& dt)
83: {
84:    std::string timeStr = dt.timeStr();
85:
86:    for (;;)
87:    {
88:      if (! editSingleLine(prompt, timeStr))
89:        return false;
90:
91:      // Convert back from string rep to DateTime
92:      if (! dt.timeStr(timeStr))
93:        std::cout << "Invalid time. Try again" << std::endl;
94:      else
95:        return true;
96:    }
97: }
```

In lines 25–27 of the edit function, we make copies of each of the fields in the
Appointment object. Then, in lines 29–32, we edit each field individually. The start
time is actually edited twice. First the date portion is edited, and then the time portion is edited. In lines 66–71, the editDate function checks to see if the user entered
the special value T, meaning "Today" for the date. If so, it sets the date to today's
date. Otherwise, it tries to parse the user's input in line 74, giving an error message
in line 75 if it is not a valid date.

After the individual fields have been edited, we need to do a consistency check.
Because the user was not given a chance to edit the date portion of the end time, we
must ensure that the end date is consistent with the start date. The code assumes
that the end time is no earlier than the start time and is less than 24 hours after the
start time. Lines 40 and 41 set the end date to be the same as the start date.
However, because an appointment might extend over midnight into the next day, we
add a day on line 45 if the end time is before the start time. After the consistency
check, all fields are written back to the appt_ member, and editing is complete.
When the editor returns to the editEntry function in Listing 10.17, line 178, the
edited record is written back to the date book using the replaceAppointment function.

Shutting Down

When a menu command such as "(E)dit" completes, it returns back to mainloop,
which returns back to main, which calls mainloop again for the active menu. When
the user selects Q from the menu, the active menu calls Menu::exitMenu to remove
itself from the menu stack. The main menu then becomes active. If the user selects Q
from the main menu, it removes itself from the menu stack as well, leaving the menu

stack empty. When this happens, the `main` function stops looping and `main` terminates. But this is not the end of the story. The `myPIMData` object, of type `PIMData`, contains `auto_ptr`s to `AddressBook` and `DateBook` objects. When `main` exits, the `myPIMData` object gets destroyed, causing the `auto_ptr` destructor to delete these objects. Similarly, the `auto_ptr`s in the `dateBookMenus` object (type `DateBookMenuCatalog`) delete the four date book menu objects.

I could have taken you down the path of a few more menu choices, but I will leave it as an exercise for you to follow the paths that you are most interested in. All the code is here as well as on the companion Web page. Your debugger program can be a valuable tool for exploring the program by single-stepping through the logic. Make sure that your debugger is powerful enough to print complex expressions such as "`*iter->first`" because this kind of expression is probably the only way to peer into standard containers, which are notoriously difficult to view in a debugger.

Next Steps

We now have version 1.0 of `TinyPIM`. In finishing the project, we needed to use most of the skills that we learned in previous chapters. We also learned how to avoid memory leaks and add exception safety using `auto_ptr`. There is plenty of room for improvement, of course. Here are some improvements you might make as exercises to help you cement the knowledge you have just gained:

1. Make the `findNextContains` functions in both `AddressBook` and `DateBook` not case-sensitive.

2. When the user selects to view, edit, or delete a record, allow her to enter the line number for the record on the same line as the menu selection itself, rather than having a separate prompt. For example, `D 5` would delete the record at line 5 on the display.

3. Allow appointments with no end time.

4. Make the year optional when entering date values. Assume the current year if not specified.

5. Design a data structure that would allow you to associate an address book entry with a date book appointment.

In the next chapter, I will give you a few pointers for building your C++ Standard Library expertise, including efficiency tips and sources for more information.

Chapter 11

Becoming Proficient with the Standard Library

If I have done my job, you now have a good grounding in the use of the C++ Standard Library. In this chapter I will touch on some topics that we haven't covered, just so that you know they are there and so that you can choose to research them more if you need these facilities in your projects. Even if you must buy another book, it is almost always less expensive to use the Standard Library than to create and debug your own version of a similar facility. In addition, many commercial and free libraries are available to help you do special tasks that were not designed into the Standard Library. When it comes to cost-effective programming practices, one rule of thumb is "buy before you build." Look for libraries that are designed to integrate with the framework provided by the C++ Standard Library.

A Few Tips

Up until now, I have presented individual features of the standard library in the context of their actual use in the TinyPIM project. Let me now diverge from this approach and give you a few tips that will help you use the standard library effectively.

Efficiency

By now, you might think that we've covered efficiency to death. It is also true that excessive concern about efficiency can cause a project to get behind schedule. However, there are times when speed or memory usage matters. Think of these tips as useful "tune-ups" that you can apply to critical portions of code.

Choose Your Containers Wisely

When more than one container type will meet your needs, efficiency might become the deciding factor in choosing one over another. If random access by index is required, use deque or vector. If a sequence that allows quick insertion or removal of elements is more important, choose list. The list container also provides functions for splicing parts of two lists together, a real CPU-time-saver if that's what you need. A deque can be used almost anywhere a vector can and is more efficient for frequent insertions because of the way memory is used. However, the C++ standard is in the process of being amended with a provision that requires elements in a vector to be stored in contiguous memory locations. This would make the address of the first element in a vector equivalent to a C-style array, which would make vector a better choice for interfacing with C.

If you must look up an element by value, the associative containers are always faster than searching through a sequence container. If you need both indexing and by-value searches (a rare case), a vector or deque can be sorted using the sort algorithm and searched with the lower_bound, upper_bound, equal_range, and binary_search algorithms in logarithmic time. If sorted order is not needed and your implementation supports it, consider using hashed associative containers. Associative containers and binary search algorithms make it unnecessary for even the laziest programmer to write very many linear searches.

Use Iterators to Avoid Duplicate Lookups

Every time you search a container, you must perform a certain number of comparison operations. Some of these operations (for example, for strings) can be quite costly if repeated too many times. If you find an item and know that you will need it again, keep an iterator pointed to that item. Thus, instead of

```
if (mymap.find(i) != mymap.end())
    mymap[i].second *= 2.5;     // performs a duplicate search for i
```

you would write

```
map<string, double>::iterator r = mymap.find(i);  // Keep the iterator
if (r != mymap.end())
  r->second *= 2.5;      // re-use results of find function
```

In the second version, we search for i only once and refer to the found item through the iterator rather than by looking it up again. However, the first version is more concise and arguably easier to read and understand. This is one example where you must weigh the trade-off and decide based on your needs. By the way, be aware that associative container functions like count and the non-iterator form of erase perform lookups, too. Erasing using an iterator is a constant-time operation, whereas erasing by value is a logarithmic-time operation.

Use the swap Function

Every standard container and string class provides a function called swap that
exchanges values of that type. There is also a swap algorithm that does the same for
arbitrary types. The swap algorithm is specialized so that it uses the containers' swap
when possible. The default swap algorithm is shown in Listing 11.1.

Listing 11.1   The Default swap Algorithm

```
template <class T>
void swap(T& t1, T& t2)
{
  T temp(t1);
  t1 = t2;
  t2 = temp;
}
```

As you can see, there are three copy operations on objects of type T. If T is a large
object like a vector, the time needed to perform the swap would be proportional to
the size of the two vectors. However, vector and all the other standard containers
have their own swap function that does not copy the elements in the vectors. Instead,
the vectors swap *ownership* of their contents. In other words, they take advantage of
the fact that, internally, each vector contains a pointer to its contents. When you
swap vectors, only the pointers are swapped, making the whole operation much
faster than even a single vector assignment. The same is true for the other standard
containers.

The fact that every standard container has an efficient swap function provides an
interesting opportunity for optimization. To illustrate this opportunity, Listing 11.2
shows a non-optimized function that takes a vector argument and modifies it. To
avoid invalidating iterators in the middle, it must not modify the original container
until the new version is complete.

Listing 11.2   A Function That Modifies a Vector

```
 1:  #include <vector>
 2:
 3:  extern bool cond(int);
 4:  extern int g(int);
 5:
 6:  void f(std::vector<int>& inout)
 7:  {
 8:    std::vector<int> result;
 9:
10:    for (std::vector<int>::iterator i = inout.begin();
11:         i != inout.end(); ++i)
12:      if (cond(*i))
```

continues

Listing 11.2   continued

```
13:         result.push_back(g(*i));   // Push a modified version of obj
14:
15:     inout = result;
16:   }
```

This function iterates through the vector (lines 10 and 11), calling cond on each element (line 12) and, if cond returns true, calling function g on the element and appending the return value from g to the result vector (line 13). In line 15, it copies the result back to inout. If the result is large, the copy could be expensive. However, line 15 would execute in constant time if we replaced it with the following:

```
15:   inout.swap(result);
```

After executing this new version of line 15, the old contents of inout end up in result and will be destroyed when the function returns. An additional benefit of using swap is that it uses no additional memory and never throws an exception. Assignment, however, can throw an exception if, for example, it runs out of memory. The global swap algorithm is specialized for the standard containers so that line 15 could also be replaced with the following, resulting in the exact same performance boost:

```
15:   std::swap(inout, result);
```

Memory Use

Sometimes using memory efficiently is as important as using the processor efficiently. In fact, inefficient use of memory can slow a program down because the processor must do constant allocations and reallocations or swap pages of memory to and from disk (in the case of virtual memory). Here are a couple of suggestions for using memory efficiently with the standard library.

capacity and reserve

The vector and string class templates provide two functions that control when and how much memory is allocated for the container. Used effectively, they can prevent excessive use of memory and excessive reallocations of memory.

The capacity function returns the number of elements or characters the vector or string can hold before additional memory must be allocated. If the vector or string grows past its capacity, the amount of additional memory allocated differs with the implementation. It is possible, therefore, to have a vector or string for which capacity() is much larger than size(), thus wasting memory. Conversely, if capacity grows too slowly, the program could spend much of its time repeatedly allocating small chunks of memory and copying the contents of the vector or string to the reallocated memory.

Using the reserve function, you can increase the capacity of your string or vector to the desired size. If you know the eventual size of your vector or string, you can use reserve once to allocate exactly the desired amount of memory, preventing wasted memory. If you don't know the eventual size, but you know that there will be a lot of growth, you can use reserve to avoid excessive reallocations. If the argument to reserve is less than the number of elements already in the vector or string, the call to reserve is ignored. Listing 11.3 shows the use of reserve to preallocate storage.

Listing 11.3   Using the reserve Function to Preallocate Storage in a Vector

```
 1:  #include <iostream>
 2:  #include <vector>
 3:  #include <cassert>
 4:
 5:  int main()
 6:  {
 7:    // Fill a vector with the squares of the first 10000 integers
 8:    std::vector<long> result;
 9:    result.reserve(10000);
10:    for (long i = 1; i <= 10000; ++i)
11:      result.push_back(i * i);
12:
13:    std::cout << "Size = " << result.size()
14:              << ", capacity = " << result.capacity() << std::endl;
15:
16:    // Assert that the size is exactly the capacity
17:    assert(result.size() == result.capacity());
18:
19:    return 0;
20:  }
```

Note that the reserve function can be used to reduce the memory allocated to a string but not to a vector. The capacity of a vector never shrinks. If you want to free all the memory allocated to a vector, a common idiom for doing this is to swap the vector with an empty vector as shown in Listing 11.4.

Listing 11.4   Using swap to Make a Vector Truly Empty

```
template <class T> void freeVector(std::vector<T>& v)
{
  std::vector<T> empty;
  v.swap(empty);
}
```

One more interesting thing about reserve is that it can be used to prevent invalidation of iterators. The push_back function in vector will not invalidate any iterators if size() is less than capacity().

11

bitset and vector<bool>

If you want to create a large array of Boolean values, but don't want to use up too much memory, the bitset class template might be what you need. A bitset acts like a fixed-length array of individual bits. So, for example, bitset<50> contains 50 bits that can be accessed with indexes in the 0–49 range. Note that the size of the bitset is a template parameter and must therefore be a compile-time constant, not a variable. A bitset cannot change size. A bitset is useful as an array or as a compact representation of a set of integers, where each integer is either in the set (bit on) or not in the set (bit off). A bitset can also be thought of as an integer mask because the bitwise *and* (&) and *or* (¦) operations work for bitsets. Bitsets are not containers in the usual sense and do not provide iterators for use in the STL framework.

If you need a container that grows and shrinks, you might be tempted to use vector<bool>. The standard defines a vector<bool> as an explicit specialization of vector that packs its elements into the smallest number of bytes possible. The decision to optimize vector<bool> in this way is very controversial and might yet be reversed. The complaint is that the packed representation of vector<bool> is slower than the unpacked representation and that the standard should not be making the decision to optimize for space instead of time. Also, because of the way the packed representation must work, a vector<bool> does not meet all the requirements for standard containers. My advice is to stay away from vector<bool>. Use deque<bool> instead if you want unpacked Boolean values. If you need really large arrays of packed Boolean values, you may need to write your own Boolean container class or find one in a third-party library.

Exception Safety

The containers in the standard library require the cooperation of the elements to do their jobs. At a minimum, a container must call the copy constructor or assignment operator for each element as well as the destructor for that element. What would happen to the container if during one of these operations the element throws an exception?

The minimal guarantee made by the standard library containers is that the container will not leak resources. In other words, every object that was in the container at the time of the exception will either remain in the container or will be properly destroyed by calling its destructor. Any memory allocated by the container will remain owned by the container or will be freed. If the container is subsequently destroyed, all objects in the container will be destroyed and all memory owned by the container will be freed. This minimal guarantee does not mean that the container will be useful after the exception, because its contents will be unpredictable.

Some operations have an additional guarantee that the container will be restored to the same state it had before the operation that caused the exception. For example, the `list` operations `push_front`, `push_back`, `pop_front`, `pop_back`, and `erase` provide this guarantee. The associative containers provide this guarantee for `insert` and `erase`. If continuing to use a container after an exception is a serious issue for you, you are best advised to stay away from `vector` and `deque`.

In order for the standard containers to provide these guarantees, the element type must be "well behaved." A well-behaved container element will never let its destructor exit via an exception and, of course, its destructor must free any resources owned by the element.

What You Don't Yet Know

As I mentioned in the introduction, I elected to cover those areas of the standard library that I feel are most useful in the widest variety of applications. I left out discussion of the more obscure or specialized facilities. One of these days, however, you are going to need one of these features, so here is a quick overview to get you started. See the section, "Additional Resources" later in this chapter for pointers to more information.

Language Support, Diagnostic, and Utilities Libraries

Several small classes, types, variables, and functions are used by the rest of the standard library as well as directly by the programmer. These comprise the language support, diagnostic, and utilities libraries within the C++ Standard Library. The Language Support Library defines components that are most tightly integrated with the C++ language or the compiler implementation. The Diagnostics Library defines some important exception classes and the Utilities Library defines miscellaneous other facilities. Briefly, the most important headers in these libraries are

- `<limits>`, `<climits>`, `<cfloat>`, and `<cstddef>` define implementation properties such as the range of an integer (`INT_MIN` and `INT_MAX`) or the type capable of holding the difference between two pointers (`ptrdiff_t`).
- `<new>` defines variants of the `new` and `delete` memory allocation and deallocation operators. Unlike older versions of `new`, the standard version will not return a null pointer on failure but will instead throw a `bad_alloc` exception, which is also defined in this header. There are also facilities that allow you to intercept an out-of-memory condition and possibly fix it. `<memory>` defines the default allocator class as well as facilities for writing your own allocator.

11

- `<exception>` and `<stdexcept>` define exceptions thrown by standard library components and provide facilities for controlling what happens in the case of unexpected or uncaught exceptions. `<cassert>` defines the `assert` macro.

- `<utility>` defines the `std::rel_ops` namespace, containing template definitions for the relational operators (see discussion of Listing 4.12 in Chapter 4, "An Alternative Implementation Using a List Container"). `<functional>` defines the `unary_function` and `binary_function` base classes as well as the standard function objects such as `less<T>` and the binders and negators.

- `<ctime>` declares the date and time functions and types.

Localization Library

The localization library, defined in the headers `<locale>` and `<clocale>`, abstracts cultural difference in order to make it easier (or even possible) to write programs for an international audience. The localization library handles things such as date/time formats, currency representation, uppercase/lowercase conversions, language-specific strings for built-in concepts like "true" and "false", and multibyte character encodings for languages that have more characters than fit in a single byte.

The C++ Localization library as defined in `<locale>` is quite complex. Fortunately, most of this complexity is handled automatically by the input/output stream library. A `locale` is an object that contains information about a specific culture. Locales are generally created by name. The name "C" is the default locale for the implementation. Other supported locales vary with the implementation. See your compiler's documentation for a list of supported locales. A `locale` is associated with an iostream by using the `imbue` function of the iostream as follows:

```
std::locale usa("C");          // Default locale (assuming a USA compiler)
std::locale france("FR");      // Implementation-specified French locale
std::cout.imbue(france);
std::cout << 3.5;              // Outputs as "3,5" (note comma instead dot)
std::cout.imbue(usa);          // Set the default locale
```

If you wanted `france` to be the default locale for all new iostreams, you could use the `locale::global` function, passing it the `france` locale. Note that calling `locale::global` does not change the locale of any existing iostreams, include `cin`, `cout`, and `cerr`. The details of `locale` are enough to fill another book, so I won't go into them here.

Compiler Note   The locale mechanism uses all the newest and most advanced features of C++ including nested templates, partial template specialization, and runtime type identification. For this reason, many compilers do not yet support the C++ `locale` class, though they usually do support the C locale mechanism defined in `<clocale>`.

Numerics Library

If you are writing scientific or engineering applications, you may have use for sophisticated mathematics. The C++ Standard Library facilities for mathematics are defined in the following headers:

- `<complex>` defines the `complex<float>`, `complex<double>`, and `complex<long double>` classes for complex number arithmetic and trigonometry.

- `<valarray>` defines a template class, `valarray<T>` (where `T` is almost always a numeric type) that works as a specially optimized vector. A `valarray` is a one-dimensional array designed for parallel numeric operations. The operations on `valarray` have been chosen so that, theoretically, an implementation could have a `valarray` class optimized for array-based hardware (for example, supercomputers). Note that a `valarray` does not have iterators and does not grow automatically, so it cannot be used like `vector` or other container classes.

Where Can I Learn More?

If you're not totally sick of the standard library by now and want to learn more, here are a few additional resources for you.

The *C++ Standard Library from Scratch* Web Page

This book is not complete without the additional materials available on the Macmillan USA Web site. In your favorite browser, visit

```
http://www.mcp.com
```

Look for the Product Support area and enter ISBN 0-7897-2128-7 to get to the support page for *C++ Standard Library from Scratch*. Here you will find a quick reference to the standard library, the code for most of the listings in this book, some exercises, errata, and some additional Web links.

The quick reference will help remind you of the names of classes and functions, their arguments, and their template parameters. It is not a full reference and does not have a whole paragraph for each feature.

The code for the listings make good starting points for experimentation. Can you get them to compile with your compiler? Can you improve on them?

As with any new skill, practice makes perfect. The exercises included here help you get comfortable using the standard library features.

11

Other Web Pages

Several Internet resources are available that contain useful information on a variety of topics relating to the standard library.

STLport

`http://www.stlport.org/`

This Web page provides access to a free version of the STL and Strings library. It also has links to several other excellent pages.

Standard Template Library Programmer's Guide

`http://www.sgi.com/Technology/STL/`

This page gives a good overview and reference for the STL portion of the standard library (containers, iterators, algorithms, and function objects).

RPI's Standard Template Library Online Reference Home Page

`http://www.cs.rpi.edu/projects/STL/htdocs/stl.html`

Note: This page has not been updated since May 1996. It is another reference for the STL portion of the standard library.

Usenet Newsgroups

The two main newsgroups for discussion of C++ are

`comp.lang.c++.moderated`

`comp.std.c++`

The former is for general discussion of C++, the latter for discussion of the recent and next standardization efforts. Neither group is specifically dedicated to discussion of the standard library, but the standard library does figure prominently among the topics discussed.

Compiler Help Files

Don't forget to look at your compiler's documentation. Commercial compilers vary in the quality of documentation that they provide for the included library. The popular compilers for Windows provide online help that lets you put your editing cursor on the name of a class or function and press one key to see information about that class or function. In addition to being a very convenient reference, the compiler's help files can alert you to compiler-specific library issues as well as provide you with a lot of other valuable information.

The ISO Standards Document

When in doubt, go to the source. The ISO C++ Standard might not be the easiest document to read, but it is the official reference source. The section about the Algorithms library is actually reasonably readable. Note that many parts of the C Standard Library are not documented in the C++ Standard. Fortunately, reference books for C have been available for some time now. You can obtain the standard from the following sources.

In the U.S.A.

American National Standards Institute (ANSI)

11 West 42nd Street

New York, New York 10036

Tel: 212.642.4900

Fax: 212.398.0023

Web: http://www.ansi.org/

ANSI sells an electronic version of the ISO standard in PDF format (about 2.5MB) in their online store at the above Web URL. The cost is $18. Whether purchasing an electronic or hard-copy version, reference document number ISO/IEC 14882-1998.

In the U.K.

British Standards House

389 Chiswick High Road

London

W4 4AL

United Kingdom

Tel: +44 (0) 181 996 9000

Fax: +44 (0) 181 996 7400

Email: info@bsi.org.uk

orders@bsi.org.uk

Web: http://www.bsi.org.uk/

11

In Australia

Standards Australia International Ltd. (SAI)

P.O. Box 1055

Strathfield—N.S.W. 2135

Tel: 61 2 97 46 47 00

Fax: 61 2 97 46 84 50

Email: intsect@standards.com.au

Web: http://www.standards.com.au/

Canada

Standards Council of Canada (SCC)

45 O'Connor Street, Suite 1200

Ottawa, Ontario K1P 6N7

Tel: 1 613 238 32 22

Fax: + 1 613 995 45 64

Email: info@scc.ca

Web: http://www.scc.ca/

Other Countries

Contact your national standards body through the ISO Web site:

http://www.iso.ch

Online

The following URLs are for the second public draft (CD2) of the C++ Standard, about 1 1/2 years before the final standard. Unfortunately, most of the changes in those 1 1/2 years are in the library portion of the standard. (The auto_ptr template, for example, changed dramatically.) However, this is a convenient reference and most of the information is still accurate.

http://www.maths.warwick.ac.uk/cpp/pub/wp/html/cd2/

http://www.cygnus.com/misc/wp/draft/

From the Author

I can be reached by email at phalpern@newview.org. I will try to answer most questions, but please be patient because it might take me a few days or longer to reply.

I have also authored training materials on the C++ Standard Library and am available to train members of your organization (one- to three-day courses, depending on the experience level of the engineers). Contact me by email for more information.

11

Index